TEACHING HISTORY IN CANADA

TEACHING HISTORY
IN
CANADA

Geoffrey Milburn

The University of Western Ontario

McGraw-Hill Ryerson Limited
Toronto
Montreal New York London Sydney
Mexico Johannesburg Panama Düsseldorf
Singapore Rio de Janeiro New Delhi Kuala Lumpur

TEACHING HISTORY IN CANADA

Library of Congress Catalog Card No. 72-3859

ISBN 0-07-092949-1

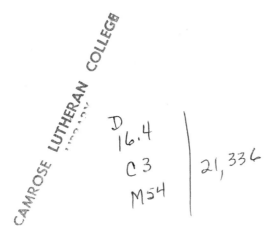

1 2 3 4 5 6 7 8 9   AP72   10 9 8 7 6 5 4 3 2
Printed and bound in Canada

CONTENTS

PREFACE

This book contains over sixty readings related to the teaching of history in Canada. They are arranged around eight themes that have appeared relevant to teachers and curriculum theorists at all levels of education. Some of these themes are theoretical in nature and others much more practical. In sum, however, they reflect some of the major problems facing the nation's history teachers in both elementary and secondary schools.

Although it is difficult to define clearly what is meant by a "Canadian" article, well over half of those included in this book have been given that label; their authors were either born or are residing in this country. Of the remainder, about seventeen were written in England and the others in the United States. It must be confessed that on some topics that have attracted great attention in recent years, scholars in Canada have not written as extensively as their colleagues in other countries. It may be argued also that an international flavour can be justified by recognizing the universality of scholarship. Since, however, the book deals with questions set in a Canadian setting, Canadian authors have, wherever possible, been included in preference to those of any other nation. A glance at the contents page will show that this was not a difficult task except in some of the earlier chapters dealing with the nature and variety of the discipline. Teaching History in Canada, therefore, is largely composed of Canadian writers, with enough comment from other countries to acknowledge our indebtedness or make comparative comment.

To keep the volume to a manageable size, the original readings have usually been edited, often severely so. Since the principal aim of the book is to provoke comment, a fairly wide net has been cast. Each theme, consequently, receives a varied treatment and the results are on occasion inconclusive or contradictory. Readers wishing to pursue topics further may consult either the selected readings given for each chapter or the suggestions contained in the introductions or the footnotes (which, except for procedural items, have been retained). This book should be considered an introductory guide, more concerned with raising questions than proposing definitive solutions.

The original concept for such a book of readings was suggested by some of my students in pre-service and in-service teacher education programs. A final version was prepared while I was working on another project supported financially by Dean Ernest Stabler and the Research and Development Committee of Althouse College of Education at the University of Western Ontario: the interrelationship between the two proved most advantageous and I would like to record my gratitude for their assistance. I have benefitted, directly or indirectly, on this occasion as so often in the past from my association with Professors R. J. Clark and D. M. Gray. My editors, firstly Mr. Garry Lovatt, and more recently Mr. Conrad Wieczorek, not only showed keen interest in the book but also played a significant role in its preparation. Finally, I owe a special debt to Mrs. Sheila Lui, Mrs. Penny Myers and Miss Margaret Zubal for their generous help with this project.

JUNE, 1972   G. MILBURN

ONE

INTRODUCTION: CURRENT TRENDS IN THE TEACHING OF HISTORY

The literature on the teaching of history is much greater in quantity today than it was two or three decades ago. Monographs, speculative discourses, texts, articles, research reports, curriculum guides and courses seem to be appearing with much greater frequency than ever before. To some extent this rapid growth can be explained in terms of greater scholarly interest in all academic matters: more is being written about every discipline, subject and topic. In the teaching of history, however, a change in the issues being investigated may be much more important than an increase in the number of investigators. Over the last twenty to thirty years, we have not been getting more of the same: the subject matter itself has been put in a new perspective by published studies.

History teachers have become accustomed to facing questions quite different from those considered important by writers of a generation ago. Examining an old "methods" book is like looking at an old map: valuable in its time, possibly still useful today, but essentially dated if not actually dangerous. Old maps are not reliable navigational aids in newly discovered territories, particularly that new world of education of which a number of writers have spoken in recent years.[1] Recent comments on the teaching of history have gone far into these previously uncharted territories and the new maps that have been drawn have led to important changes in the way history teachers approach their task.

Teachers could hardly fail to be affected, for example, by what John Higham has called the "inpouring of speculative thought"[2] about the nature of history over the last thirty years. Such scholars as E. H. Carr, Pieter Geyl, Sir Herbert Butterfield, R. G. Collingwood and Henri Marrou have reflected upon definitions, interpretations, objectivity, causation and generalizations within the discipline and, in addition, they have examined the relationship of history to other disciplines in the humanities and social sciences. This vastly increased attention[3] given to philosophic questions has produced a rich, controversial and far from simple literature. Despite the complexity of these investigations, educators recognized at an early date that they could not be excluded from the classroom. Many teaching questions are philosophic in nature. How a teacher defines his discipline is revealed in his daily lessons. His stand on historical truth may be shown in the questions he asks or the replies he gives to students. What he thinks about the nature of the subject or its relationship to other disciplines may be deduced from his methods and curriculum. To test their own approaches, therefore, and to improve the quality of their instruction, teachers have begun to employ more widely than ever before the theoretical discussions of philosophers and historians.[4]

The second major development that has influenced the curriculum in schools is the increased interest in what may be called the methodology of the subject. Sensitive to criticisms of rote memorization, historians at all levels of education have looked within the discipline itself for alternative approaches. In recent years great interest has

[1] For example, Jerome S. Bruner, Toward a Theory of Instruction (Cambridge, 1966), W. Kenneth Richmond, The Teaching Revolution (London, 1967) and Marc Belth, The New World of Education (Boston, 1970).

[2] John Higham et al., History (Englewood Cliffs, New Jersey, 1965), p. 143.

[3] Higham notes that "when the American Historical Association thirty years ago published a Guide to Historical Literature (1931), it listed just ten works on the philosophy of history, only one of which had appeared since 1875. Presumably nothing written in the late nineteenth or twentieth century, except Spengler's Decline of the West merited the attention of a professional historian. A comparable section of the new Guide to Historical Literature that the AHA brought out in 1961 included 59 titles, almost all published in recent decades." Ibid. p. 142.

[4] The work of such pioneers as Henry Johnson, Teaching of History (New York, 1915; Revised edition, 1940) ought not be overlooked.

been shown in the ways in which a historian uses his sources and tests his evidence for authenticity. If a young person is to be taught to evaluate his data, the questions posed by historians and the methods used in their work may be appropriate models for the student. These techniques and those borrowed from sister disciplines have begun to find a place within the history curriculum. Some historians such as Richard H. Brown, Co-Director of the Amherst Project, have identified as an immediate challenge the task "to produce history courses in the schools that are a good deal closer than traditional courses have all too often been to what history is as an intellectual discipline — closer in nature, in design, and in purpose."[5]

Nevertheless, many critics of the current system have pointed out the dangers of using academic models developed by a highly trained profession. In his now famous study of the teaching of Canadian Studies in schools, A. B. Hodgetts found at least some academic historians "clinging to what must be regarded as a nineteenth-century philosophy."[6] Even if all historians were exemplary practitioners of their craft, it is unlikely that their example would suffice to solve all the problems of the young student. Rather than look to subject specialists for inspiration, some curriculum theorists, impressed by advances in psychology and related disciplines, have begun to apply to the history curriculum some of the lessons learned in these fields.

Consequently, great attention has been paid to how students learn. Although older conceptions based on such theories as faculty psychology or the school of mental discipline may still be very much alive in some of our daily practices, they have been largely dismissed by scholars. Classroom procedures stressing problem solving, divergent thinking and creativity have been far more attractive alternatives. In particular a large number of scholars have advanced theories based on "inquiry" although they have disagreed on the meaning to be attached to that word. Most of them have assumed that the learner has the ability to relate a problem to its context, suggest possible solutions or hypotheses, select relevant data, weigh alternative answers and propose a tentative generalization. By following such procedures recitation and memorization will be replaced by higher level thinking. "Inquiry," as Byron G. Massialas and Jack Zevin define it, "is behaviour which is characterized by a careful exploration of alternatives in seeking a solution to a problem. Although such cognitive tasks as construction of hypotheses, definition of terms, and validation of propositions are critical to the intellectual process, creative ideas and conjectural thinking are

[5] Richard H. Brown, "The Historian and New Approaches to History in the Schools," Teacher's College Record, Vol. 72(1), September 1970, p. 75.

[6] A. B. Hodgetts, What Culture? What Heritage? (Toronto, 1968) p. 21.

essential ingredients as well."[7] Working with such theories, curriculum designers have produced an impressive range of experimental courses of study that have had a remarkably swift ripple effect in countries on both sides of the Atlantic.

Very rarely, however, have these courses relied entirely upon the written word. Well aware of the reading limitations of many students (and familiar with the advice of communications experts) most curriculum designers have skilfully blended a variety of audio-visual materials. Some scholars have made very expensive investments in films while others have relied upon video-tape or slide-audio-tape support. Some research has been conducted with computer-assisted instruction even to the extent of placing a coordinated selection of print and audio-visual materials in a computer bank. These new forms of media are not being used as "aids" in the old-fashioned sense: they are designed to be integral parts of a course of studies, to involve the student in a process of active inquiry or to convey an entirely new impression of the subject at hand.

Other scholars have been reluctant to accept without reservations the "inquiry" approach to history. Mark Krug has pointed to what he regards as the de-humanizing features of the new social science projects. He claims that the possible contributions of history to the school curriculum have been dismissed, often in favour of procedures that would prove boring in the classroom. "The study of history," he writes, "results in the emotional involvement of the writer because it deals with man who is good or evil, or both, who has the capacity to distinguish between right and wrong, who can rise to great heights, create beautiful works of art, and perform good acts, but who also can be an agent of destruction and the cause of evil."[8] Opinions of this kind have attracted a great deal of support.

In recent years, therefore, there has been a swing towards the study of values in the curriculum. Important work has been done in showing how attitudes towards minority groups in society may be formed or confirmed. A number of philosophers have asked significant questions about the relationship of a student's value system to the types of procedures adopted in class discussions. During the last five years, rival claimants have disputed the role of national as opposed to international history in the formation of what they consider to be desirable patterns of thought. A. B. Hodgetts has told us that in his opinion Canadians will continue to face a series of serious social problems "as long as we fail to use fully the tre-

[7] Byron G. Massialis and Jack Zevin, Creative Encounters in the Classroom (New York, 1967) p. 6.

[8] Mark M. Krug, History and the Social Sciences: New Approaches to the Teaching of Social Studies, (Waltham, Massachusetts, 1967), p. 13.

mendous power of education."[9] The curriculum implications of such statements have not yet been unravelled.

There can be little doubt, however, that the exchange of ideas between historians, philosophers and psychologists has had a number of interesting results. New approaches and techniques that originated in scholarly inquiry or in the experimenter's laboratory have been transferred to educational settings. Practices that have been traditionally accepted in one discipline have been challenged by concepts drawn from another. Criteria from a number of disciplines are being considered before the history curriculum is established. Consequently, W. K. Richmond's observation that "it is possible to discern the broad outlines of a new pedagogy"[10] may well apply to history as to other subjects.

The work of a number of formal curriculum projects may be helpful in our understanding of the nature of this new pedagogy. In Canada, Great Britain and the United States comparatively well-funded investigations — although rarely on the scale to which science studies have become accustomed — have studied particular problems and concepts in the history curriculum. In the last few years they have published a remarkable quantity of theoretical volumes, reports and actual courses that may well serve as models for the classroom teacher.

The significance of these projects — both formal and informal — is indicated in the types of problems that have been studied. W. H. Burston at the University of London, using as his guide the work of both practising historians and philosophers of history, such as R. G. Collingwood and W. H. Walsh, has explored the curriculum implications of such matters as the relationship between fact and interpretation and the nature of objectivity. At Carnegie-Mellon University in the United States, Edwin Fenton has most successfully applied concepts of historical inquiry to a variety of high school courses. He has drawn his inspiration from the practice of historians and from the findings of psychologists. Fenton, however, has not gone as far towards social science models of the proof process as have certain other scholars interested in formal methods of inquiry. Cousins, for example, has developed a four-part mode of inquiry that begins by asking students to understand and interpret materials, proceeds to the development and testing of insights and concludes with the exploration of if-then-always generalizations. Others such as Donald Oliver at Harvard have investigated the role of various disciplines in forming the value systems of students. Lawrence Stenhouse in Great Britain has studied the relationship between the content of history and the social sciences and the concept of good citizenship. In Canada a number of scholars have studied the effect

[9] A. B. Hodgetts, op. cit., p. 14.

[10] W. Kenneth Richmond, op. cit., p. 3.

of certain materials in teaching undesirable racial attitudes or, alternatively, not teaching directly enough certain desirable stances on national or international issues.

The first victim of this unparalleled commitment to curriculum research in history was the old "methods" course. Since the new work presumes a fairly extensive historical knowledge in addition to a broad familiarity with basic concepts in educational philosophy and psychology, traditional types of training thought appropriate for history teachers have become obsolete. The professional education that has replaced it focuses upon the study of issues as well as the observation of practical examples.

The second victim was the concept of one curriculum pattern that could be applied to many students in many jurisdictions: in short, the official course of study. So many variables exist that no single design seems workable, at least in the foreseeable future. "The accumulated evidence," note the authors of the 1971 Report of the Canada Studies Foundation, "clearly indicates that the knowledge, understanding and intellectual skills needed in Canadian society are not likely to be achieved through generalized textbooks and provincially-designed curricula such as most schools are using at the present time."[11] Consequently theorists are beginning to speculate about the existence of a series of curriculum models that weave together selected strands from the body of available theory. Current research may be directing us to a variety of designs that draw upon different philosophic, psychological and historical principles, each distinct in itself and capable of achieving different goals. These models may serve as research tools, instruments for curriculum analysis and, perhaps most importantly, useful paradigms for professional training.

All of these developments have profound implications for Canadian schools. Relating new ideas, particularly if they include radically different features, to accepted educational patterns is never an easy task. In Canada difficulties that can normally be expected may have been accentuated by the fact that many of the newer curriculum proposals have originated in foreign countries, particularly, although by no means wholly, the United States of America. Some Canadian nationalists doubt whether curriculum proposals developed within a foreign context can be applied to history courses in this country. Others feel that insufficient information is available to be able to assess adequately the effectiveness of current models. Influential sections of the academic and educational community consider it essential that Canada should generate its own solutions, either by careful reflection in the community at large, especially among teachers, or by establishing formal or informal centres where national curriculum problems can be investigated.

[11]The Canada Studies Foundation, Annual Report 1971, (Toronto, 1971), p. 6.

Yet it would be unwise to reject the experience of others in developing new materials and approaches. Many of the concepts in educational theory are able to cross international boundaries although care must be taken not to assume too much similarity between educational systems. A large number of curriculum projects being implemented in Canada could be improved by careful consideration of examples in other countries. At the very least, Canadian researchers will be able to avoid the many mistakes made by their foreign counterparts!

Over the last two decades, therefore, a number of important issues have been brought to the attention of the history teacher. Perhaps these questions, taken singly, are not new: each of them has a well-established historical or pedagogical genealogy. But, taken in their entirety, they represent a formidably new challenge. Modern teachers are being asked to reflect upon the nature of the discipline, its varieties and methodology, the question of truth in historical narratives and the part played by broad interpretations in telling a national story. Against this historical background they are examining current practices in Canadian schools and the applicability of new theories to their own curriculum planning. This type of rigorous self-analysis calls for contributions from scholars in many related disciplines, especially philosophy and psychology. The final result of these debates — which we can confidently expect will be handled with restraint and caution — may be a scholarly and meaningful reappraisal of curriculum design and teaching in history and its related disciplines.

TWO

HOW HAVE HISTORIANS DEFINED HISTORY?

Teachers are very worried about student perceptions of the nature of history. To put it bluntly, the discipline seems dull and dreary to Canadian youngsters. A. B. Hodgetts, for example, tells us that about half of the group he sampled were hostile towards Canadian Studies. A girl in British Columbia reflected the opinions of many of her own age group when she told him that history appeared to be "memorization of old treaties and so on."[1] In other countries, feelings are much the same. A few years ago a group of American scholars reported that many high school students shared Henry Ford's opinion that history was "bunk" and an "anachronism."[2] It

[1] A. B. Hodgetts, What Culture? What Heritage? (Toronto, 1968) p. 23.

[2] Maurice G. Baxter et al., The Teaching of American History in High Schools (Bloomington, Indiana, 1964) p. 50. See also M. B. Booth, History Betrayed? (London, 1969).

is difficult to resist the conclusion that the majority of students are committed to definitions of the subject that are at best oversimplified and at worst misleading or incorrect.

It is clear that scholars do not share these views. To them, history seems to be a dynamic, growing and ever-changing discipline, complex in its structure and infinitely varied in its appeal. They speak eloquently of its ability to reveal the human condition through imaginative reconstruction and sympathetic understanding. Rather than use such words as dull, dreary and laborious they dwell on such adjectives as mind-enlarging, thought-provoking and humane. Some see the subject as the queen of the disciplines, the subject that above all others integrates knowledge, and, in effect, the foundation of the modern curriculum.

The reasons for this tragic difference in perceptions of the subject are not difficult to find. Until very recently, a characteristic feature of school courses was their comparative rigidity: history for students appeared to be neatly parcelled bodies of factual knowledge. Textbook writers have assumed more often than not that their principal function has been to outline content or to narrate what has happened in history. Although there have always been outstanding exceptions, teachers have not raised in class questions related to what history is or how it is to be defined. Students, therefore, have answered those questions from the only evidence they had, the books they read or the methods they witnessed.

It would be irresponsible to suggest that a student will detect in a discipline the same features as those seen by a scholar. The latter brings to the study of the past an awareness that comes only to the mature and creative mind. The student, however, is immature and young; he lacks a frame of reference and often seems to have not even a rudimentary knowledge of the subject. Despite these differences, educational theorists point to the importance of attitudes in the learning process. Making the student aware of the point of view of the scholar may be as important as making the scholar more sympathetic to the plight of the child.

Teachers are asking the question that E. H. Carr posed to historians in a dramatic fashion ten years ago: what is history?[3] They are anxious to learn its unique contribution to humane studies, the nature of its appeal, its relevance to everyday life and its value as a source of ideas. Although they are more interested in modern comments, they are not ignoring the origin of the subject, its development through the centuries and the changes that have taken place in the last seventy years. Their source is the fertile mind of the professional historian. One of the principal starting points for curriculum theorists is the definition written by the scholar.

---

[3] E. H. Carr, What Is History? (London, 1962).

They do not expect scholars to agree. The dimensions of history are so vast, the work of historians so personal and the approaches so varied that definitions of the subject necessarily differ. There may not be as many definitions as there are historians but occasionally it must appear so. Yet it is in this variety, this willingness to describe the subject from many points of view, that some of history's strengths may lie. The opinions expressed in the readings in this chapter not only have been powerful determinants in new curriculum guidelines but also offer a direct challenge to that girl from British Columbia and the many thousands of youngsters now in the nation's classrooms who share her point of view.

1. Canadian historians have not specialized in a study of the nature of history. Although they have made brilliant contributions to interpretations of the national experience, they have not devoted similar energy to the philosophy of the subject. There are, of course, a number of exceptions, among whom must be included Dr. Richard M. Saunders, a member of the faculty at the University of Toronto since 1931. In the following reading, he compares history to the "memory" of society and shows how the subject can be a challenge for each individual.

We have all read accounts of those unfortunate persons who through some terrible concussion have found themselves face to face with a complete loss of memory. Plaintively they ask, "Who am I?" "Where am I?" "Where do I come from?" and countless other pathetic questions, trying always to establish their identity, to get back into their place in society, to feel secure, somehow to belong. If they succeed, well and good; if not, they must begin anew, building another identity, making connections with people, growing roots in society until after a long and painful process they once more can think of themselves as persons with a known identity, as beings among fellow beings, with relationships and connections that have been slowly created over the years, and which can be remembered. They have, in other words, acquired a personal history which enables them to place themselves in the world.

In reading of such tragic cases we might well ask what it would be like to be living in a land where all the people, ourselves included, were suffering from amnesia, the result, perhaps, of some incalculable atomic explosion, or of a hitherto unknown disease? Who then could answer the queries, "Who are we?" "Where do we come from?" "What are we doing here?" What an enticement to some aggressive nation, avid for power, this situation would be. How easy to impose upon the anxious, frustrated

[1] From R. M. Saunders, "Some Thoughts on the Study of History," *Canadian Historical Review*, 37(2), June 1956, pp. 109-110, 117-118. Reprinted by permission of the publisher, University of Toronto Press.

people the welcome bonds of slavery, with its security and certainty. Incredible, ridiculous, it may be said. Possibly. Yet we may not have been too far from something of this sort these latter years. However, let us leave the imaginary, and come to reality. What, in fact, have we been considering if not a people that has lost its sense of identity, of being. Why? Because of their loss of memory. Now a people, no more than an individual, can *be,* can exist, without memory. If they live they can at best be but animals, stripped of all social and human aspect. But a people's memory, like an individual's, is history. We are, then, thinking of a people without history.

It is significant that in order to think of a people without history it has been necessary to dream up an imaginary cataclysm. In the ordinary course of events peoples without history do not exist. As we look around the world, or back into the record of man, we find no people without a sense of history, from the most primitive to the most civilized. To the primitive tribe history may be oral tradition, legend and myth, but it informs the tribe that holds it with a sense of being, as surely as the most cultivated history does the most civilized societies of men. The very universality of the sense of history wherever we encounter human society makes it reasonable to conclude that man in society and some sort of historical-mindedness are inseparable. Indeed, it looks as though man could not exist in society without history, for history provides at least partial answers to those essential questions, "Who are we?" "Where do we come from?" "What are we doing here?" Without answers to these questions there can be no cohesion, no organization, no purpose in society. If this be so then the first use of history is to provide any society with a sense of unity and being, lacking which it would die.

*   *   *

We come to realize, as we think about history, that in the pages of history we can, if we will, see human life in all its richness, its variety, and its colour. In the study of this subject we can broaden our experience, enrich our lives, deepen our understanding, sharpen our judgment, even find sympathy and tolerance for our fellow men, for if we look carefully we shall find in them, ourselves. We discover that the greatest, the over-arching use of history, is to give to men a vision of man.

What the student of history will do, if and when he catches sight of this vision of man that may be found in the pages of history, what use he will make of his knowledge, is a decision that has to be made by each individual. He may, if he will, sell his knowledge, or use it to exploit his fellowmen. He may find in it a perennial source of pleasure, a satisfaction of curiosity and an aesthetic delight that will last him all his life long. He may be inspired to extend our knowledge and understanding still further, to become a worker himself in the field of history. He may be led to use his knowledge to work for a better understanding amongst the peoples of the world, or to bring about reform and betterment in the society of which he is a member. He may even find himself impelled through the study of history to a deeper worship of God.

Whatever decision is made it will in the last analysis be founded on the student's personal philosophy and religion. Now the study of history does not impose belief in any particular philosophy or religion, for history is no more deterministic than human life itself. None the less, there is a point where, if a student of history press his enquiries that far, he must enter upon a consideration of questions of a philosophic and religious import. He asks himself, for instance — and this is the point at which history and philosophy merge — what is the meaning of these facts of history that I am studying? Most, perhaps all, the answers given will find their source in the philosophy or religion which the student brings to the study of history, but they must, even so, be given in the light of the new knowledge of man that comes through that same study. Because of this, although the study of history does not automatically force a person to hold any one set of beliefs, few students can go very far in this study without either finding in history an illustration of their own beliefs, or being led to a revaluation and clarification of their philosophy of life. The study of history, in other words, has its own part in the formulation of that philosophy on the basis of which the student will finally decide what use he will make of his knowledge of history.

To know history, then, is not only to know man better, it is to know oneself better, one's relations to mankind as a whole, one's own outlook on life. The knowledge of history is one doorway to wisdom.

2. *George Macaulay Trevelyan (1876-1961) Regius Professor of Modern History at Cambridge University until 1940, is one of the most popular historians of the present century. Author of many books on Italian and British history, he became widely known for an essay in which he refuted the then commonly-held opinion that history was a science.* Rejecting any version of the subject based on an -ology, Trevelyan re-established history for the ordinary reader as a branch of literature. His narratives are effortless, dramatic and moving. In an essay entitled "History and the Reader" he described the purpose of history and the nature of its appeal.*

In itself history raises and attempts to answer two great questions — (1) what was the life of men and women in the past ages? and (2) how did the present state of things evolve out of the past? The reader can be interested in the past for its own sake, for the value or instruction he finds in former states of society, and former habits of thought which have passed away and left little or nothing behind. Or else the reader may be interested chiefly in the explanation which history alone can afford of the

*G. M. Trevelyan, Clio : A Muse (London, 1913).

[2] Reprinted from G. M. Trevelyan, "History and the Reader," in
An Autobiography and Other Essays, 1969, pp. 59-60, 62, 65-66, with
the permission of the publishers, Longman Group
Limited, Essex, England.

origin of the institutions, beliefs, habits and prejudices of the various peoples of the world at the present day. In other words, he can be interested in the past, either for its own sake, or as the parent of the present. Similarly, he may be interested in static views of various past scenes and happenings, or he may be interested principally in the moving stream of events, the causal and evolutionary aspect of the history of mankind.

I will say a little about these two aspects of history separately. First, the value to the reader of discovering what life was like in various ages and countries of old: this kind of intellectual curiosity can in our day be satisfied more fully and more correctly than in any previous age, because of the wonderful work of modern scholarship. It is a relief to escape from our own mechanical age into a world when the craftsman was more and the machine less, when imagination was more and science was less. Nor is this mere hedonistic escapism. It enlarges the mind and imagination, otherwise imprisoned in the present. We get glimpses of other worlds, human and faulty like ours, but different from our own, and suggesting many things, some of great value, that man has thought, experienced and forgotten. Indeed, I know of no greater triumph of the modern intellect than the truthful reconstruction of past states of society that have been long forgotten or misunderstood, recovered now by the patient work of archaeologists, antiquarians and historians. To discover in detail what the life of man on earth was like a hundred, a thousand, ten thousand years ago is just as great an achievement as to make ships sail under the sea or through the air.

How wonderful a thing it is to look back into the past as it actually was, to get a glimpse through the curtain of old night into some brilliantly lighted scene of living men and women, not mere creatures of fiction and imagination, but warm-blooded realities even as we are. In the matter of reality, there is no difference between past and present; every moment a portion of our prosaic present drops off and is swallowed up into the poetic past.

The motive of history is at bottom poetic. The patient scholar, wearing out his life in scientific historical research, and the reader more idly turning the pages of history, are both enthralled by the mystery of time, by the mutability of all things, by the succession of the ages and generations.

*   *   *

Besides the contemplation and study of the Past for its own sake, there remains the second great value of History, namely the light it throws on the present. You cannot understand your own country, still less any other, unless you know something of its history. You cannot even understand your own personal opinions, prejudices and emotional reactions unless you know what is your heritage as an Englishman, and how it has come down to you. Why does an Englishman react one way to a public or private situation, a German another way, a Frenchman in a third way? History alone can tell you.

In this stage of the world, when many nations are brought into close and vital contact for good and evil, it is essential, as never before, that their gross ignorance of one another should be diminished, that they should begin to understand a little of one another's historical experience and resulting mentality. It is a fault of the English to expect the people of other countries to react as they do themselves to political and international situations. Our genuine good will and good intentions are often brought to nothing, because we expect other people to be like ourselves. This would be corrected if we knew their history, not necessarily in detail but in broad outlines of the social and political conditions which have given to each nation its present character.

*　　*　　*

I hope I have begun to make out to your satisfaction my case for the twin propositions, (1) that it is part of the duty of historians to present history in a readable form, or rather, in a variety of forms readable by various sections of the public. And (2) that the general reader ought to study history. If he knows no history he is not properly educated either as a citizen or as an intellectual and imaginative being. But few readers will study history because they think it a patriotic duty to do so, or even because they want to improve their minds. Readers read because they like reading, and the books they choose will be those that interest or delight them. People will read history if it fascinates them. It is therefore the duty of historians to make it as fascinating as possible, or at any rate not to conceal its fascination under the heap of learning which ought to underlie but not overwhelm written history.

And how fascinating history is — the long, variegated pageant of man's still continuing evolution on this strange planet, so much the most interesting of all the myriads of spinners through space. Man's evolution is far more extraordinary than the first chapter of Genesis used to lead people to suppose. Man's history, — prehistoric, ancient, mediaeval and modern, — is by far the most wonderful thing in the Universe of which any news has come through to us. It contains religion; it contains science; at least it contains their history. It contains art and literature. The story of man is far more wonderful than the wonders of physical science. It is a mystery unsolved, yet it is solid fact. It is divine, diabolic — in short, human. "The proper study of mankind is man," more proper to him than even the study of beetles, of gases, and of atoms. And this wonderful pageant can be viewed both in rapidly revolving films of large expanse of time and space, and in 'close-ups' of single people and single scenes.

3.　R. G. Collingwood (1889-1943), although a leading authority on the archaeology of Roman Britain, was primarily a philosopher, becoming Waynflete Professor of Metaphysical Philosophy at Oxford University in 1935. In a book published after his death, he put for-

[3] Reprinted from R. G. Collingwood, "Human Nature and Human History," in *The Idea of History,* 1946, pp. 213-214, 215-216 with the permission of the Clarendon Press, Oxford.

*ward the thesis that history is concerned with human "thoughts" rather than events, and that the historian recreates those thoughts in his own imagination.**

The historian, investigating any event in the past, makes a distinction between what may be called the outside and the inside of an event. By the outside of the event I mean everything belonging to it which can be described in terms of bodies and their movements: the passage of Caesar, accompanied by certain men, across a river called the Rubicon at one date, or the spilling of his blood on the floor of the senate-house at another. By the inside of the event I mean that in it which can only be described in terms of thought: Caesar's defiance of Republican law, or the clash of constitutional policy between himself and his assassins. The historian is never concerned with either of these to the exclusion of the other. He is investigating not mere events (where by a mere event I mean one which has only an outside and no inside) but actions, and an action is the unity of the outside and inside of an event. He is interested in the crossing of the Rubicon only in its relation to Republican law, and in the spilling of Caesar's blood only in its relation to a constitutional conflict. His work may begin by discovering the outside of an event, but it can never end there; he must always remember that the event was an action, and that his main task is to think himself into this action, to discern the thought of its agent.

In the case of nature, this distinction between the outside and the inside of an event does not arise. The events of nature are mere events, not the acts of agents whose thought the scientist endeavours to trace. It is true that the scientist, like the historian, has to go beyond the mere discovery of events; but the direction in which he moves is very different. Instead of conceiving the event as an action and attempting to rediscover the thought of its agent, penetrating from the outside of the event to its inside, the scientist goes beyond the event, observes its relation to others, and thus brings it under a general formula or law of nature. To the scientist, nature is always and merely a "phenomenon", not in the sense of being defective in reality, but in the sense of being a spectacle presented to his intelligent observation; whereas the events of history are never mere phenomena, never mere spectacles for contemplation, but things which the historian looks, not at, but through, to discern the thought within them.

*   *   *

The processes of nature can therefore be properly described as sequences of mere events, but those of history cannot. They are not processes of mere events but processes of actions, which have an inner side, consisting of processes of thought; and what the historian is looking for is these processes of thought. All history is the history of thought.

*A critical review of Collingwood's theory can be found in W. H. Walsh, Philosophy of History : An Introduction (New York, 1960), pp. 48-59.

But how does the historian discern the thoughts which he is trying to discover? There is only one way in which it can be done: by re-thinking them in his own mind. The historian of philosophy, reading Plato, is trying to know what Plato thought when he expressed himself in certain words. The only way in which he can do this is by thinking it for himself. This, in fact, is what we mean when we speak of "understanding" the words. So the historian of politics or warfare, presented with an account of certain actions done by Julius Caesar, tries to understand these actions, that is, to discover what thoughts in Caesar's mind determined him to do them. This implies envisaging for himself the situation in which Caesar stood, and thinking for himself what Caesar thought about the situation and the possible ways of dealing with it. The history of thought, and therefore all history, is the re-enactment of past thought in the historian's own mind.

This re-enactment is only accomplished, in the case of Plato and Caesar respectively, so far as the historian brings to bear on the problem all the powers of his own mind and all his knowledge of philosophy and politics. It is not a passive surrender to the spell of another's mind; it is a labour of active and therefore critical thinking. The historian not only re-enacts past thought, he re-enacts it in the context of his own knowledge and therefore, in re-enacting it, criticizes it, forms his own judgment of its value, corrects whatever errors he can discern in it. This criticism of the thought whose history he traces is not something secondary to tracing the history of it. It is an indispensable condition of the historical knowledge itself. Nothing could be a more complete error concerning the history of thought than to suppose that the historian as such merely ascertains "what so-and-so thought", leaving it to some one else to decide "whether it was true". All thinking is critical thinking; the thought which re-enacts past thoughts, therefore, criticizes them in re-enacting them.

It is now clear why historians habitually restrict the field of historical knowledge to human affairs. A natural process is a process of events, an historical process is a process of thoughts. Man is regarded as the only subject of historical process, because man is regarded as the only animal that thinks, or thinks enough, and clearly enough, to render his actions the expressions of his thoughts. The belief that man is the only animal that thinks at all is no doubt a superstition; but the belief that man thinks more, and more continuously and effectively, than any other animal, and is the only animal whose conduct is to any great extent determined by thought instead of by mere impulse and appetite, is probably well enough founded to justify the historian's rule of thumb.

4. Sir Lewis Namier (1888-1960) created a new school of historians by subjecting events and institutions to microscopic analysis. Two of his finest works, The Structure of Politics at the Accession of George III *(London, 1929) and* England in the Age of the American

[4] Reprinted from L. B. Namier, "History" in *Avenues of History* pp. 7-8. Copyright © 1952 by L. B. Namier (Hamish Hamilton, London).

Revolution (London, 1930), redrew the picture of eighteenth-century English history by a painstaking review of details of the period. His writings have been so influential upon historians at large that one observer has written that "not only the generation which closed with his death in 1960, but the one which is beginning now, may well be called by historiographers of the nineties 'The Age of Namier'." In the following extract he reflects on whether we can learn from the past and stresses the importance of analytic insight and selection.*

In certain disciplines, such as diplomacy, military art, politics, or finance, individual experience is obviously and necessarily inadequate: men have to draw on history, which is vicarious experience, less vivid and formative but much wider. Can men learn from it? That depends on the quality and accuracy of the historian's perceptions and conclusions, and on the critical faculties of the reader — on the 'argument', and on the 'intellects' to comprehend it. When erudition exceeds intelligence, past results are rigidly applied to radically changed situations and preparations are completed for fighting the previous war. Conclusions drawn primarily from experience in the narrow theatre of the Crimean War gave rise to Frossard's doctrine of systematic defence; next, the German victories of 1870 made military opinion swing back in favour of relentless attack; the price paid for it in the trench-warfare of 1914-18 produced in turn the Maginot mentality among the French public and politicians, though much less among the soldiers who continued to plan offensive action: but in the slow-motion style of 1918. The Germans in 1914 neglected Clausewitz's injunction, if there is one enemy to go for his capital, but if two, for their line of communication. In 1940 they correctly went first for the Channel ports, and only next for Paris; but in 1941 they perhaps unduly neglected a new factor in warfare: had their main initial offensive been directed against the Caucasus, they might have cut off Russia's oil supply and immobilized her armies. The time lag in disciplined military thought is aggravated on the victorious side by the glory which attaches to past successes and by the prestige of their ageing artificers. Yet in all spheres alike, even in the freest, false analogies, the product of superficial knowledge and reasoning, are the pitfall of history as *magistra vitae*.

Human affairs being the subject matter of history, all human pursuits and disciplines in their social aspects enter into it. But as no human mind can master more than a fraction of what would be required for a wide and balanced understanding of human affairs, limitation and selection are essential in the historian's craft. Analytic insight into the tangle of human affairs coupled with a consciousness of his own limitations is the mark of the real historian, and maturity is attained perhaps later in his work than in any other discipline.

*John R. Hale (ed.), The Evolution of British Historiography from Bacon to Namier (Cleveland, 1964) p. 79.

As history deals with concrete events fixed in time and space, narrative is its basic medium — but guided by analytic selection of what to narrate. The function of the historian is akin to that of the painter and not of the photographic camera: to discover and set forth, to single out and stress that which is of the nature of the thing, and not to reproduce indiscriminately all that meets the eye. To distinguish a tree you look at its shape, its bark and leaf; counting and measuring its branches would get you nowhere. Similarly what matters in history is the great outline and the significant detail; what must be avoided is the deadly morass of irrelevant narrative.

5. *Historians have different opinions about the relationship of past to present. Most would agree with G. M. Trevelyan's statement in an earlier reading in this chapter that the study of history throws light on the present. A few critics, however, have argued that the emphasis placed by historians and students on the history of Western Europe has narrowed their vision and circumscribed their thoughts. Most outspoken has been Geoffrey Barraclough, an expert in both medieval and contemporary international history, who has called for a reassessment of the subject to meet the needs of a changing world. Professor Barraclough's books include* Origins of Modern Germany *(Oxford, 1946) and* An Introduction to Contemporary History *(London, 1966).*

The past impinges at every turn on the present; and the question of its relevance, the task of ensuring that the relationship of past and present shall be a right relationship, is therefore a practical question, which may well contribute to the shaping of the future. That does not mean that we should make ourselves slaves of the past, forgetful that every day something happens which no man ever foresaw and probably no man ever wanted. Historical knowledge can blind as well as illuminate; and it is at least as important to be aware of what does not survive as to perceive what lives on. The assessment of relevance has become more difficult; the 'old smooth generalizations' no longer fit; and it has become evident that the wider our view over the past, and the better we are able to scan the horizons, the less likely are we to be deceived by what we know. As I have tried to indicate, it is only a history that is universal in spirit — a history that looks beyond Europe and the west to humanity in all lands and ages — that can serve our purposes. That statement, of course, is not meant to imply that more specialized historical investigation is redundant or of an inferior order: only that *alone* it is not enough, because it deals with less than 'the whole system of reality' which, as Bury perceived, is and must remain history's supreme objective. If we are to know where we stand in a changing world, and if history can help us to know where we stand, we must look beyond this island, and beyond the lands

[5] Reprinted from Geoffrey Barraclough, "The Historian in a Changing World" in *History in a Changing World*, pp. 26-28, 29-30, with the permission of Basil Blackwell, Publisher, Oxford.

associated with it; we must look beyond the continent of which it is a part. History will not, as is sometimes feared, lose meaning that way, as though only the history of the homeland or (some modern historians seem even to suggest) of the parish-pump has relevance to our habits and daily lives and modes of thought. On the contrary, it will gain in relevance, because it will be nearer to the conditions of modern life, in which — in spite of political divisions — the whole world is one, and — whether we like it or not — the fortunes of every one of us are linked to the fortunes of all the others.

*   *   *

Many who are not historians feel dissatisfaction, and even disenchantment and disillusionment, when they survey the field of history to-day. It seems to have betrayed the high hopes that were placed in it; it offers no sure guidance among the dilemmas of a changing world. What is its use for the practical man who is not an historian? What is its contribution to the understanding of the present?

In part the criticism implied in these questions is justified; in part it is based upon mistaken notions of the scope of history, which historians of an earlier generation too often took it upon themselves to foster. The expectation that history would be able to provide clear-cut answers for the conduct of present and future affairs, was false; and to ask the historian to provide such answers is, often, to require him to betray his integrity. The historian has too long been encouraged to pursue abstruse research in the confident belief that 'a complete assemblage of the smallest facts of human history will tell in the end.'[1] To-day we have good reason to be less certain than men of Bury's generation of the truth of this assertion. . . .

*   *   *

It is still, I believe, true that the historical approach — though not the only approach — has much to offer which cannot be acquired in any other way, to all those who are faced by the task of working out a philosophy of living in an unstable world. But if it is to contribute towards an intelligent, well-informed and critical judgement of the problems of modern society, radical revision is necessary. In the first place, we must combat the fragmentation which has overtaken history, and accustom ourselves, once again, to look at the past as a whole; for unless we have a positive ideal of universal history, our history will inevitably tend to be less than universal. Secondly, we must seek for history an end outside itself — as it had, for example, when it was viewed as a manifestation of the working of God's providence. That statement is not intended to imply a return to a theological view of history (which, whether desirable or not, I regard as impracticable to-day); but it does mean that its study should have a constructive purpose and a criterion of judgement, outside and beyond the historical process. Thirdly, we should not evade the test of relevance; for although the past may have existed for itself, history — the attempt to discover, on the basis of fragmentary evidence, the significant things about

[1] Cf. J. B. Bury, *Selected Essays*, 17.

the past — exists for us. And finally, and above all else, we must make a determined effort to revive the connexion between past and present, between history and life, which — owing to the mistaken ideals historians have pursued — is in evident danger of perishing. The twentieth century is still in search of a history liberated from the preconceptions of an age which has passed, and adequate to itself;[2] but the foundations are there — if we will but use them — for a new structure of history, which will serve us, and serve us well, in a world which has radically changed and is still changing.

[2] I adapt here the formulation ('Twentieth-century thought in search of a historian') used by Emery Neff for the concluding section of his interesting book, *The Poetry of History* (1947).

6. *When explaining why history is studied in our schools and colleges, a historian may stress the subject's intellectual benefits. It is worth studying, we often hear, "for its own sake". "Content," we are told is not so important as "learning how to think." Since the purpose of studying history is to develop the mind, writes G. R. Elton, "it matters little what particular sections of it are taught."* Dr. J. H. Plumb has taken issue with these objectives. Complaining that the subject has lost essential qualities it once possessed, he calls for history that has a social purpose, that will, in essence, benefit societies of the future. Dr. Plumb, an expert on eighteenth century history, is currently Professor of Modern English History in Cambridge University.*

For any historian, it seems to me, who can bring himself to believe that the past exists outside his own head, the fact of human progress remains undeniable. The material and intellectual progress in the last 7,000 years is staggering not only in its complexity but in its increasing rapidity. Put a flint knife by a computer or a handloom by a sputnik. And surely it ought to be the prime duty of the historians to investigate this process, to describe it, to attempt an explanation of how it came about, and for this theme to be their social purpose. It ought to be the historian's duty to lay bare these processes by which social progress has taken place, in the hope that knowledge and understanding may lead to their acceleration and development. So, too, should they concern themselves with those factors in society which have inhibited growth and change and, even at times, led to retrogression, so that these might, in the future, be avoided. Such preoccupations would not mean, as Geyl would have us believe, that history would become unimaginative, blinkered, and insensitive and concerned entirely with success.[3] Because one believes that the most important

[3] See P. Geyl, *Debates with Historians* (The Hague, 1955), pp. 18-34.

*G. R. Elton, The Practice of History (New York, 1967) p. 150.

[6] Reprinted from J. H. Plumb, "The Historian's Dilemma," in *Crisis in the Humanities*, pp. 42-44. Copyright Penguin Books Ltd., 1964.

feature of human history is the story of man's progressive control over his environment, this does not mean that one throws overboard all one's imagination, insight, and judgement or one's sympathy for what fails and what is destroyed. But to ignore the implication of the concept of progress seems to me to lead to disintegration, nihilism, and to the proliferation of meaningless investigations. In so doing historians turn their back on their social function. Their investigations of the past should lead to an explanation of it for their time and generation, so that, by explaining, man's control over his future may be increased.

Now, the failure to do this exists not so much in our historical work as in our historical teaching. Much historical work in progress is deeply concerned with historical change or with the major forces that have moulded society. Nor is the failure so complete in the teaching of history to historians, although this is often terribly disorganized, at times superficial, and, frequently, concerned with tertiary issues. Nevertheless anyone with imagination and some scholarship can deepen his experience about the nature of man in society and the historical processes of change. He will not, of course, in my own University of Cambridge be led directly to such considerations. He will, for example, be expected to know far more about Tudor Chamber finance than the impact of the geographical discoveries, or the scientific revolution. Instead of being central to his education, the idea of progress will be incidental to it. What we can be certain about is that the social purpose of history will neither mould his studies nor help him to form his attitude to the past. He will be taught inexorably to distrust wide discussions and broad generalizations, to eschew any attempt to draw conclusions or lessons from history. He will be encouraged to read history and treat history as an intellectual pastime, with little rhyme and less reason. Those who go off to teach in schools go to instruct and not to educate. And worse still history fails to fulfil its social function, in government, in administration, in all the manifold affairs of men.

7. *Very rarely do historians examine the relationship between history and religion. To many scholars, indeed, the ways of the Deity are, by definition, not part of their professional concern. The designs of God are best left, in their opinion, to priests or mystics. One person who has entered this forbidden territory is Sir Herbert Butterfield, formerly Regius Professor of Modern History in Cambridge University.*

Those who say that everything in history can be explained without bringing God into the argument would be doing no more than walking round in a circle, even if it were true that anything in history — or even a blade of grass — had yet been fully explained. A world of blind men

[7] Reprinted from H. Butterfield, "Providence and the Historical Process" in *Christianity and History* 1954, pp. 107-109, 111-112 with the permission of the publishers, G. Bell & Sons Ltd., London.

might equally maintain that their universe was explicable to them without the introduction of a foreign concept like the notion of light. Whatever the claim the natural scientists might make, it is clear that the historian can never be sure that he has collected all the relevant factors into his hands. He has been able to set out the story of the sixteenth century in a way that seemed self-complete and self-explanatory, and then it has been discovered later that he had left out of account one of the most important and widely operative factors in modern history, namely the remarkable price-rise that affected so many aspects of that period. There is no such closed and interlocking system in history as forbids us to believe that some totally new factor may not be discovered to alter our interpretation of a given episode. There is no such self-contained intellectual system as would forbid a man who was an historian to believe that God Himself is a factor in history — all the harder to discover perhaps if His hand was in operation everywhere. And of course no historian can deny the power of religious faith in history, even though that faith might be dismissed as a delusion or a form of inebriation.

When we are concerned with that kind of history-making which goes on over our heads in the way I have tried to show, it is remarkable how often we do our thinking in symbols, or by means of patterns; but I think we are deceived by our own devices unless the symbols are personal ones, and that is why I have . . . said of this kind of history-making that it was as though History herself had decided to stand up and take a hand in the game. Some people have seen the course of this history-making as a spiral; they point for example to civilisations which seem to come in cycles, developing and decaying, each new one beginning its cycle a little higher up than the previous one. Some think of history almost as though it were a mechanistic system — interests colliding with one another, with diagrams of forces, and everything interacting like the parts of a great machine. Others, having in mind the growth of society or the evolution of a branch of knowledge, have drawn their analogies from organisms in biology. Such symbols or patterns, however, have reference only to selected parcels of historical events, isolated from the rest of the complex fabric of historical happening. They are dangerous, for none of them is sufficiently flexible, and history as a whole must be very subtle in pattern — for it must be subtle enough to include and combine all these other partial patterns. Those who — thinking in pictures somewhat, or in diagrams — imagined in 1919 that history was an ascending process, or that, having taken a curve in the nineteenth century it would continue that curve in the twentieth century — those who in 1919 thought that since the world had become more liberal and democratic for a century it could now only become more liberal and democratic still — were actually handicapped in their historical knowledge, because they had run it into too rigid a pattern. They did not remember what a live thing history is, and how wilfully it may break away from the railway-lines which the prophets and pedants may have set for it.

*　　　*　　　*

When we think of the action of God in history — and present it to ourselves in pictures, as we are almost bound to do — we need not imagine a heavy hand interposed to interfere with the working of a heavy piece of machinery. Perhaps a better picture of our situation would be that of a child who played her piece very badly when she was alone, but when the music-teacher sat at her side played it passably well, though the music-teacher never touched her, never said anything, but operated by pure sympathetic attraction and by just being there. Perhaps history is a thing that would stop happening if God held His breath, or could be imagined as turning away to think of something else. Lord Acton surrendered unduly to the spirit of his age when he said that without progress there could be no Divine Providence, and complained that Cardinal Newman could not see God in this kind of pattern in history, but only in biography, in the intimate interior of personalities.

To a religious mind all those providential dispositions which I have attempted to describe must appear as Divine, as the orderings of God Himself; and in the workings of history there must be felt the movement of a living God. Combined with [other] things . . . they constitute a kind of history the end of which does not lie in history itself or in any of the patterns and schematisations which appear in our textbooks — patterns and schematisations which are sometimes presumed to be the very purpose of the whole human drama. These dispositions constitute a kind of world which is a discipline for the soul and they provide for men an end, an object to strive for, which is not merely laid up for the last generation that may happen to live on the earth. They imply also that history, by the very fact that it is so personal, is essentially a moral affair —in so far as we take a purely mundane point of view — moral, not intermittently (as when we resort to morality for the purpose of exposing the character of our enemies), but through and through, in the way that the Old Testament was developing its interpretation. The patterns that matter in history are patterns that end in personalities, who are the blossom and the fruit — they *are* posterity, they *are* the heirs of all the ages, whom creation groaned through so many astronomical eras and such long geological epochs to produce. Men work for progress, but without regarding it as the end which gives meaning to history. They are subordinate only to the glory of God.

8. *During the last few years, history has been attacked by a number of critics on the grounds that it is irrelevant to the problems of today or the needs of the student in the future. "We are bound," wrote Jerome Bruner, "to move toward instruction in the sciences of behaviour and away from the study of history."* The movement to*

*Jerome S. Bruner, Toward a Theory of Instruction (Cambridge, 1966) p. 36.

[8] Reprinted from William H. Cartwright, "The Enduring Relevance of History" in *View* 1(1), Winter 1970, pp. 1-2 with the permission of the author and Ginn and Company, Lexington, Mass.

which he refers has become so powerful that many teachers seem to be bewailing the imminent death of the subject. (See, for example, Dr. Trueman's article in Chapter 7). Although many historians are uncomfortable with the word "relevance," considering it over-used and befuddled by controversy and careless thinking, few of them are prepared to admit that the discipline is useless. "We neglect," wrote J. S. Bromley, "the past at our peril: as a lesson in humility, tolerance, and compassion; as the only way to explain ourselves to ourselves and to understand some of the dark forces which ride in our lives without our knowing it; as a source of vitalizing inspiration; and, in a measure, as a prophylactic against foolish action."† In the following reading, Dr. W. H. Cartwright, for many years a Profes-sor at Duke University, considers in more detail some of the same ideas and directly refutes the charge that history is irrelevant.

It is fashionable in some quarters these days to point with scorn at the study of history being unrelated to problems of the present. There are those who would abolish it in favor of contemporary studies that are assumed to be more "relevant." The recent expansion of contemporary studies in the curriculum was long overdue. They have important contributions to make to the education of people who must deal with terrible problems in the present and the future. But it is no derogation of those studies to assert that an adequate social education cannot be achieved without substantial attention to history. It is true that too much of the history that has usually been taught has consisted of unimportant details that bear little relation to the modern world. However, this charge is also valid for much of what is offered in the name of relevance today but is really only transient or pe-ripheral to the real concerns of society. History is not only relevant to these concerns; it is indispensable.

No social institution, development, or event can be understood without consideration of history. The crises of the Middle East have little meaning unless long-standing associations and values of Arabs, Jews, and great powers are comprehended. The problems of minority groups are not likely to be solved without serious attention to the long history of oppression of subject peoples by dominant ones. Indeed, blacks, Mexican-Americans, and American Indians insist that their history must be taught as part of the solution to their problems.

History offers a means of studying peoples and persons. Through it the pupil should see people at work on matters of universal and enduring im-portance in different times and settings. Thus, he should come to sympa-thetic understanding of peoples different from his own and persons differ-ent from him. And he should gain an appreciation of the essential unity of humankind.

It is in its capacity to sift out of the mass of knowledge those elements which have enduring value that history has unique importance in the social

†J. S. Bromley, History and the Younger Generation (Southampton, 1962) p. 9.

studies. In times of troubles, the concept of permanence that can come only from history is especially important. The knowledge that people in other times and places have endured similar trials should help establish a sense of stability. History for a society is like memory for a person, and without it stability cannot be achieved. A colleague, R. Baird Shuman, has observed that the Red Guards of China demonstrated the evil that can be done by young people who have a sense of destiny and a total commitment but no sense of history. "Present-ism" is something to be feared; it is a common saying that usually nothing is as old as last week's headlines.

No society has thrived or existed long that has not employed knowledge of a common past as a bond. History has been essential to the maintenance of religions and states. Similarly, it is necessary to all other organized groups — political parties, youth organizations, and schools.

Historical study should be a guide to social action. Statesmen and ordinary citizens, employers and workers, cannot make wise decisions about government, international relations, trade, production, race relations, or any other matter of social significance without considering similar decisions made by people in other times. The study of history teaches skills in gaining and using information. These skills, applied to consideration of the past, are essential in arriving at all kinds of social decisions throughout life.

Because its principal approach is narrative, history has an advantage over other social sciences in the development of social understanding in the elementary school. A story can be followed more easily and can be more interesting to children than the kinds of analyses that are the main devices of the contemporary and behavioral social sciences. Of course, the story should be interesting to children and relevant to matters of enduring importance. Making it so is one of the important tasks of curriculum makers, textbook writers, and teachers.

Human beings are unique in their use of history. Other species which have existed through countless generations have not changed their ways of life through social means. Human beings alone have altered their condition from generation to generation by learning from the past. If they were to ignore history, they would be little different from the brutes. But they cannot ignore history. This being so, it is important that they make conscious use of it.

The study of history is especially important to the citizens of a democracy, for they must determine their own future. This fact was recognized by those who led in the creation of the United States. In drawing up plans for school instruction, both Franklin and Jefferson provided an important place for history. If they chose other words than "relevance" in emphasizing the importance of historical study, they made it clear that they considered such study relevant. Jefferson would have made it the principal study in the elementary school. In his *Notes on the State of Virginia,* written toward the end of the Revolutionary War, he explained the legislation that he had proposed for the establishment of universal education. After setting forth some of the values to be derived from such education, he wrote:

But of the views of this law none is more important, none more legitimate, than that of rendering the people the safe, as they are the ultimate, guardians of their own liberty. For this purpose the reading in the first stage, where they will receive their whole education, is proposed, as has been said, to be chiefly historical. History by apprising them of the past will enable them to judge of the future; it will avail them of the experience of other times and other nations; it will qualify them as judges of the actions and designs of men; it will enable them to know ambition under every disguise it may assume; and knowing it, to defeat its views.

THREE

VARIETY IN APPROACHES TO THE PAST

That there should be a great variety in approaches to the writing of history should not be surprising. Such huge quantities of historical data have survived that even large teams of scholars can read only a small portion of it. Consequently, the organizing patterns for the study of history are as varied as human experience itself. Some writers make general statements covering many centuries while others study individual men, particular nations or special aspects of the past. Writers differ widely in their training, background and method of presentation. "Clio's house," observed Crane Brinton, "is indeed a spacious one, with many different dwelling places, planned and furnished in many different styles."[1]

Nevertheless there are some approaches which are more respected, more common or more enduring than others. Narrative histories, for example, have a long tradition within the profession stretching back to Greek times. Studies of particular nations or

[1] Crane Brinton, "Many Mansions," The American Historical Review, 62(2), January 1964, p. 310.

significant institutions have an honoured place on every historian's bookshelf. The reading public has long been attracted to biographies and a life of a famous politician or statesman is very often on the best-seller list.

Although there have always been mavericks among historians who have rejected the usual or customary approaches, diversity in recent years has become more common and more acceptable. Whereas constitutional history was at one time given a pre-eminent position, historians are now as likely to be studying the arts, social customs and technology of former societies. New dimensions of the past are being explored by the application of techniques and skills developed in other disciplines. Mark Krug has remarked that the new "lenses" of contemporary historians are giving us a different outlook on former societies.[2] A recent panel of experts studying the contribution of new techniques and approaches to the discipline observed that "the nature of history is to thrive on diversity. The various approaches nourish and stimulate one another and the inquiries and findings of any one section are ignored by the others only at their peril."[3]

[2] Mark M. Krug, History and the Social Sciences: New Approaches to the Teaching of Social Studies, (Waltham, Massachusetts, 1967) p. 82.

[3] David S. Landes and Charles Tilly (eds.), History as Social Science, (Englewood Cliffs, New Jersey, 1971) p. 36.

1. Richard Hoggart (b. 1918), a British educator and author, has been a Professor of English at the University of Birmingham in England, and an Assistant Director-General of UNESCO in Paris, France. Although he is an expert on the writings of the English-born poet W. H. Auden, he is noted for his wide interests in cultural studies. In this extract he comments upon the insights that literature can bring to our understanding of the nature of society.

Many students of society, who are historians, social scientists, political scientists and philosophers, find the study of works of literature useful and readily say so. They do not feel threatened by a different kind of discipline or seek to acquire stature from stressing their subject's special mysteries. More important, the high degree of imagination necessary for really distinguished work in any of the humanities or social sciences ensures that men with such powers do not mistake the necessary technical boundaries between academic disciplines for divisions within human experience.

Yet still it is not easy to define exactly in what ways literature illuminates society. One is pointing to something more than the use of literature as

[1] Reprinted from Richard Hoggart, "Literature and Society" in Norman Mackenzie (ed.), *A Guide to the Social Sciences*, 1966, pp. 225-228, 230 with the permission of George Weidenfeld & Nicolson Ltd., London.

documentary illustration, a source of raw material from whatever period one is studying. If one uses it as a quarry to be raided for "background", a mass of evidence which interestingly shows the life of an age but acts only as illustration of the judgements one then makes about a society, one is working *from outside literature* — as a historian or philosopher or social scientist, rather than allowing literature to provide in its own right a form of new and distinctive knowledge about society.

It would be foolish to deny or underestimate this documentary use of literature. Literature can serve such a purpose, most usefully. Imagine a long line of books, all of them normally studied in courses on literature. At one end might be books felt by historians or political scientists or philosophers to belong to their fields as much as to that of the literary student — memoirs, works of philosophy, diaries, letters, essays (and writers such as Defoe, Bunyan, Swift, Pepys, Burke, Newman). Towards the middle are mixed kinds of writing such as philosophical poetry, for instance Pope's *Essay on Man,* and those novels which most evidently illustrate elements in their age. There is a huge range within a range here, from Sterne through Samuel Butler's *The Way of All Flesh* to much of Charles Dickens. Right at the other end of the line are works which seem more 'purely literary', in the sense that their value to students of society is not at first obvious. T. S. Eliot's *Four Quartets* would be a recent example.

Not all these works will have to anything like the same degree that 'something more' than illustrative value I have so far only hinted at. How much of this value they have depends on two things: on their intrinsic power, their power as works of literature; and on our ability to read them as works of literature, rather than to use them as quarries for extraneous building. Properly read — read in and for themselves, with an openness to the author's imagination and art — works of literature give an insight into the life of an age, a kind and intensity of insight, which no other source can give. They are not a substitute for these other sources, and to think so would be foolish. But it is just as foolish to think that these other sources can be sufficient in themselves. Without the full literary witness the student of society will be blind to the fullness of a society's life.

What are these "intrinsic", these peculiar qualities of literature to which a good reader attends? Good literature recreates the sense of life, its weight and texture. It recreates the experiential wholeness of life — of the life of emotions, the life of the mind, the individual life and the social life, the object-laden world. It creates these things all together and interpenetrating, as they do in the lives we live ourselves. Tolstoy knew that a whole range of dissatisfactions felt by an upper middle-class Russian woman in the nineteenth century would suddenly find their focus and demand action when she saw, as though for the first time, the hair sprouting from her distinguished husband's ears. Conrad never ceased to wonder (even more than other novelists) at the way a little gesture, something about a man's clothing or a woman's voice, could focus a whole personal and social situation. Experience is much more complicatedly, much more fluidly, inter-involved than we like to remember; literature makes it harder for us to forget.

Good literature recreates the immediacy of life — the sense that life was and is all these things, all these different orders of things, *all at once.* It embodies the sense of human life developing in a historical and moral context. It recreates the pressure of value-laden life so that — to the extent of the writer's gifts and art — we know better what it must have meant to live and make decisions in that time, at that place, to have thought and felt, to have smelt roast beef, been troubled by falling hair and wondered what one was making of one's life .

Most important of all, literature seeks a new kind of wholeness — to trace the pattern or movement which can lie behind the apparently inchoate details of life. Henry James's novels, for example, often work out polarities between innocence and experience in the lives of individuals and between societies (innocent America and experienced Europe), polarities not 'objectively' evident but nevertheless — he believed — at work deep within the psyches of individuals and the consciousness of societies.

Through literature "we know better what it must have meant . . .", I said a few paragraphs back. Perhaps I should have said "we *feel* we know better". For is our response to literature really a form of knowledge, and if so in what sense?

Some people say it is not. Novels are all very interesting, they may say, and admit that they enjoy reading them. But, they continue, they do not confuse them with *knowledge*. Novels are inventions, fabrications, imaginings. They don't tell us "what it must have meant" or, if they are about contemporary life, "what it really means"; they tell us what someone imagines it must have meant or must mean. They tell us something about him — the writer, in there; not about them — other people, out there. They have no representative significance or meaningful outer reference. They do not therefore belong to the pursuit of knowledge as these people define it, which is the effort after and the considered interpretation of objectively verifiable material, independent of the personality of the enquirer.

As a deliberately adopted professional position (a technical stance) this can, in certain circumstances, be admirable; as a general statement about human life it is one-eyed. In some disciplines one must act as though all knowledge were scientifically verifiable (and in some subjects it can be so defined). In the study of society it cannot be verified in the same way. Sociological and social-psychological techniques are already immensely sophisticated and rightly grow more sophisticated every day; they are still crude in comparison with the complexity of what an unskilled labourer feels on his pulses every day of the week.

*   *   *

A good writer can give us a sense of the formative but largely submerged currents in an age's life. From Jane Austen's books, quite apart from their considerable value as social documents, one of the great re-

wards is this sense of the way life was lived 'in the bone' at her time —
that behind people's actions and reactions lay *this* particular sense of
England's destiny, *these* assumptions about the relations between the sexes,
about class and money and duty. Similarly though more broadly we gain
from the great nineteenth-century Russian novelists a wonderfully close
sense of the inwardness of Russian life at the time—mercifully, in view
of the much more prescribed access one has today to Russian life. The
earlier insights give at any rate some imaginative perspective.

*2. The relationship of biography to history has always been very
close. Books such as Donald G. Creighton's two-volume study of Sir
John A. Macdonald or William Kilbourn's poetic study of William
Lyon Mackenzie have been considered models of both brilliant
biography and fine history.* "Biography," Allan Nevins tells us,
"is the indispensable ally and supporter of history."†*

*Nevertheless, there have been occasions in recent years when
biographers and historians seemed to drift apart. On the one hand,
some biographers, such as Lytton Strachey, used methods that were
unacceptable to historians: on the other, the interest taken by the
historical profession in the social science aspect of their craft alien-
ated biographers. In an address to the Canadian Historical Association, John M. Gray surveyed the common ground between these two
forms of writing. Mr. Gray, President of the Macmillan Company
of Canada since 1955, is a distinguished figure in Canadian letters,
being the author of, among other works,* Lord Selkirk of Red River
(Toronto, 1963).

It seems that at least there was a time when historians moving towards
more scientific history were right to distrust biography; and when biography, whatever else it was, was not a method of writing history that anyone could approve. One cannot now imagine a serious biographer —
whether trained as an historian or not — leaving any available channel
undredged for sources. The change from 1907 to 1947 has produced an
attitude that biographers of the last century would not easily believe in.
Yet the change does not wholly answer our questions. For if history is
a science, then biography is not history — and will never be. That isn't
to say that in serious biography anyone should condone inaccuracy, or
that biography has nothing to contribute to historical studies. It is simply
that biography's highest requirement is to present the living image, the

*Donald Creighton, John A. Macdonald, 2 volumes, (Toronto, 1952, 1955)
and William Kilbourn, The Firebrand: William Lyon Mackenzie and the
Rebellion in Upper Canada, (Toronto, 1956).

†Allan Nevins, The Gateway to History, (New York, 1962) p. 369.

[2] Reprinted from J. M. Gray, "Biography as History," *Canadian
Historical Association Report 1965*, pp. 148-149, 152, 153 with the
permission of the author, John Morgan Gray.

re-creation of a man, and this may demand the exclusion of much historically useful information that would clog the narrative or otherwise interfere with that purpose. It may also require the inclusion of much that is historically trivial, in the process of making the narrative live. For if it does not live it is not biography. The biographical form has its roots deep in literature, and we have yet to discover that it can flourish in any other soil.

To many historians it will seem that the biography I approve is under-researched and over-written. But I talked about the deliberate exclusion of information. It is one thing to exclude facts and quite another to be unaware of them. The biographer who would produce a convincing likeness must know everything he possibly can — however seemingly trivial — about his subject. Then, out of the great heap of crude ore he has mined, he must smelt the pure metal that is to his purpose, and out of it shape the likeness that will persuade us of its truth to life. Have I to an extent described also the process of writing history? I presume I have, but I have not at the same time convinced myself or you that biography and history occupy the same room; difficulties remain. Let me suggest an example. I believe that David Cecil's *The Young Melbourne* has been rightly praised as a fine example of the art of biography, though as history I think it is not wholly satisfactory. It is a moving and intensely interesting account of an historical figure, set against a lightly but carefully sketched background of the Regency period in England. It gives a surprising insight into the times without telling us a great deal about them. It gives great depth of understanding of the character of a public man while telling us almost nothing of his public life. What has the bewitching and tragically foolish Lady Caroline Lamb to do with early-nineteenth-century England — she who occupies about half this book? Almost nothing. But she had a great deal to do with the making, and almost the breaking, of a future prime minister. Is this to the purpose of history? I believe many of you would say that it is; yet I also believe that few historians could have written this book, and fewer still would have attempted it in this way. I wonder why?

The answer may lie in the historian's unwillingness to recognize both the opportunities and the limitations of the biographical form. It can do some things supremely well, and others it should not attempt; it cannot encompass all the materials of history. History takes all time and all place for its province; not that all periods of history are equally important, but none defy being written about except as source material may be limited. Yet, not all people are fit subjects for biography — not even all the people who have shaped history. History has to concern itself with material whether it is of general interest or not. Biography does not have to, indeed should not — and that is perhaps enough to make it suspect. Because, what do we mean by "general interest"? The highly personal aspect of the selection of topic, the highly personal point of view, are enough to make the scholar wary. The necessity to provide interest is obviously full of traps: the danger of heightening a scene and thus shading its truth; the danger of over-simplifying a character or his motives, when character and motives are seldom simple.

*   *   *

In the end the argument over the values and weaknesses of biography as history seem to me little more than an aside in the continuing debate between — in whatever form — a scientific and literary approach to history. Apart from the demands of art, biography with its necessarily narrow-angled lens will produce some distortion; but it is a distortion that is well understood and easily corrected; and the lens can bring out detail as well as provide the warmth of a burning-glass.

*   *   *

In all this I have nowhere intended to suggest that good biography can ever be unassailable history — any more than good history can in our day be unassailable history. But good biography is not the more assailable by reason of its literary form. Truth in biography and in history is subject to much the same conflicts or deficiencies of evidence, and to that host of human failings that seem likely to outlast and outsmart the computer: unrecognized prejudice, inadequate capacity, failure of imagination and patience and nerves. Apart from these, biography may be more subject to error in the extent to which individuals remain even more mysterious than events. This risk seems to me offset by its greater reach, that quality referred to by Trevelyan of being "more personal, human and intimate". That is not to say that it is a greater or lesser accomplishment, only that it can do for history (if indeed they are separate and distinct) what history can hardly do for itself. It can more easily reach the reading public. It can awaken a taste for history, and bring you readers more prepared to make the effort to deepen their knowledge and broaden their perspectives. It can help to answer for you that maddening and largely uninformed cry that "Canadian history is dull". History, it seems to me, fights always on two fronts — or should : one is the battle to expand the bridgehead of truth: the other is a battle for attention, to communicate the truth as it appears. In both battles biography can be history's strongest ally.

3.   One of the ways in which historians differ is the scale *upon which they write. Some, such as William H. McNeill in his re-markable* The Rise of the West *(Chicago, 1963), take the entire story of man as their subject. Others prefer to reflect upon the story of one nation or to deal with an entire continent or a small part of one country. They recognize, however, key differences in writing each of these types. Organizing evidence or formulating generalizations*

[3] Reprinted from H. P. R. Finberg, "The Local Historian and His Theme" in H. P. R. Finberg and V. H. T. Skipp, *Local History: Objective and Pursuit,* 1967, pp. 10-13, 14-15 with the permission of the author and the publisher, David and Charles (Holdings) Ltd., Devon.

may be quite a different matter for a multi-national history as compared to the history of a small region. Every form that history takes poses its own definitional problems.

Take, for example, the case of local history. Thirty or more years ago when many historians were deeply committed to studying the workings of the nation, local history tended to be left to amateurs or antiquarians. A number of pioneers, including the author of the following reading, have devoted a large proportion of their lives' work to changing this image. The first Professor of English Local History in that nation's Universities and author of many brilliant local studies, Mr. Finberg has tried to explain to his colleagues and to the general public the particular differences of his own special field.

The business of the local historian, . . . as I see it, is to re-enact in his own mind, and to portray for his readers, the Origin, Growth, Decline, and Fall of a Local Community. If this principle is accepted, it becomes possible to define with something like precision the relationship between his study and other disciplines, whether academic or non-academic. The sources he must consult will be part written, part unwritten. In so far as he deals with unwritten evidences, we may style him an archaeologist. He is also a geographer, since part of his task is to elucidate in detail the process of *défrichement* — we have no English word for it — whereby the soil of his parish has been subdued to human purposes by gradual conquest of the primeval marsh or woodland. He is not a geologist, but he interrogates the geologist on the character of the soil and the structure of the underlying rocks, because without this knowledge he cannot rightly interpret the effects of human action upon the landscape. His contribution to historical geography demands an intensive observation of fields, hedges, roads, and water-courses. Much of his time is thus spent out of doors; but since field-work must be controlled and amplified by documentary research, he is also an assiduous visitor at libraries, record offices, and muniment rooms. He is an economic historian because the greater part of man's life is spent in gaining a livelihood, and a historian of art and education and religion because man does not live by bread alone. Though he never, I hope, utters the fatuous word 'medieval', which has even less meaning for local than for national and ecumenical history, he is perforce a medievalist because the so-called Middle Ages were the formative period in the life of most English towns and villages, and indeed covered something like two-thirds of their whole existence. But he is also a modernist, if that is the right word, because many of them survived as local communities into the age of railways and motor transport. He is thus not a specialist in any one period; nor is his an antiquarian pursuit. Antiquary is a word of fluid meaning, but I take it to mean one who studies the monuments of antiquity — usually a single class of monument — for their own sakes. For the antiquarian the sculptures on the west front of Barchester cathedral, or the cross-legged effigies in the parish churches, are objects to be studied in relation to each other and to similar monuments elsewhere. For the historian they are particular manifestations or expressions of a social life which he is trying to reconstruct in its entirety.

It is sometimes held that local history provides a useful method of approach to national history. And it is true that sometimes a train of momentous happenings is found to have been touched off in some village whose chronicler, by revealing this fact, teaches the national historian something he might not have discovered for himself. It is also true that if the histories of all our parishes were written as they should be written, the history of England would need to be revised at many points. It may be, also, that a teacher who wishes to give his pupils something more than a 'notional apprehension' of English history will find it helpful to illustrate the Wars of the Roses by showing them the tomb of Sir William in the parish church, or the strife of Cavalier and Roundhead by pointing out the ruins of Sir Lionel's mansion. But I am quite sure that to esteem local history only or chiefly for its propaedeutic value is to underestimate it, and that to treat it as an introduction or a contribution to national history is to invert the true relationship between them. We may grant that the history of Meryton or Mellstock will help us to understand the history of England, just as the history of England will help us to understand the history of Western Christendom; but it remains true that a study of the whole will do more to enlighten us about any single part than vice versa. In other words, when we are sufficiently familiar with the European past to read English history intelligently, and when we are thoroughly well grounded in the history of England: then, and not till then, can we begin to think of writing the history of Liverpool or Lydiard Millicent or Saffron Walden. Local history is not an elementary study. It is one to which the amateur or the young student can, and often does, make a valuable contribution; but in its higher reaches it demands mature scholarship and a wide background of general culture.

Another claim that I will venture to make for it is that local history is pre-eminently a humane discipline. Let me recall here the well-known little rhyme:

> *The art of biography*
> *Is different from geography.*
> *Geography is about maps,*
> *But biography is about chaps.*

History too is "about chaps," and local history brings us nearer to the common run of chaps than any other branch of historical study. It gives us, in the language of the films, a close-up of them on their farms and in their workshops and behind their counters. It studies them as social beings, as members of a rural or urban community; but by seeking them at their home address it enables us to see them as flesh and blood, and not just as pawns on the national chessboard. The national historian, dealing with some vast agglomeration which he labels villeins, Puritans, the lower middle-class, or what you will, tends to lose sight of the human person.[1]

*   *   *

The standpoint of an angel, gazing with pity and comprehension at the antics of mortal men, is of course beyond our reach, but one can think of several purely human standpoints from which national history could be studied more intelligently than from that of the group which has contrived to make itself, at a given moment, master of the state. Local history brings us face to face with the Englishman at home, and reminds us that it is he who foots the bill his rulers have run up for him. By so doing, it restrains the propensity to worship mere power and success, a propensity which loses none of its baseness from being carried back into our study of the past.

[1] Even in the study of history a kind of acquired simplicity is needed just to see things as they really are, just to see things naked, instead of envisaging them in the categories which historians have created to fit them into—attributing things to the Renaissance.

4. Our view of the past is often changed by the kinds of questions that we pose to our evidence. Many of these questions are inspired by work in other disciplines. In the following extract, for example, Dr. John H. Trueman revises the traditional interpretation of the "Dark" Ages by examining their achievements in technology. Author of many highly commended high school history texts, Dr. Trueman is particularly interested in medieval history. Currently he is a Professor in the Department of History and Associate Dean of Humanities at McMaster University in Hamilton, Ontario.

First, what is technology? It may be defined as the application of science to industry — if we understand the terms "science" and "industry" as being used very broadly. Technology may involve the way a cave man produces his flint axes, shaping them by trial and error until he knows exactly how to do it and can manufacture axes by the handful. Or technology may involve more complex developments, such as manufacturing clay bricks, or bronze shields, or iron swords.

The interesting thing to note in studying history is that technology and its accompanying inventions cannot be forced into the ancient, medieval, and modern compartments which we use to chronicle political and cultural history. In fact, as a distinguished American historian has written, there "is more historical continuity in the progress of European technology in the last 3000 years than in art, literature, philosophy, or scholarship."

[4] Reprinted from John H. Trueman, "New Light on the Dark Ages," *Canadian Journal of History and Social Science,* 1(4) May 1966, pp. 8-9, 9-10, 11-12 with the permission of the publishers.

There was, as Lynn White has incisively demonstrated in his *Medieval Technology and Social Change*,[1] a steady progress in technology even after Rome fell. For, strange as it may seem, adverse conditions — political disintegration and confusion, even economic depression — have been known to stimulate technological developments. The barbarians that flooded into Western Europe brought with them a number of articles and customs that the Romans did not have: trousers, fur garments, the easily heated house as contrasted with the Mediterranean patio type, the use of soap, the ski, barrels and tubs, the stirrup, and a number of other things which we take for granted, but which the ancient world lacked. Most important of all, they brought with them a new type of plough.

* * *

As you can understand, a heavy wheeled northern plough had a number of advantages over the light scratch-plough. It eliminated the necessity of cross-ploughing, thereby decreasing the peasant's work and increasing the area of land he could cultivate. It also changed the shape of the fields. Since the new plough needed only to plough in one direction, the squarish field of the scratch-plough became the long, narrow field of the heavy wheeled plough. But the mouldboard was fixed and not reversible. Hence ploughing could not be done one furrow beside the other, coming and going, because the furrow-slice would always fall to the same side. With the fixed-mouldboard plough, the first furrow had to be cut down the middle of the field, and then the other furrows were ploughed alternately on the left and right sides of it. The result was the "high-ridged" field, which in cross-section developed an arched appearance. The arch, in turn, had its advantage: even in the wettest years a crop could be raised on the crests of the ridges, while in dry times the depressions between the crests retained moisture and promoted growth. The third advantage of the heavy plough was the most important of all. The peasant could now cultivate the heavy rich soils of the bottom land, and raise on them far better crops than he could ever hope to get from light upland soil. The result, of course, was that productivity rose in northern Europe.

The introduction of the heavy plough had one further consequence. Because it required more than one yoke of oxen to pull it, the peasants had to pool their oxen in order to assemble the three or four yokes needed to pull the plough. To make use of the plough teams effectively it was apparently decided to distribute the land in a sequence of strips to the various peasants who owned the plough and the oxen. Thus a single peasant's holdings were divided up into scattered strips in the two or three large unfenced or "open" fields of the manor. It did not make sense to let each peasant plant whatever he pleased; so the custom grew up of planting all the strips in one large open field at the same time, while letting all the strips in one other large open field lie fallow.

[1] Oxford, 1962; paper-back edition, 1964.

Thus you can see how the wide use of the heavy plough in northern Europe turned out to be a revolutionary technological innovation which changed the peasant's whole way of life.

Along with the use of the northern heavy plough came three other startling innovations. The Greeks and Romans had been unbelievably inefficient in their use of horses. Horseshoes had not been invented, with the result that many an animal became useless because of broken hooves. Secondly, only the yoke system of harness was used — a system well suited to oxen but not to horses. For it consisted of two straps encircling the belly and neck of the animal, and, when a horse pulled, the neck-strap pressed on its jugular vein and windpipe, tending to choke it and restrict the flow of blood to its head. And finally, the ancients harnessed their teams side by side, a method that resulted in a smaller force in a forward direction than if the teams were harnessed one behind the other by an extension of the traces.

*   *   *

When we add together all this information on ploughs, open fields, horseshoes, horse collars, and tandem harnessing, the sum total is a medieval agricultural revolution. The horse moves more swiftly than the ox, and can work an hour or two longer each day. In northern Europe, where the climate is temperamental, such staying-power was important since often the success of a crop depended on ploughing and planting under favourable circumstances. But there was one drawback. The horse might be rapid — but it was also expensive. For it burns an expensive fuel, grain, while its slow cousin the ox can subsist on a cheaper food, hay. To use horses it would be necessary to have surplus grain left over to feed them. Was there such a surplus?

For southern Europe the answer was no. The two-field system provided not much more than enough to feed man and ox. One field was ploughed in the fall and planted with winter wheat or rye that would be harvested the next spring. The other field lay fallow, but was ploughed twice to turn under the weeds. No summer planting was done at all, because summer rain was too scarce.

But in the north where the climate was temperate, two crops a year were possible. By dividing up the land of the manor into three main fields, there could be one fallow field (ploughed twice), one field ploughed once and planted in the fall with winter wheat or rye to be harvested the next spring, and one field ploughed once and planted in the spring with oats, barley, peas, or beans, to be harvested in the fall. The result of the three-field system, then, was less ploughing for more crop. The three-field system could not possibly work in southern Europe because of the lack of summer rainfall. In the north, however, the climate was suited to it. Combine with this climate the heavy plough, which made it possible to cultivate rich northern European soils, and the new harness, which allowed the horses to exert more power to pull the plough, and you have the necessary elements for greatly increased food production.

The three-field system had, as you can see, marked advantages over the two-field system. It distributed the labour of ploughing, sowing, and harvesting more evenly over the year. It reduced the possibility of famine by diversifying crops. And, most important of all, the spring planting allowed the production of certain very important crops. Although grass or hay provide sufficient calcium for bones, the phosphorus and protein necessary for muscle growth must come from grains. This phosphorus and protein is best provided by oats; hence oats is the best possible food for horses. Now the three-field system gave northern Europeans a surplus of oats for their horses, while peas and beans, also planted in the spring, furnished the people with protein to balance the carbohydrates already provided by the wheat and rye of the fall planting. The effect of more and better food on northern Europe was marked. There was a population explosion.

And what follows? By about the year 1000 the focus of Europe had shifted from the Mediterranean Sea to the plains of the north. It was on those well-watered plains with their summer rainfall that the heavy wheeled plough was pulled by horses whose diet consisted of oats. It was on those plains that slavery died out quickly after the year 900, as the cumulative effects of animal-power supplemented by water- and wind-power (the latter two of which there has been no time to discuss here) replaced human by non-human energy. It was on those northern plains that towns sprang up, towns fed with the new surplus crops.

So it came to pass that for the first time in history there arose a complex civilization which was not supported by the bent backs of slaves or coolies. Such a civilization — a civilization not dependent on slaves — had never been seen before. Egypt, Greece, and Rome had had their power and their glory. But it was in the "Dark Ages", on the northern plains of Europe, that slavery died out.

How dark were the "Dark Ages"? Not dark at all from the technological point of view. It is true that men forgot Greek, and their Latin would have scandalized Cicero. Nevertheless, the rough peasants of the Middle Ages worked a noiseless revolution on the plains of northern Europe.

---

5. In a perceptive article included in Sociology and History: Methods, *the late Richard Hofstadter noted that the barriers between history and sociology were visibly melting. Historians, he said, were becoming more sensitive to the importance of social mobility, kinship, the social role of ideologies, acculturation and life styles.* In the following reading, Fernand Ouellet, Professor of History at Carleton University, illustrates how collaboration between the two*

*Seymour Martin Lipset and Richard Hofstadter, Sociology and History: Methods (New York, 1968) pp. 14-15.

[5] Reprinted from Fernand Ouellet, "Histoire et Sociologie: Le point de vue d'un Historien," *Canadian Historical Association Annual Report, 1966,* pp. 170-173 with the permission of the author.

disciplines can be fruitful. Dr. Ouellet *is the author of* Histoire économique et sociale du Québec: Structures et conjoncture *(Montreal, 1966) a brilliant example of the application of new questions from related disciplines to a study of the past. (See Appendix for translation of this article.)*

Histoire et sociologie, c'est d'abord au niveau de l'histoire sociale que les échanges seront sans doute les plus fructueux. C'est davantage sur le plan d'une conception historique qui accorde moins d'attention à l'individuel, au singulier comme tels qu'au groupe et au collectif. Lucien Fèbvre définissait ainsi l'histoire: "Histoire, science de l'homme, ne l'oublions jamais. Science du changement perpétuel des sociétés humaines, de leur perpétuel et nécessaire réajustement à des conditions neuves d'existence matérielle, politique, morale, religieuse, intellectuelle. Science de cet accord qui se négocie, de cette harmonie qui s'établit perpétuellement et spontanément, à toutes les époques, entre les conditions diverses et synchroniques d'existence des hommes: conditions matérielles, conditions techniques, conditions spirituelles."[8]

Assumer cette définition de l'histoire, c'est admettre l'inter-dépendance des différents paliers où évolue l'homme vivant en société. Certes l'histoire économique est intéressante en elle-même, mais elle l'est davantage dans sa résonance sociale, voire dans ses implications politiques, même mentales. De même l'histoire sociale à l'état pur, si elle est possible, n'a qu'une valeur limitée et elle n'acquiert de perspective véritable qu'en s'alimentant en plus aux réalités économiques, démographiques, politiques et mentales. Cette approche nous paraît tout aussi évidente pour l'histoire politique et la démographie historique que pour l'étude des idées. Car la réalité historique ne se laisse pas aisément ranger sous une seule étiquette, si évidente soit-elle en apparence. Elle est variée et complexe. Les travaux d'Ernest Labrousse, de Georges Lefèbvre et d'Albert Soboul sur la Révolution française[9] illustrent le caractère fécond d'une acceptation de l'histoire comme "totale".

Une telle perception du métier d'historien, loin de réduire les exigences concrètes du travail de l'historien, les accroît. En effet l'histoire tend à passer du stade qualitatif pour essayer de devenir quantitative. A ce niveau, au reste, le document individuel a beaucoup moins de sens que les grandes séries: les collections et les fonds d'archives. Il est évident, d'autre part, que l'introduction de la mesure est plus facile en histoire économique que dans les autres domaines. Là encore il faut se garder de toute illusion.

[8] L. Fèbvre, Combats pour l'histoire, p. 31 et suiv.

[9] Signalons ici livre récent d'Albert Soboul, The Parisian Sans-Culottes and the French Revolution, 1793-94, Oxford Press, London, 1964, 280 p. Les titres de chapitres suffisent à indiquer l'approche globale: Mentality and Social Composition, Social Aspirations, Political Leanings, Practical Applications of Sans Culottes Politics, Political Organization, Daily Life of the Mlitant Sans-Culotte, Popular Movement and Bourgeois Revolution. Les livres de Labrousse et Lefèbvre sont trop connus pour qu'une mention détaillée soit nécessaire.

Car le chiffre n'avait pas la même importance autrefois qu'aujourd'hui. En tête de leur vaste étude sur *Séville et l'Atlantique* pendant le siècle qui suit la découverte de l'Amerique, Huguette et Pierre Chaunu écrivent: "Est-il vrai qu'il n'y ait de science que du mesurable et que l'histoire puisse et doive, dans ce sens même, prétendre à une promotion scientifique . . . il est évident qu'on ne peut pas atteindre à une connaissance satisfaisante d'une économie présente ou passée, si on ne la réduit à la mesure. Et sans connaître la réalité matérielle, que saurait-on du temps passé? . . . Et puisque l'on parle couramment d'un Ancien Régime politique et économique, il est commode de parler, à l'intérieur même de ce système périmé, d'un Ancien Régime de la mesure, désignant par là les siècles pour lesquels l'historien doit être son propre statisticien.[10]" Placer l'histoire sous le signe de la mesure, non seulement pour une meilleure connaissance des économies mais aussi des autres secteurs, c'est déjà faire le pont avec les autres sciences de l'homme. Il est vrai que la mesure n'est pas une fin en soi mais, grâce à elle, il devient possible d'approfondir le passé dans sa totalité. Frédéric Mauro, au début de son histoire quantitative du *Portugal et de l'Atlantique au XVIIe siècle,* affirme à propos de son entreprise: "Cependant il a voulu répondre aux exigences de la science historique contemporaine: essai d'histoire économique, il a voulu être à la fois géographie, sociologie et théorie économique du passé. Il a cherché à utiliser les ressources de la technologie et de la statistique et les concepts que la science sociale du présent mettait à sa disposition. Il ne les a, certes pas, appliqués brutalement, car les mots et les systèmes ont leur temps et ceux d'aujourd'hui ne doivent pas suggérer au chercheur ceux qu'il crée pour l'investigation et la compréhension du passé[11]." Ces ambitions quantitatives et cette ré-orientation progressive des perspectives suggèrent de plus en plus à l'historien d'aborder l'étude du passé selon deux dimensions fondamentales: les structures et la conjoncture.

Découvrir les cadres, les systèmes et les éléments durables à l'intérieur desquels évolue l'homme, tel est certainement un des objectifs de l'historien désireux d'expliquer adéquatement le passé. Pas plus que les déterminismes géographiques n'échappent à son investigation, les structures économiques ne doivent demeurer étrangères à l'historien. Car l'économie n'est pas une accumulation d'activités disparates, livrées aux fantaisies individuelles et dénuées de rapports entre elles. Des hiérarchies existent, des dépendances s'affirment entre les différents secteurs qui tendent à se regrouper autour d'une ou plusieurs activités dominantes. En somme l'aménagement de l'espace, même sans être formellement planifié, ne s'opère pas au hasard. Il est la résultante d'une certaine ordonnance quand il n'est pas le produit d'un système. Il en est de même de la société.

Sans doute celle-ci est-elle formée d'individus, jouissant d'une autonomie plus ou moins grande, mais elle est en même temps composée de groupes,

---

[10] Pierre et Huguette Chaunu, Séville et l'Atlantique, 1504-1650, volume d'introduction méthodologique, p. 6.

[11] F. Mauro, Le Portugal et l'Atlantique au XVIIe siècle, 1570-1670, p. 1.

de classes, parfois de castes, ayant leurs intérêts propres et leurs valeurs particulières. Dans toute société, même dans celles qui prétendent avoir réalisé un certain nivellement des conditions, il existe des élites qui ont tendance à s'identifier à l'ensemble de la société et à modeler celle-ci en fonction de leurs intérêts et de leurs valeurs. L'équilibre de la société dépend certes de facteurs proprement sociaux mais trouve en outre son support dans l'arrière-plan économique aussi bien que dans les réseaux institutionnels qui la fondent et l'expriment. Cette solidarité entre économie, société et institutions est loin d'être absolue: des désaccords plus ou moins profonds existent et des décalages s'inscrivent qui indiquent que même les structures les plus fermes sont en perpétuelle évolution. La création de la Commission internationale d'histoire des mouvements sociaux et des structures sociales illustre bien cette nouvelle préoccupation des historiens. Les mêmes rapports étroits subsistent entre les structures sociales et les mentalités, au point que la notion de structure mentale, comme celle d'idéologie, commence à entrer dans le vocabulaire des historiens. Robert Mandrou, au terme de son livre sur la France moderne défini comme un essai de psychologie historique, écrit : "Cette reconstitution de visions du monde individuelles prend sa pleine valeur dans la mesure où elle débouche sur une typologie, où elle permet de reconstruire des visions socialisées: c'est le groupe qui est important, car il pèse toujours de tout le poids des conformismes sociaux sur les individualités[12]." Si l'historien est entraîné à penser en termes de structures, qu'elles soient économiques, sociales, politiques ou autres, c'est que la compréhension du passé dans sa complexité l'y incite fortement. C'est aussi qu'il est impossible de saisir adéquatement une évolution sans avoir une connaissance suffisante du tout organisé qui évolue.

Les structures, quelles que soient leur résistance ou leur durée, se font et se défont, soit en raison de nécessités internes, soit sous l'effet de conjonctures particulières. L'idée de conjoncture, puisée chez les économistes, tend à acquérir dans le langage des historiens une signification beaucoup plus vaste. Pierre Chaunu écrit à ce sujet: "L'inexorable conjoncture, dont on sait maintenant qu'elle transcende sociétés, continents et systèmes politiques . . . d'autant plus inexorable qu'elle est moins extérieure à l'homme, mais bien l'expression la plus profonde du rythme propre de toutes les sociétés humaines[13]." Ainsi envisagée la conjoncture n'est pas

[12] R. Mandrou, Introduction à la France moderne. 1500-1640. Essai de psychologie historique, p. 351. Voir aussi son livre: Classes et luttes de classes en France au début du XVIIe siècle, 125 p.

[13] P. Chaunu, op. cit., p. 22. Dans l'énorme volume consacré aux structures atlantiques dans la même série, l'auteur écrit: "Tout élément isolé du Social global, pour être soumis à l'analyse scientifique, possède une certaine durée. La répartition des phénomènes socio-économiques entre structures, ce qui dure et conjoncture, ce qui passe, n'est en rien immuable. Parler de structures et de conjoncture ne signifie, donc, pas autre chose qu'une volonté de classement autour d'un axe temps. Dans la mesure où le temps est la dimension de l'histoire, celle qui confère son originalité au milieu des sciences de l'homme et sa supériorité dans la hiérarchie dans les sciences du Social, la classification entre structures et conjoncture convient admirablement à tout travail d'histoire." P. Chaunu, Séville et l'Atlantique. Les structures, p. 12.

seulement économique, démographique, militaire et politique, elle mobilise en même temps la société et les mentalités. En un mot, elle possède un caractère global. Il est vrai que les rythmes et les tendances de l'économie sont particulièrement significatifs. Car la conjoncture économique, parce qu'elle affecte le statut des groupes et des classes, qu'elle confirme ou remet en question certains réseaux institutionnels, et qu'elle déclenche des réactions psychologiques, agit directement ou indirectement sur la société. Peu ou point de tensions, de conflits ou de mouvements sociaux ou politique qui ne soient d'une façon ou d'une autre liés aux conditions économiques. C'est souvent à l'intérieur des crises que mûrissent les prises de conscience les plus décisives. L'inverse est d'ailleurs vrai. Les changements même passagers dans la société se répercutent au niveau économique. Le contexte démographique toujours très important en arrive, à certains moments, à exercer une action décisive sur les groupes et les psychologies. Qui oserait nier les implications multiples et profondes de l'immigration loyaliste, des arrivages massifs d'immigrants britanniques après 1815 et du surpeuplement des seigneuries dans le Bas-Canada à la même période? Les inter-actions entre économie, société et démographie sont continuelles, assurant selon les moments la primauté l'un ou l'autre de ces facteurs.

6. *The relationship between history and geography has always been close. "We can discern no high walls between them, no defensive moat, no tariff frontiers," H. C. Darby tells us.* More than one historian, indeed, has suggested that for some purposes sturdy boots are more useful than reading desks.†*

In the following extract, Dr. George Tomkins discusses the contribution of historical geography to Canadian Studies. An Associate Professor in the Faculty of Education at the University of British Columbia, Dr. Tomkins spent the year 1971-1972 as Director of the Canada Studies Foundation.

It should be said right away that there is a certain inevitable ambiguity about a sub-discipline that occupies the boundary between history and geography. From one viewpoint, the historical geographer uses the data and materials of the historian, as well as the latter's method, for geographical purposes. That is to say, he seeks to reconstruct the geography of the past, to ascertain distributions, spatial relationships or regional character at some previous time.

As an example of the approach, we may imagine the teacher who wishes his pupils to gain some appreciation of the evolution of the rural landscape

---

*"Historical Geography" in H. P. R. Finberg, (ed.), Approaches to History (Toronto, 1962) p. 156.

†A. L. Rowse, The Use of History (London, 1946) pp. 41-43.

[6] Reprinted from G. S. Tomkins, "Historical geography: An Approach to Canadian Studies," *Monday Morning,* Volume 3(9), May 1969, p. 40, with the permission of the author.

of Southern Ontario. He might turn to an historical document in the form of extracts from a letter written home by Thomas Radcliff, a young Irish immigrant who had settled in Upper Canada in 1832. The letter is available in an interesting collection, *Authentic Letters from Upper Canada* (Pioneer Books, Macmillan):

We are now, thank God in perfect health . . . and absolutely enjoying . . . a comfortable residence in our own loghouse, the timbers of which, about three months ago, displayed their leafy honours in the wild forest. It consists of a cellar, three rooms and a small store-room in the principal story and two bed-rooms in the roof . . . The edifice is thirty feet by twenty-five, from out to out. For the five rooms we have three flues and two stoves and mean to be very snug and warm . . . I have discovered limestone . . . for building the stack of chimneys and plastering the interior of the house . . . and it may answer very well . . . till I can build a frame-house of greater dimensions which I mean to do . . .

Radcliff then explains that his land has a rolling surface except for some 'flats' where it is drained by a creek or small rivers. It is well forested, and he aims to remove all trees except for some 'ornamental timber' and a few maples. His letter continues:

The quality of the timber denotes the richness of the soil. Ours consists of maple, beech, butternut, elm, white ash, hornbeam, a sprinkling of oak, and some cherry and basswood . . . I find [the soil] to be, in surface, five inches of black vegetable mould, over a few inches of clay loam . . . and almost all my land of this description, is an extended level of wheat soil, without the least unevenness. The knowing ones who have seen it say it will give wheat forever; and speak of fifty bushels to the statute acre . . .

I bought a young milch cow and calf for twenty-four dollars — she gives a good supply of milk and cream . . .

I have been occupied in getting as many acres as I can cleared and prepared for cropping. Sixteen are already under operation which will make a good open about the house . . .

Radcliff then describes various methods of removing the trees which were burned to produce ashes, the first 'crop' on a pioneer farm in Upper Canada. An acre of his timber produced about 60 bushels of ashes, to be sold to the nearest ashery. There potash was made, for use in manufacturing glass, soap and other commodities.

Use of the above documentary material, in conjunction with appropriate pictures of pioneer settlement, would enable pupils to understand some aspects of the economic history of Upper Canada and to reconstruct the landscape as it must have appeared in Radcliff's time. Skilful questioning should bring out such points as the type of building materials used, the various uses made of timber, the pioneer attitude towards the forest, the type of woodland that covered Southern Ontario at the time, the quality of the soils, land use and sources of income and so on. Other points to be brought out would include: ashes as a first 'crop'; wheat as the characteristic pioneer crop; the influence of wheat on commercial development, notably on the development of transportation; reasons for the decline of wheat in Upper Canada later in the century; the development of dairy farming and, by 1900, the first appearance of specialized agriculture (such as Niagara fruit) in Southern Ontario.

What makes this material historical *geography* (as distinct from economic and social history which it also is) is the use the teacher and pupils make of it. That is to say, the focus is on the landscape and on its essential character. To be sure, the historian does not necessarily neglect these, but his focus is more likely to be on men, their institutions and the society they created. The geographer is more interested in how these interacted with the natural environment to create past and present landscapes. His enterprise is essentially a study of the geography of change. Every landscape is in the process of becoming different from what it is at a given moment.

7. To conclude this chapter on varieties of history, it may be useful to examine a bold statement of how history differs from other disciplines. In the following reading, Dr. Gordon Leff, Professor of History at York University in England, argues forcefully for the recognition of certain essential features in history.

I want to argue that it is precisely the dynamic, relative character of history, its preoccupation with the specific and the concrete, its lack of regularity, that makes it indispensable to all social and human understanding; and that the rejection of the old notion of historical destiny for that of the future as open gives history a greater importance now, when so much more depends upon our conscious choices, than in the past. In my view the present unsatisfactory state of the social studies, including much history, is directly attributable to the failure to recognise this. What we need is to reinstate the historical dimension into our thinking, not to escape from it into a world of non-temporal abstractions.

I have two grounds for saying this. The first is the opposite of the traditional defence of history: namely, that as the study of the past it offers us precedents for the present. I don't deny that it may, or that there is an obvious connection between the past and present. It is rather that this is largely irrelevant to understanding either the past or the present. No doubt, in certain situations, parallels with the past can provide a moral boost, as with the parallels drawn in 1940 between Britain's situation then and in 1800. But most of history does not revolve around such comparisons, and when it does the result is usually history at its most jejune. Why? Because history, although it is directed to the past, is essentially about the new. It is read and written as the unfolding of events which by definition have not occurred before. That is the only reason for their having a history.

[7] Reprinted from Gordon Leff, "The Past and the New," *The Listener*, 81, 10 April 1969, pp. 485-486, with the permission of the author.

If Hitler's invasion threat in 1940 had been identical with Napoleon's in 1800, no separate study of Hitler's would be needed: we should merely say: "For Hitler in 1940 see Napoleon 1800." We don't do this, precisely because they were different, even if the circumstances were in each case similar.

Now the very need for precedents is evidence that we are confronted with something outside our previous experience, and the fact that we rarely find them beyond the most superficial and formal resemblances in history is no less evidence that history is the record of difference rather than of similarity. Let me develop that. Of course in one sense there is an overall similarity in history since it is about men; but this doesn't give it continuity. Indeed what distinguishes history and the human studies is that they are built around change, whether of a culture, a language, a system of law or institutions. Only when they are treated as abstractions can they be regarded as constant. But to see social phenomena exclusively in abstract and static terms does not make for superior knowledge: indeed often quite the reverse.

That is where history, indeed all social knowledge, is different from the natural and formal sciences. Where these last pre-suppose determinism, the repetition of the same processes given the same conditions, history pre-supposes contingency: that no two individuals or their circumstances will be exactly the same. Men's human history, as opposed to their natural history, is not the repetition of endless life cycles of individuals, but of repeated changes, which break the cycle and give it a new direction. History is written around these. Not every occurrence has to be a turning-point to be significant; but history can only be conceived in terms of difference, even if it is only the formal differences of one king succeeding another. And when it is only formal, so is the history written about it. Even the old-fashioned history books passed rapidly over the reigns of the unimportant kings to get to the highlights. We may not now agree with their criteria, but we make the same assumption that something is historically important in the degree to which it makes a difference. Whether this was for change or conservation is secondary to whether it represents something new. The so-called Carolingian Renaissance of the ninth century, for example, aimed merely at reviving education, not creating new knowledge; but this in itself was a striking development, even though it did not survive.

The presence of something that was not there before gives history its meaning. Charlemagne without his empire and his reforms would have been just another Frankish king. Through them he marks a new phase in the history of the earlier Middle Ages. We read and write the history of his reign in this light.

The same applies to any history. Its point is still to tell a story, or at least unfold a sequence. Like any sequence it is orientated to the future, which by definition is not revealed in the present, because there is no set way in which men are bound to act, even if they tend to act in certain ways at certain times. It is precisely in considering the possible alternatives within any situation that its history lies. Even if the predictable result is the one that emerges — say, that a strong army beats a small one — the result has still to be considered within the context of the other countervailing possibilities, which, until they were overcome, were part of the situation. No amount of knowing about Edward I's achievements can tell us how they turned to nothing in Edward II's reign, any more than we can know about Napoleon from knowing about the outbreak of the French Revolution in 1789. We cannot do so because at the time the future remained open. That is what makes us turn to history to understand how it came to be. Were we able to deduce Edward II's reign or Napoleon independently of the events which led to them, we should no more write their history than we write the history of the kettle which boils, to account for its boiling. It is the difference between determinism and contingency. The one gives the universal conditional laws of nature and the natural sciences; the other, in having a future which is different from the present, demands history to make it intelligible: to enable us to discover how and perhaps why men took one course rather than another when more than one course remained open to them.

But history doesn't just provide a context to what would otherwise be merely a shapeless succession of events: it enables us to measure what is common down the ages and what is peculiar to men at different epochs; to distinguish between what men are and have to suffer in virtue of being men, and what they can do and what they can become as individuals and members of diverse societies. This antinomy between the universal and the epochal is central to historical understanding. It doesn't take place in a void. It is we who put the questions about a particular segment of history, just as the scientist tests his hypothesis about a particular segment of nature. Neither is just an observer; both are actively involved in manipulating their data to bring order to it.

But with this difference: that the historian is concerned not just with facts but also with values. That is what makes his, and all social knowledge different from that of nature and the natural sciences. To know about a rock crystal entails grasping the universal scientific laws under which it can be subsumed, and which therefore hold for all similar cases; knowledge of any kind of social phenomenon, on the other hand, from religion to banking, demands grasping the system of values to which it belongs; it is not enough to describe its operations, we have to penetrate to its meaning for those who operated it. I deliberately use the word 'penetrate', which has come to have pejorative associations with some kind of mystical or non-intellectual intuition, because this is what human actions involve. Just as we cannot understand an argument unless we know the meaning of the words used, so we cannot understand the way in which men act unless we know the ideals and interests which actuate them.

FOUR

THE HISTORIAN AT WORK

Judging by the stocks of major bookstores, history books are best sellers. In many countries the names of famous historians are well known to the educated classes. Samuel Eliot Morison in the United States, George Macaulay Trevelyan in Great Britain, Donald G. Creighton and Guy Frégault in Canada have influenced the intellectual development of generations of their countrymen. Their works may not rest on every lady's boudoir table, as Macaulay claimed for his books, but they are able to attract a degree of attention not shared by many scholars in other disciplines. A superb style, a jargon-free prose and a magnificent range of subject matter are some of the qualities that explain their popularity among the reading public.

These qualities are not, however, peculiar to historians; they are treasured by novelists, poets and, indeed, any person who takes pride in writing readable prose. Consequently some have said that no specialized training is necessary for writing history. In one respect they are right: the gifted amateur has always been welcomed into the profession (although more reluctantly in recent years) and many of the greatest names in historiography had no formal training. From another point of view, however, the distinction between amateur and professional appears to be quite clear. An antiquarian lacks not only discipline in organizing his data but also an understanding of the nature of history. That sense of perspective is highly prized. Literary style is not the only asset a novice should develop: he must also master the historian's craft.

A wide range of techniques is used by modern historians. The search for documents is a characteristic pursuit of the trade and when found they are subjected to precise and careful criticism. Scientific discoveries of the last few decades have revolutionized the content and methodology of early history in particular. Historians have learned to analyze societies using techniques borrowed from kindred disciplines, especially anthropology, sociology and psychology. Their command of great quantities of data has been broadened by the application of computer technology to historical problems. On technical grounds alone, history is much more of a profession than it was twenty years ago.

In addition, scholars have begun to reappraise theoretical issues within the discipline. They are concerned about how to order data and interpret events, how to group topics into periods and how to make evaluative statements. When explaining this happening or giving the causes for that event, they are sensitive to the theoretical issues inherent in explanation and causation. They are aware also of the uncertainty of historical truth and the dangers of dogmatic statements about the past. Finally, historians would readily admit that the language and tone of a piece of historical writing can be at least as persuasive as the application of even the most modern scientific method.

1. Historians spend much of their time looking for and assessing what is called "raw data," the surviving evidence upon which their final judgments are based. They spend innumerable hours in such familiar places as archives or government offices or in any number of strange locations where some record of the past may be found. As soon as they begin to collect their data, they must reflect upon the inter-relationship of individual pieces and weigh their importance. This task bears a marked resemblance, Professor Robin Winks tells us, to that of a detective. Dr. Winks, a Canadian-born historian now working at Yale University, speaks from the experience of one who

[1] Reprinted from Robin W. Winks, "The Historian as Detective,"
The Texas Quarterly, 9, Winter 1968, pp. 47-48. Copyright © 1969,
Robin W. Winks. Permission of Julian Bach Literary Agency.

has written extensively on the history of many nations within the Commonwealth. His most recent book, The Blacks in Canada: A History *(Montreal, 1971), is based upon a detailed study of a wide range of materials related to an important minority in Canada.*

Much of the historian's work, . . . like that of the insurance investigator, the fingerprint man, or the coroner, may to the outsider seem to consist of deadening routine. Many miles of intellectual shoe leather will be used, for many metaphorical laundry lists, uninformative diaries, blank checkbooks, old telephone directories, and other trivia will stand between the researcher and his answer. Yet the routine must be pursued, or the clue may be missed; the apparently false trail must be followed in order to be certain that it is false; the mute witnesses must be asked the reasons for their silence, for the piece of evidence that is missing from where one might reasonably expect to find it is, after all, a form of evidence in itself.

Precisely because the historian must turn to all possible witnesses, he is the most bookish of men. For him, no printed statement is without its interest. For him, the destruction of old cookbooks, gazetteers, road maps, Sears, Roebuck catalogues, children's books, railway timetables, or drafts of printed manuscripts, is the loss of potential evidence. Does one wish to know how the mail order business operated, or how a Nebraska farmer might have dressed in 1930? Look to those catalogues. Does one wish to know whether a man from Washington just might have been in New York on a day in 1861, when it can be proved that he was in the capital on the day before and the day after? The timetables will help tell us of the opportunity. Does one wish to see the growth of new highways, the spread of asphalt into a neglected corner of Colorado, or Indiana, or Maine during the depression years? Oil company roadmaps will help. Does one wish to know what kinds of ideas a Theodore Roosevelt, or a Clement Attlee, or a John F. Kennedy may have fed upon as children? Back files of *St. Nicholas,* or *Boy's Own,* or even *Superman* will be relevant. And thus one also needs to know who collects what: that the University of Syracuse houses children's literature, that Cornell holds on to its railway timetables, or that Yale keeps old road maps.

Of course one applies these notions of relevancy outside booklined rooms too, and the historian needs to be the most practical of men as well. One historian of my acquaintance worked with Marine intelligence during World War II. He was asked to help judge how many Japanese had dug in on one of the strategically crucial South Pacific islands, an island which the Marine Corps planned to make its own, whatever the losses, within a few days. No Japanese could be seen from aerial reconnaissance, for the camouflage was nearly perfect. This historian provided an accurate figure, however, for he noted from aerial photographs that particularly dark patches could be identified as latrines, and upon consulting a captured Japanese army manual, he learned how many latrines were to be dug per unit of men. The rest was so simple a matter of calculation that even the historian could provide an answer without the aid of a computer.

Clearly, then, the historian needs to assess evidence against a reasonably well-informed background. Is one writing of the Pullman Strike of 1896? One must, obviously, know quite a bit about general labor conditions, about business management, about employment opportunities and the nature of economy, about Chicago and its environs, and about the railroad industry. But since many of the strikers were Welshmen, one also needs to know something of contrasting work conditions in that part of Wales from which the workmen came. Since the strike was compounded by inept police and militia work, one needs to know about the nature of such work in Illinois and, comparatively, elsewhere. One needs to investigate the judicial system, the role of President Grover Cleveland, the powers open to Governor John P. Altgeld, the ideas of Eugene V. Debs, and the effects of the Chicago World's Fair, which brought hundreds of drifters into the metropolitan area to contribute to the violence associated with the strike. Since the strike disrupted mail service throughout the nation, forcing letters north onto Canadian tracks, one needs to investigate at least briefly the Canadian rail network, the relationship with railway men elsewhere, and the applicability of the secondary boycott. One needs to know much of the general climate of opinion at the time to assess the meaning of the strike. One needs to look at company, city, union, judicial, militia, post office, presidential, legal, and gubernatorial records; at the private papers of Cleveland, Altgeld, Pullman, Debs; at the papers of the judges, magistrates, and strikers, if they can be found and, when found, if one can gain access to them. Much that one learns on such journeys will never appear in the final book but every nuance, every sentence, will be better informed, closer to the truth, more protected against one's own biases (which can never be totally blocked out, and no responsible historian claims that they can be), than if such journeys were not taken at all.

2. *In recent years historians have been using with greater frequency techniques borrowed from kindred disciplines. Methods developed by demographers, for example, have changed our views of seventeenth-century population patterns in England and the social structure of a Canadian city two hundred years later.* Scholars trained in both sociology and history are examining general themes such as revolution and violence which older historians have tended to study only as particular cases or episodes.† In an issue of the London* Times Literary Supplement *entitled "New Ways in History," Mr.*

*Peter Laslett, The World We Have Lost (London, 1965) and Michael B. Katz, "Social Structure in Hamilton, Ontario," in Stephan Thernstrom and Richard Sennett (eds.), Nineteenth-Century Cities: Essays in the New Urban History (New Haven, 1969) pp. 209-241.

†David S. Landes and Charles Tilly, History as Social Science (Englewood Cliffs, New Jersey, 1971), pp. 39-48.

[2] Reprinted from Keith Thomas, "The Tools and the Job," *The Times Literary Supplement,* April 7, 1966, pp. 275-6. Reproduced from *The Times Literary Supplement* by permission.

K. V. Thomas, an authority on pre-modern primitive beliefs,‡ has outlined the nature of these new techniques and assessed their long term effects upon the discipline.**

Future histories of English historical writing are likely to reveal the first half of the twentieth century as a time when most historians temporarily lost their bearings. The academic study of history which they inherited had been shaped by Victorian pride in the great English institutions of Parliament and the Common Law. The majestic narratives of Stubbs and Gardiner exemplified a preoccupation with the growth of English liberty, while Froude and Seeley expatiated upon the unparalleled ascendancy of the British overseas. In such a climate it was natural that the subject-matter of history should be primarily political and constitutional: history was a training for politicians and administrators, and the constitution was England's greatest contribution to the world. The sociological tastes of the eighteenth-century Scottish school of philosophic historians had left little impact, for their lineal descendants were not historians but classical economists. On the Continent more unsettled conditions had stimulated the sociology of Marx and Durkheim, while the melting-pot of the United States had generated the social self-consciousness of Veblen. But English intellectual life was largely innocent of these preoccupations. The early twentieth century saw the revival of British sociology, but it was sociology at a distance — the study of primitive tribes, a subject which had its uses in Imperial administration, but which no one thought had anything to do with the understanding of European history.

*   *   *

Politics and the constitution therefore remained the central concern of academic historians, though the multiplication of historical knowledge made it increasingly impracticable for them to emulate the long narratives of their predecessors. Their characteristic art-form became the learned article in the *English Historical Review,* scholarly and precise, but cautious in its conclusions, so as to delay its inevitable fate — supersession by another article, even more scholarly. History was seen as a craft, not a cumulative science, and there was no greater indictment of a practitioner than to say that he had built upon the work of his predecessors. Nor was history a seamless web. Rather, it proliferated into separate specialisms with their own learned journals — economic history, ecclesiastical history, or military history. Progress was to be made, not by reflective synthesis, but by the discovery of new facts, or better still new sources. The intellectual energy devoted to writing this disintegrated history was of an unprecedented dimension. It involved rigorous handling of documentary evidence and an aversion to jargon or woolliness of expression. It invoked no recondite

‡Religion and the Decline of Magic **(London, 1971).**

****G. R. Elton has said that "the whole of [Thomas'] article, and indeed of the issue of which it formed part . . . , is shot through with an engaging arrogance and historically invalid assertions."** The Practice of History, **(New York, 1967), p. 7, fn.**

conceptual tools, for commonsense and good judgment were all that was needed to understand the workings of human beings, and theory was profoundly distrusted. A course in palaeography, and perhaps six months in Germany to learn the language, were all the professional training required by the clever undergraduate to follow in the paths of his masters.

It did not need the collapse of the British Empire or the other shocks engendered by the upheavals of the twentieth century to make it clear that academic history, for all its scholarly rigour, had succeeded in explaining remarkably little about the workings of human society or the fluctuations in human affairs. In a renewed attempt to find meaning behind the apparently aimless accumulation of factual knowledge, many British historians turned to Marxism, which they found seductive perhaps less for its political implications than for its demonstration of the interrelatedness of social phenomena. It seemed the only way of countering the prevailing fashion of splitting up history by topic which seemed to impede the understanding of society as a whole. Under Marxist influence great advances were made towards fitting the pieces together again. Writers like R. H. Tawney or Harold Laski illuminated the links between religion, political thought and economic development. They pioneered the study of social structure and the sociology of knowledge. The last decade has witnessed the apotheosis of this tradition, and it is worth reflecting how impoverished the contemporary historical scene would be without Dr. Christopher Hill's studies of Puritanism and society, Professor C. B. Macpherson's interpretations of seventeenth-century political thought, or Dr. E. J. Hobsbawm's learned and astringent sorties into social and economic topics.

*   *   *

Lately, however, sociological interests have outgrown their original source of inspiration. The stereotyped social vocabulary of Marxism has been found increasingly inadequate to convey the complex realities of historical development, while its economic determinism seems to obscure the diversities of habit and sentiment which in fact bind men to each other. At this point of intellectual development the increasing number of British historians who are not content to grub away in the old empirical tradition have turned to see what help can be derived from the new sciences of society which have sprung up elsewhere — sociology, social anthropology, demography, and social psychology.

In so doing they are decades behind their colleagues in other countries. In France the *Annales* school, founded by Marc Bloch and Lucien Febvre, has long urged the historical study of *la psychologie collective*. Britain has no medievalist to compare with Bloch, no monument of demographic study to rival Goubert's great work on Beauvais. In the United States, the home of the social sciences *par excellence,* it has become common for historians to draw upon sociological techniques and terminology. To realize how much it has been left to Americans to apply new techniques to English history one need only recall such works as Professor G. C. Homans's portrait of medieval agrarian life in *English Villagers of the Thirteenth*

Century, Professor Neil Smelser's systematic application of sociological theory in *Social Change in the Industrial Revolution,* Professor W. K. Jordan's statistical analysis of charitable endowments, or Professor Aydelotte's employment of refined statistical techniques to illuminate voting patterns in the House of Commons of the 1840s. Other American scholars have analysed such social groups as the merchants of medieval London and the domestic servant class of the eighteenth century. Whether the reader seeks information on medieval population or seventeenth-century suicide it is to works published in North America that he must go. Of course there have already been important English contributions to historical sociology, but most of them have been in the old empirical tradition and owe no explicit debt to theory. The practitioners of the biographical study of M.P.s enshrined in the *History of Parliament* would probably disown any affinity with American political sociology and "career-line analysis". Neither are the distinguished studies of English land ownership initiated by Professor H. J. Habakkuk, or the local history pioneered by Professor W. G. Hoskins, any more self-consciously sociological in inspiration. Historical sociology may be thus haphazardly begun, but it is unlikely to be sustained without a more systematic indoctrination in the social sciences.

* * *

The first benefit to be expected from such a training is a refinement of the historian's social vocabulary. The lack of conceptual precision underlying abstractions like "class", "feudalism" or "revolution", in which historians so frequently deal, has tended to generate protracted historical controversies which are primarily semantic in character. One need only recall the ambiguities inherent in such notions as "the rise of the gentry" or "Thomas Cromwell's establishment of bureaucratic government" to see how acute the problem is. If the analysis of the past is to be rigorous, then the construction of an historical typology, a means of classifying and comparing, is an urgent *desideratum.* It cannot come from sociology alone, but an education in the concepts of sociology seems the quickest way of attaining it.

A further advantage will be the introduction of more demanding techniques of verification. A great proportion of the statements made in a history book are ultimately statistical in their implications. When historians generalize about the behaviour of social classes or individuals, when they speak of "public opinion" or "the climate of the age", they are implying regularities of a numerical kind. In the past they have tended to arrive at such conclusions by "feel" rather than by figures, and their findings have been illustrated impressionistically rather than demonstrated by statistics. A growing awareness of the intellectually unsatisfactory nature of such procedures has coincided with the development by social scientists of new techniques of what is unappealingly called "quantification". The historian cannot use the sociologist's polls, interviews and Rorschach tests, but he can employ his elaborate methods of sampling and measuring. A more self-conscious statistical approach will enable him to be objective when the facts are available, and to refrain from unverifiable pronouncements when they are not. Georges Lefebvre's maxim has proved prophetic: *Pour faire de l'histoire il faut savoir compter.* It seems certain that the computer will replace the "stout boots" worn by the advanced historians of the past generation. In America the new econometric history, less than ten years old, is already sweeping all before it. Resting upon an alliance between mathematically sophisticated tools of measurement and the construction of elaborate theoretical models, it promises a definitive solution to such problems as the economic efficiency of slavery or the contribution of the railways to American economic growth.

* * *

But it is not only the economic historian who will be driven into the use of mechanical aids to the handling and analysis of his evidence. All historical propositions relating to the behaviour of large groups, for example, about illiteracy or religious activity, are susceptible of treatment in this way, and indeed permit of no other. The problems in social history to which Tawney called attention will be solved by different methods and in a different style of historical writing. The appearance, first of Professor G. E. Aylmer's study of office-holding, and now of Professor Lawrence Stone's *The Crisis of the Aristocracy,* marks the transfer of the long-protracted "gentry" controversy to a different intellectual plane. For, although superbly written, often in a traditionally impressionistic way, Professor Stone's case rests upon his voluminous statistics. These may well be challenged, but the days when the introduction of impassioned rhetoric was thought to advance the understanding of social change are clearly over.

Nowhere has the importance of the new numerical techniques been more obvious than in the historical study of population. Here a genuine breakthrough can be saluted, for the difficulty of establishing population trends for the centuries before the modern censuses may now be overcome by the methods devised for the exploitation of parish registers by the Institut National d'Études Démographiques and brought to England by the new Cambridge Group for the History of Population and Social Structure.

It would be a pity if the importance of this latter venture were underrated because of the over-eagerness of its sponsors to peddle their wares, for the techniques of family reconstitution outlined in their *Introduction to English Historical Demography* will certainly revolutionize the study of English population in the pre-industrial period, even if the limits to its potentialities are still unclear. Population movements help to explain such economic developments as the price-rise of the sixteenth century. They also concern such matters as harvests and food-supply, epidemics and medicine, the age of marriage and the size of families. That is to say, they illuminate not just impersonal trends but the lives of real people. Mr. Peter Laslett is right to stress the indispensability of this numerical study of society for the reconstruction of the social structure and mental environment of the past. Meanwhile some less advertised contributions to this type of history should be remembered: the painstaking examination by Mr. J. A.

Banks of the factors leading the Victorian middle classes to take up birth control; the important essays in *Population in History*; and the most impressive piece of demographic scholarship to date — Mr. T. H. Hollingsworth's *The Demography of the British Peerage*.

*   *   *

A different source of inspiration is to be found in the writings of the British social anthropologists. Their unique advantage is to have studied at close quarters the working of primitive societies which often approximate closely to those the historian tries to reconstruct from inadequate documents. Under their influence has arisen a disposition to take more seriously the "primitive" features of European society, and to discover the logic behind some apparently barbarous practices. Stimulated by African analogies, for example, Mr. Wallace-Hadrill has been able to show that the Frankish blood-feud did not involve incessant warfare, but was a useful mechanism for the settlement of disputes. Soon the judicial ordeal, hitherto dismissed by legal historians as irrational, may be revealed as a less clumsy procedure for identifying the guilty than might have been supposed. The witchcraft accusations of seventeenth-century England are coming to be seen as a reflection of hostilities engendered by the breakdown of the old village community. Work currently being carried out on this subject has benefitted directly from the stimulus of the anthropological studies initiated by Professor Evans-Pritchard's *Witchcraft, Oracles and Magic among the Azande,* where emphasis is laid upon the explanatory function of witch beliefs and upon the importance of the social relationship obtaining between accuser and accused. In the same way, Professor Max Gluckman's analysis of conflict in African societies has thrown light on such superficially remote topics as the medieval law of treason, and the Wars of the Roses. Englishmen are now disposed to see analogies between their history and that of "under-developed" African countries in a way the Victorians could never have done. The gain in understanding and comparative sense is incalculable.

Anthropologists and sociologists alike share a concern in the microscopic analysis of social structure. The next few decades will see many comparable historical studies of small communities — manors, villages, parishes — in which social structure and inheritance practices are likely to be a central preoccupation. From the new Urban History Group should come more studies like Mr. H. J. Dyos's history of Camberwell, *Victorian Suburb*. For this subject, as Professor Asa Briggs remarks in his *Victorian Cities,* the work of the Chicago urban sociologists is "as relevant as the writing of any school of history". Indeed the social surveys made by contemporary sociologists will be the basis of the social history of the future. The same microscopic approach is likely to advance the study of religious history. There is no English counterpart to the French historical school of religious sociology, with its regional studies and its *Archives de Sociologie des Religions*. But work on the religious censuses of the nineteenth century has begun, and it cannot be long before we have studies in which the largely untapped records of the Church are combined with secular sources to produce a history of religious practice which is firmly related to the structure of local communities.

The findings of social psychology, however, still await incorporation into the writing of history. The widespread rejection of commonsense assumptions about human motivation, initiated by Freud, was enormously stimulated by the spread of fascism. The atrocities of Hitler's regime could not be explained by old-fashioned rationalist psychology, and the rash of postwar studies of such subjects as the authoritarian personality or behaviour in concentration camps were strongly historical in their implications. In America their findings have been effectively deployed, notably by Stanley Elkins, whose *Slavery* sets out to explain the so-called "Sambo" personality of the Negro slave. In England the lone pioneer has been Professor E. R. Dodds, whose splendid essays on *The Greeks and the Irrational* showed that new ideas could be introduced without any loss in scholarly power or literary elegance. There has, however, been distinguished work by Richard Cobb and George Rudé on mobs, riots, and other manifestations of *la mentalité collective,* and by Professor Cohn and Dr. Hobsbawm on popular millenarianism. It is likely that the next decade will see interesting research into such forms of collective paranoia as rumours and Catholic scares. Meanwhile the greatest gap in the psychological field is a historical study of methods of child-rearing at different periods.

The social history of the future will therefore not be a residual subject but a central one, around which all other branches of history are likely to be organized. This dethronement of politics will encounter much resistance. Sociological thinking has usually been pioneered by rootless intellectuals, foreign observers and immigrants. It does not come easily to the English academic, who has always been more closely involved with the established social order. It involves cooperative scholarship and organized research, a world of seminars, workshops and graduate programmes, which is alien to the individualist, prima donna tradition in which most English historians have been reared. It brings with it the risk of jargon and obscurity, whereas history has always been regarded as a subject which should be intelligible and attractive to laymen. In the age of the historical factory some nostalgia is inevitably felt for the simpler days of the domestic system. But it is misguided to resist what Professor Trevor-Roper has called "the creeping paralysis of professionalism". If history is to maintain a deserving place in the affections of the reading public it is essential that those with a gift for popular exposition should master the new techniques, so that, even if they do not themselves contribute to knowledge, they may at least be able to evaluate the contribution of others.

Meanwhile the coming revolution threatens to ossify some well-established institutions. As a vehicle for current historical opinions, the *English Historical Review* has already been eclipsed by *Past and Present,* whose subscribers hold conferences on such sociological topics as work and leisure, social mobility, or popular religion. In its final volume the *Oxford History of England* gives out a brilliant swansong for the dying concept of real history as past politics, and social history as an undemanding subsidiary. School history courses will discard such traditional boundary-posts as 1485 or 1714 as elementary outlines of economic and social history come to seem more "basic" than the names of the kings of England. Some agonizing re-appraisals will occur in those universities where historians of the future are still reared on a traditional diet. At Oxford recently, out of seventy-six members of the history faculty invited to propose other subjects to be combined with history at the undergraduate level, there were only two who regarded either sociology or anthropology as potential candidates. Lack of technical training in economics has already debarred many ex-Oxford historians from contributing effectively to the study of economic history. Similar conservatism may prevent them from participating in these new intellectual enterprises. It thus remains to be seen whether the prevailing system of historical training can generate the intellectual flexibility necessary for the new history to sustain itself. The tools of reconstruction are at hand, but the will to use them may be lacking.

3. *Some historians have an uncanny knack for forming inspired generalizations from essentially incomplete and fragmentary data. They can, as it were, see the shape of the puzzle with amazing accuracy from a careful assessment of two or three pieces. Others have been dubious about the validity of results obtained in this manner, or unwilling to make judgments without a much more methodical, even scientific, examination of the evidence. "The facts surpass common sense," said Charles Tilly when describing his work on nineteenth-century French conflicts. "They cry for systematic verification."* In order to tame the sheer quantity of material that exists on significant historical topics, scholars have made greater use of statistics, mathematical processes and, more recently, computers. Techniques for quantitative analysis promise what G. Kitson Clark calls "a most interesting revolution in history."† One scholar who has both used and studied these techniques is Dr. William O. Aydelotte, Professor of History at the University of Iowa since 1950. In his article on "Quantification in History" he points out some of the strengths of the method.*

*Charles Tilly, **"In defense of jargon,"** Canadian Historical Association Annual Report 1966, **p. 185.**

†**G. Kitson Clark,** The Critical Historian **(London, 1967), p. 176. For a survey of the use of quantitative methods in a particular field of Canadian history see Peter J. George and Ernest H. Oksanen, "Recent developments in the Quantification of Canadian Economic History,"** Histoire Sociale/Social History, 4 **(Novembre, 1969), pp. 76-95.**

[3] Reprinted from William O. Aydelotte, "Quantification in History," *The American Historical Review*, 71(3), April 1966, pp. 805 (1.28)-806, 809 (1.15-28), 824 (1.20)-825 with the permission of the author. Reprinted in 1971 by Addison-Wesley, Publishing Company Inc., Reading, Mass.

A quantitative presentation of the available information can help to direct the student's attention to the questions most worth investigating. Since it brings the whole of the evidence, on the point it covers, into intelligible focus, the general character of the findings can be more readily perceived and relationships and differences emerge that could not so easily have been observed without this reduction of the data. Such an analysis reveals what events or issues were of special interest, in the sense of involving change through time or departure from the norm, and hence might particularly repay investigation. It can, in this manner, help in defining or restating the historical problem to be studied.

Beyond this, a quantitative analysis offers a systematic means of testing hypotheses. It establishes how many examples there are to support each side of the argument and thus reveals not only the main features of the evidence but also, more important, the exceptions to them, the nuances, the degree to which the emerging generalizations need to be qualified. Measurement locates the defect in the original hypothesis and registers "the departure from theory with an authority and finesse that no qualitative technique can duplicate." A quantitative discrepancy between theory and observation is obtrusive. "No crisis is . . . so hard to suppress as one that derives from a quantitative anomaly that has resisted all the usual efforts at reconciliation."[3]

The general overview of the whole evidence obtained by quantitative means can also be a powerful stimulus toward the reformulation of one's ideas. When anomalies occur, the student can direct his attention to the cases that do not fit the original theory, try to find out why they are exceptional, and, by rearrangements of the data, test alternative hypotheses that may account for a larger proportion of the evidence. Such manipulations of the data, would take an immense amount of time to do by hand, but, ordinarily, they can readily be performed by machines. I advise my students, if they are working with fifty cases or more, to punch the information. This is easily done, and, once it is done, there is no great difficulty about trying additional correlations. By the same token a quantitative analysis can even, in some cases, point the way to the formulation of new hypotheses that will make the findings more intelligible.

The case for quantification might be made in still a different way by saying that it is a method of reasoning, one that involves number. As one of my colleagues at the University of Iowa has put it, quantification adds, to whatever factual or historical premises may have been established, the premises of mathematics as well. "Arithmetic is a vast treasure house of additional premises, or, what amounts to the same thing, of patterns of deductive inference. Quantification is the key to the treasure."[4]

The advantages of this approach have been appreciated by a number of present-day historians. G. Kitson Clark suggests as appropriate advice to

[3] Thomas S. Kuhn, "The Function of Measurement in Modern Physical Science," in *Quantification: A History of the Meaning of Measurement in the Natural and Social Sciences,* ed. Harry Woolf (Indianapolis, 1961), 50, 52.

[4] Gustav Bergmann, *Philosophy of Science* (Madison, Wis., 1957), 69.

someone who wishes to generalize about a group or a class: "do not guess, try to count, and if you can not count admit that you are guessing."[5] Lawrence Stone writes: "Owing to the obstinate perversity of human nature, it would no doubt be possible in England of 1958 to find, if one tried, declining manual labourers and rising landed gentry. To have any validity at all, conclusions about social movements must have a statistical basis."[6]

In the next extract from the same article Dr. Aydelotte lists some of the objections that have been raised to the use of quantitative analysis and tries to put the entire debate in perspective.

Furthermore, much hostility to quantitative methods still remains among some members of the historical profession. Despite what might seem the obvious advantages of these methods for certain kinds of problems, despite their notably successful application in many historical projects, and despite their long acceptance as a matter of course in several related disciplines, some historians still object to them vociferously and consider them altogether inappropriate for historical research. Questions have been raised regarding: (1) the value of the work that has been done; (2) the feasibility of this approach in view of the admittedly limited materials available to historians; (3) the reliability of the results obtained by these techniques; and (4) the usefulness or significance of the results. These objections are not wholly without foundation. It would be pointless to deny either the limitations of the method or the lapses of some of its practitioners. To concede this, however, is not to tell the whole story.

* * *

In general, the discussion of quantification in history has involved much talking at cross-purposes. Many of the common objections to this approach seem to arise from a misconception of its function. They appear to assume that claims have been made for it that no responsible statistician would make. No one well versed in this line of work would argue that all historical materials can be quantified, that the figures provide any final demonstration of the broader inferences derived from them, or that the figures tell the whole story. Such assertions are clearly improper. If they are not made, however, as by informed workers in this line they are not, much of the current offensive against quantitative techniques fails. The central point around which discussion of the subject has in part revolved is not an intellectual issue but a problem of communication.

The use of quantitative methods for history presents substantial difficulties not always appreciated by enthusiasts or neophytes. Those who have employed them are likely to be less starry-eyed about their possibilities than those who have merely commended them without trying them. Indeed, quantitative projects may be more glamorous in the planning stage than

[5] G. Kitson Clark, *The Making of Victorian England* (London, 1962), 14.

[6] Lawrence Stone, letter to editor, *Encounter, XI* (July 1958), 73.

they are after the results have been gathered; the findings sometimes turn out to be flatter and less revolutionary than had been hoped.

Though the difficulties are real enough, however, it is not clear that they constitute objections specifically to a quantitative approach, or that they can be resolved by dispensing with it. The standard objections are misconceived or placed out of context when presented as grounds for rejecting these methods altogether. Properly understood, these reservations serve not to discredit quantification but to mark the boundaries of what it can accomplish. Indeed, the apparent disadvantages of quantitative research, the impediments to generalization that it presents, are actually advantages for they call attention to limits in knowledge or to flaws in reasoning that might not otherwise be perceived or fully appreciated. When all reservations have been made, quantification has still shown itself, in the light of the considerable experience we now have, to be a powerful tool in historical analysis. It helps to make the work both easier and more reliable, and, in some cases, it provides a means of dealing with questions that could not be attacked in any other way. Those wrestling with problems for which this approach is appropriate can ill afford to dispense with it. In the general intellectual twilight in which historians are condemned to spend their lives, even some small effort to render the darkness less opaque may be advantageous.

4. Although historians differ widely in their choice of subject and even the means by which they approach it, they share a number of common philosophical problems. One of these, the relationship of fact to interpretation, is considered by E. H. Carr in a later reading in this chapter. Others include the nature of bias, the making of moral judgments and the nature of causation. This last problem — how do historians explain the causes of an event? — has been analyzed by Jacques Barzun and Henry F. Graff. Dr. Graff is a specialist in American history at Columbia University, while Dr. Barzun has gained an international reputation for his studies in many disciplines at the same University.

Though we have steadily strengthened our defenses against the skeptic and shown how documentary evidence and its handling — the balancing of probabilities, the making of objective judgment, and the seeking out of competent testimony — successively raise our certitude about the past higher than any imaginable certitude about the present, this favorable comparison itself spurs the skeptic to his last effort: "Granted that you may know enough to tell a reliable story, full of significant detail, you really know nothing unless at every point you also know the causes."

The challenge takes one into deep waters. Whole books have been written about Causation. Their contents could not be reviewed in a few pages even if all the questions were finally settled in the minds of men. Only a sketch of the question can be given. The chief difficulty lies in what is meant by Cause. Neither philosophers nor scientists agree on what causation is or does. In the mid-eighteenth century, the philosopher David Hume showed that the conception of Cause as a compelling push that produces an effect is an illusion. Man has no immediate sense of the necessity that makes one billiard ball propel another after striking it; he has only an expectation of the event, an expectation that has been bred in him by habitual experience. Ever since Hume, theories of causation have been numerous but none has proved universally acceptable. All that is agreed upon is that where Cause is, there is Regularity.

Everyone nevertheless continues to believe in causes that compel. We say: "The manager's behavior caused X to resign," and we think we know what we mean. But as soon as we try to say precisely what we mean our confidence breaks down. A psychologist will show how inadequate is our grasp of the cause: the alleged cause was a mere pretext; the manager's offensive behavior was imaginary — a "projection" on the subordinate's part. Or again, the latter's behavior may have provoked the other's — hence the man himself was the cause of his own resignation. Or possibly his wife caused it, unknown to herself and to him.

These speculations are meant only to show that when we speak of causes in human affairs we are usually dealing with a variety of elements that stand at different degrees of depth from the observed event and that are not easily touched or separated. Judge Hand called them incommensurables because they cannot be measured and sometimes cannot even be discerned. If a man kills himself sixteen days, five hours, and twenty-three minutes after receiving a piece of bad news, what is the cause of his suicide? In ordinary speech we say either "Things became too much for him," or "A man's vitality is lowest in the early morning," or "A man of John's tradition and character could not face bankruptcy." In other words we ascribe his death either to an unfathomable psychological state, or to a physiological fact, or to a recognizable idea born in response to a situation. We are not likely to ascribe it to the bullet and the gun, because that cause does not interest us: it interests only the coroner.

Generalizing from this we infer that what history reveals to mankind about its past does not uncover *the* cause (one or more indispensable antecedents) of any event, large or small, but only the *conditions* (some of the prerequisites) attending its emergence. Not only can we not isolate the cause, but we cannot properly define of what sort it would be. When Pascal said that if Cleopatra's nose had been shorter this would have changed the face of the world (to say nothing of her own), he was pointing out that personality plays a role in History. He did not mean that Cleopatra's nose was *the* cause of Mark Antony's defeat at Actium: it was at best one of the antecedent conditions. In short, when we give an account of human events we fasten upon those points that seem to us suitable to connect believably with our present concerns and previous experience. If these connections are duly brought out we say we "understand."[37]

The thought occurs that we might come closer to a real cause, and obtain results akin to those of physical science, if we could only deal with well-defined kinds of events, such as, say, automobile accidents. We do in fact classify these and learn that mechanical failure caused so many percent, speeding so many, and intoxication so many. Can this possibility of classification and statistical measurement be extended throughout the realm of History so as to conquer and annex it to science? Some argue that this is impossible because the facts of History are unique and its personages also; they do not recur, or as the popular saying has it: History never repeats.

To this it is answered that *all* events are unique, even the "same" experiment done twice in a laboratory. All the individuals of the brute creation are distinct also, even the sheep in a field. This suggests that in both realms

there are facts that have nothing in common with other facts — for example, the geological formation of the earth — and of these facts we say that they do not recur; and there are facts which more or less resemble other facts — a lion that resembles other lions, a person who goes to school like millions of other persons — and of these facts we say that they repeat themselves.[38]

From this the writer goes on to argue that a large part of history is scientific in the sense of being based on description and classification of similar instances, just like zoology. In deciphering ancient inscriptions or studying Roman law, "the historical sources present the same sign for the same idea;" hence comparison and definition and exact analysis are possible.[39]

There is another sense in which history is a part of the realm of science, and which should prevent us from thinking of the two as opposed or widely removed from each other: the events of history occur in the same universe and follow the same material "laws" as the objects of science. Men are subject to gravitation and decay, statesmen in transit are no different from other moving bodies, and what is most important, men's minds work upon historical data with the same perceptions and logical rules as they do in science.

A difference remains, of course, which most observers feel intuitively even when they find it difficult to assess. History cannot, like physical science, pare down events and reproduce them at will in the simple forms and favoring conditions that we call experiment. Nor . . . can the

---

[37] For a subtle and authoritative account of causation as it is conceived in physical science today (and as it must be conceived in the "historical" realm which includes all that is not science), see Henry Margenau, *Open Vistas,* New Haven, 1961; esp. 191-214.

[38] Gaetano Salvemini, *Historian and Scientist.* Cambridge, Mass., 1939, 91.

[39] *Ibid.,* 94.

historian sort out his materials into independent units that will stay put long enough for him to measure and relate them as constants and variables.[40] Even when we count automobile accidents we pursue our practical interest at the expense of strict causal analysis. The *immediate* error that caused the drunken driver's accident interests us no more than the remote cause that led him to drink.[41]

Every attempt in historical writing to formalize causal description or make a show of exactitude by assigning one "paramount" cause and several "contributory" causes ends in self-stultification. Any such distinction implies a measurement that we cannot in fact make . . . .

[40] We can of course achieve this relation intuitively through historical *judgment*, as Garrett Mattingly has pointed out: "Conscious that every human situation contains certain elements of uniformity and certain elements of uniqueness, we scrutinize each new one and compare it with everything we can find out about similar situations in the past, seeking to assign values to constants and to isolate the variables, to decide which factors are significant, what choices are actually present, and what the probable consequences are of choosing course A and rejecting B." ("The Teaching of History," Princeton University Bicentennial Conference [unpublished], Feb. 20, 1947, 5).

[41] For an admirable discussion of the logic of historical analysis, see an article under that title by Ernest Nagel in *Scientific Monthly,* LXXIV (March 1952), 162-69.

5. Despite his libraries, techniques and skills, the historian is often unable to tell us what we want to know about the past. The Muse of History seems more willing to disarm us with new questions than satisfy us with her answers. Many people find this uncertainty or ambiguity unsettling or intolerable; but others see the pursuit of history's elusive clues as fascinating and mind-enlarging. In the following reading Allan Nevins clearly demonstrates that he belongs to the latter school. Dr. Nevins published more than sixty books in the period from 1914. Although perhaps best known for his studies of the Civil War period, he also wrote a justly famous introduction to the study of history, entitled The Gateway to History, *in which this discussion of the role of problems appeared.*

The most important part of history is clearly a series of problems, and more than half of the historian's work is to make a statement of attempted solutions. Obviously a great part of these problems can never be settled. Some are insoluble because they are too vast and complex — the problem of the causes of the fall of the Roman Empire, for example. Others are insoluble because of the loss or suppression of historical evidence. We shall never know whether the visit of the high Jesuit official Francis Borgia to the French court just before St. Bartholomew's had any connection with the massacre, for the evidence has been destroyed. We shall never penetrate many another secret for the same reason. Still other problems

[5] From "Problems in History" in *The Gateway to History* by Allan Nevins, pp. 229-230. Copyright 1938, 1962 by D. C. Heath and Company. Reprinted by permission of Doubleday & Company Inc.

are insoluble because they involve psychological motives of extreme difficulty. What was the nature of Burr's conspiracy? Was it a conspiracy against the United States or against Spain? Claude G. Bowers and Thomas Perkins Abernethy declare that it was treason, but Walter F. McCaleb has written a monograph to prove that it was not. In the last analysis, the answer rests upon what was in Burr's mind in 1804-6. How much real danger existed in August 1862, that the British Ministry would recognize the Confederacy? In the last analysis, the answer rests upon what was in Palmerston's mind. Still more completely insoluble are those problems which involve the psychology of whole peoples. Why did the people of the Lower South determine upon secession in 1861? It is always difficult to say what public opinion is, and it is certainly impossible to produce any clear determinant of social psychology — to say what was dominant in the mind of millions of people at a given hour.

The array of unsolved if not insoluble problems is innumerable; and indeed it is their endless variety, their constant challenge to fresh research, their changing aspects as time throws them into new perspective, which makes history so fascinating. We meet problems of time: What are the true dates for those of semi-mythical character in the Anglo-Saxon calendar? When did the desire for independence take firm root in the American colonies? We have problems of identity: Are present-day Armenians the descendants of the ancient Hittites? Who was King Arthur? There are problems of character and personality, like that met by Paul Van Dyke's study of Catherine de' Medici, or Garrett Mattingly's fascinating book on Katherine of Aragon. There are problems of motive: for example, the analysis by George Otto Trevelyan of General Howe's reasons for not going to the aid of Burgoyne, or the sifting by M. Coquelle of Napoleon's reasons for breaking up the Peace of Amiens. There are problems in the origin of ideas — such as Charles A. Beard's argument upon the economic roots of ideas written into the American Constitution, and John N. Figgis's discussion of the divine right of kings. There are problems of place: Where is the battlefield of Bannockburn? Just how far east did Alexander the Great penetrate toward India? We encounter problems of specific cause: Compare Tenney Frank's view of the reasons why Carthage entered upon the First Punic War with Ferrero's view. We face problems as minute as the unanswered question whether Swift married Stella, and as broad as the inquiry into the effect of the moving frontier upon the mind of the American people.

6. One of the most fascinating questions for layman and student alike is how famous historians actually write their histories. In the following extract Edward Hallett Carr, a distinguished and extraordinarily productive historian of the Soviet Union, tells us some-

[6] Reprinted from E. H. Carr, "The Historian and His Facts" in
What Is History? (London, 1962), pp. 22-24, with the permission
of Macmillan, Basingstoke.

thing of his own methods, and shows us how facts and interpretation
come to be interrelated in his own writing.

How ... in the middle of the twentieth century, are we to define the
obligation of the historian to his facts? I trust that I have spent a sufficient
number of hours in recent years chasing and perusing documents, and
stuffing my historical narrative with properly footnoted facts, to escape
the imputation of treating facts and documents too cavalierly. The duty
of the historian to respect his facts is not exhausted by the obligation to
see that his facts are accurate. He must seek to bring into the picture all
known or knowable facts relevant, in one sense or another, to the theme
on which he is engaged and to the interpretation proposed. ... But this,
in turn, does not mean that he can eliminate interpretation, which is the
life-blood of history. Laymen — that is to say, non-academic friends or
friends from other academic disciplines — sometimes ask me how the historian goes to work when he writes history. The commonest assumption
appears to be that the historian divides his work into two sharply distin-
guishable phases or periods. First, he spends a long preliminary period
reading his sources and filling his notebooks with facts: then, when this is
over, he puts away his sources, takes out his notebooks and writes his book
from beginning to end. This is to me an unconvincing and unplausible
picture. For myself, as soon as I have got going on a few of what I take
to be the capital sources, the itch becomes too strong and I begin to write
— not necessarily at the beginning, but somewhere, anywhere. Thereafter,
reading and writing go on simultaneously. The writing is added to, sub-
tracted from, re-shaped, cancelled, as I go on reading. The reading is
guided and directed and made fruitful by the writing: the more I write,
the more I know what I am looking for, the better I understand the significance and relevance of what I find. Some historians probably do all
this preliminary writing in their head without using pen, paper or type-
writer, just as some people play chess in their heads without recourse to
board and chess-men: this is a talent which I envy, but cannot emulate.
But I am convinced that, for any historian worth the name, the two processes of what economists call "input" and "output" go on simultaneously
and are, in practice, parts of a single process. If you try to separate them,
or to give one priority over the other, you fall into one of two heresies.
Either you write scissors-and-paste history without meaning or significance;
or you write propaganda or historical fiction, and merely use facts of the
past to embroider a kind of writing which has nothing to do with history.

Our examination of the relation of the historian to the facts of history
finds us, therefore, in an apparently precarious situation, navigating deli-
cately between the Scylla of an untenable theory of history as an objective
compilation of facts, of the unqualified primacy of fact over interpretation,
and the Charybdis of an equally untenable theory of history as the subjective product of the mind of the historian who establishes the facts of history
and masters them through the process of interpretation, between a view of

history having the centre of gravity in the past and a view having the centre of gravity in the present. But our situation is less precarious than it seems. We shall encounter the same dichotomy of fact and interpretation again ... in other guises — the particular and the general, the empirical and the theoretical, the objective and the subjective. The predicament of the historian is a reflexion of the nature of man. Man, except perhaps in earliest infancy and in extreme old age, is not totally involved in his environment and unconditionally subject to it. On the other hand, he is never totally independent of it and its unconditional master. The relation of man to his environment is the relation of the historian to his theme. The historian is neither the humble slave, nor the tyrannical master, of his facts. The relation between the historian and his facts is one of equality, of give-and-take. As any working historian knows, if he stops to reflect what he is doing as he thinks and writes, the historian is engaged on a continuous process of moulding his facts to his interpretation and his interpretation to his facts. It is impossible to assign primacy to one over the other.

The historian starts with a provisional selection of facts and a provisional interpretation in the light of which that selection has been made — by others as well as by himself. As he works, both the interpretation and the selection and ordering of facts undergo subtle and perhaps partly unconscious changes through the reciprocal action of one or the other. And this reciprocal action also involves reciprocity between present and past, since the historian is part of the present and the facts belong to the past. The historian and the facts of history are necessary to one another. The historian without his facts is rootless and futile; the facts without their historian are dead and meaningless. My first answer therefore to the question, What is History?, is that it is a continuous process of interaction between the historian and his facts, an unending dialogue between the present and the past.

7. *It is not by chance that histories, unlike the works of many other disciplines, are often best-sellers in the marketplace. One of the most prized features of historical works has been their readability. Scholars have consciously striven to reach the highest standards of literary grace. "The sense of form," writes Dame Cicely V. Wedgwood, "the capacity to weigh and to use words correctly, the shaping of sentences, and the structure and presentation of a scene, a fact, or an exposition are the natural concomitants of the clear, inquiring, disciplined and imaginative mind which is needed for historical research."* To describe how to achieve excellence in narrative form is by no means easy: such a virtue resists dissection. One of the few*

*C. V. Wedgwood, Truth and Opinion (London, 1960), p. 74.

[7] Reprinted from W. L. Morton, "The Art of the Narrative," *Culture* 20 (1959), pp. 395-399, 401-402 with the permission of the publishers.

Canadians who has tried is W. L. Morton, Professor of History at Trent University. His stress upon the "art of history" adds a new dimension to the task described by E. H. Carr in the previous reading. Dr. Morton's published works include The Progressive Party in Canada *(Toronto, 1950),* The Kingdom of Canada *(Toronto, 1963) and* The Critical Years: The Union of British North America *(Toronto, 1963).*

Of what, we may . . . ask, consists the art of history? The three elements, it is suggested here, are selection, arrangement and narration.

Selection is, in fact, twofold: first the selection of a subject, and second, the choice of facts to be presented in the development of that subject. With respect to subject, I do not refer to the historical paper, or essay; these, as in science or in other forms of literature, are confined to the exposition of an idea. They are analytical, and lack the true historical element of narrative. By a subject I mean an area of study extensive enough to permit the development of events in time, with broad description, with building of climaxes and with fluent narrative. A subject ought to have a beginning, middle and end. It ought to possess form; in a historical subject, the form must be a natural one. Much of the skill of the competent historian consists in having an eye for a subject, a sense of contours beneath, and the knack of pointing them up in analysis and narrative.[12]

Selection as a matter of determining the facts which are to be used is partly a matter of research, partly one of incipient composition. One begins research with a question to be answered, perhaps with an hypothesis to be tested. These govern the selection of one's first notes. Then, by a process the most mysterious and exciting in historical work, a subject, an exposition, begins to form, dissolve and reform in the researcher's mind. It is a process that continues during research and during the long culling, sorting and arranging of the notes. It does not completely end until the writing is finished.

The process is one which may be described, but is difficult to analyse. What are its sources and its determinants? It arises, I suggest, from the desire to find out what really happened. The determinants are the impact of actual fact discovered, tested and established, on the historian's questioning mind. The question demands an answer which shall be, not only factual, but also coherent, logical, formal. Thus the process of selecting the significant and revealing facts is very deep-seated; it arises in the historian at his most scientific and anticipates, in embryonic flutterings and strivings, the formal completion of his task.

The next of the trinity, arrangement, comes into play when the process of research is completed, and the transitional process of selection has passed its climax. Arrangement is the internal economy of the subject, the marshalling in outline of the chosen fact. The subject is arranged in periods or topics. A balance is struck between the need to drive ahead

[12] See C. V. Wedgwood, *Velvet Studies,* pp. 10, 11.

with the narrative and the necessity to pause to analyze a situation: as Carlyle wrote, "narrative is linear, action is solid."[13] The treatment of events is determined; when they are to march in straight line development, when a bird's eye view is to be taken, when the march is to be checked for block or cross section analysis, or whether two or more interweaving lines of advance must be attempted. The straight line advance is the normal choice, of course, and usually the most effective.

Arrangement must also take account of the element of personality. There are kinds of history which are not concerned with personality, but most history must find a place, even the chief place, for personality. An historical person is a fact or an event, but is not to be equated with an impersonal one. I do not speak now of the problem of how to recreate a personality, but only of that of managing the introduction, presentation, and development of the play of a personality in action. It is a very difficult matter, and may be treated in diverse ways. The simplest is to introduce the person at the opportune phase of the narrative, establish the character in isolation, and thereafter treat him as an acquaintance. More difficult and more effective is to arrange a grouping of personalities, also at an opportune phase. This is a favourite practice of Macaulay. Most exciting is the presentation of contrasted personalities, when such are afforded by the history. Macaulay loved to do this, and, of course, the contrasting personalities and careers of Gladstone and Disraeli are a gift for all time to the historians of Victorian England. Most effective, and the highest art, is to present the personality recurrently as the narrative and the personality develop reciprocally. Personalities which merit the exercise of such art are, however, comparatively few; in this, it is also to be noted, history is trenching on biography.

In the third member of the trinity, narration, we find the one definitely literary element in the art of history. The historian, I suggest, ought to study the elements of a good narrative style. The prime element is exposition. The root meaning of narration is to tell what one knows. A good narrative style is therefore a simple expository one, which never comes between the narrator and his audience. It should be above all things plain, though not pedestrian, and on occasion capable of variation, of elevation, of colour. It should abstain from rhetoric, in which form may supersede truth.

The next element in narration is pace. A narrative must march. By the cumulative use of tense, temporal adverbs and motive adjectives, of dates, of sweeping or hurrying rhythms, the historical writer may create a sense of motion in time, of events steadily building up in time sequences. This effect can be increased by judicious and well marked changes in speed.

A clear style and a good pace are to be achieved at the various levels of chapter, paragraph and sentence. In narration the chapter is the big wave which carries the story forward. The opening of the chapter begins the

---

[13] Thomas Carlyle, "On History," *Critical and Miscellaneous Essays,* II (London, 1869), p. 351.

lift of the wave, the main body delivers its rush, the close comes in the wash and the stir of the incoming force of the next. This phase of the historian's craft is, of course, closely related to arrangement. Macaulay, the master among English historians of arrangement, is also master of the handling of the chapter in narration.

If the chapter may be likened to the wave, the paragraph is the stride in narration. It is the swing of the whole body from one foot to the other and back again. The whole is carried forward a definite distance; so in narration, the paragraph must definitely carry the whole narrative, or at least that part of a complex narrative which is in play. It follows that the main body and close of a paragraph is, in proportion, as important as the handling of the same elements of the chapter.

The chapter and the paragraph, however, yield to the sentence as the main vehicle of narrative. If it cannot be said that an historical narrative is no stronger than its weakest sentence, it is true, at least, that the general quality of a narrative is determined by the average quality of its sentences. To me it seems that among the makers of historical style, two kinds of sentence are in favour. One I would dub a standard rhythmic sentence. It is a sentence which by phrase and rhythm balances in the structure of one statement contrasting or complementary elements. The supreme example is Gibbon's; majestic, moving, controlled, it marches across the centuries, carrying its imperial burden as steadily as the legions strode carrying the fate of Rome. So great is its power that it sweeps narrator and reader over the thin places where the records were scanty and doubtful and where interest flags. Edgar McInnis, among our own Canadian historians, to cite a contemporary example, employs a standard rhythmic sentence of much force and staying power. The other kind I would designate a flexible narrative sentence. This is essentially a simple, positive statement. As used by a master, however, as in J. A. Froude's description of the martyrdom of St. Thomas a Becket in *Short Studies on Great Subjects,* or by A. R. M. Lower in *Colony to Nation,* it is capable of much power, charm and precision. Its chief virtues are that it never betrays its employer or deceives the reader, and that it has a good narrative run.

None of these elements of narrative composition is, of course, used in isolation. As already indicated in the comments on the handling of the chapter, much of the narrator's art lies in taking up the thread from the preceding unit, spinning it through its own course, and casting it out to the next. Indeed, the quality of an historian's art may be quickly judged by examining his use of connectives. The linking of chapter to chapter, paragraph to paragraph, sentence to sentence is a very large part of the art of narration, by which the finest effects of sequence, run and tempo may be achieved.

*   *   *

Finally, in employing the re-creative and preservative properties of literary art, the historian may exercise the full freedom of the literary artist to give a sense of immediacy and to bring out the authenticity of his material. The historian, if he is capable, can make his history truer by judicious descriptive writing.[18] Parkman has conserved the now devastated American forest in his great history as it was before axe and fire had done their work, and that part of his work will remain true, whatever later research may do to the balance. This he did by the imaginative incorporation into his histories of his own experience of the American forest as it survived in his own day. Parkman was a master of the use of detail not recorded, but as Allan Nevins comments, "inherent in the situation."[19] To create a similar effect, the historian may pile on detail, like a Dutch master, as Donald Creighton does in the description of the women's dresses at the political picnics in *Macdonald: the Old Chieftain*.

In history when all is said, method is primary and art secondary. Yet art is important to history. It is necessary to win an audience, and without an audience, history will surely perish, not only for want of reward but for want of stimulus. History, as distinguished from antiquarianism, can never be content to talk to itself. Art in history is also important, because, properly understood and properly used, it is an aid to truth, demonstrable truth, in that it makes it more possible to recreate what actually happened. And the art of history is the art of narrative.

[18] Butterfield, *The Historical Novel* (Cambridge, 1924), p. 16.
[19] A. Nevins, *The Gateway to History* (Boston, 1938), p. 48.

8. Historians claim that the "scholarly attitude" encouraged by the reading of the subject is important. "It is not what is studied but how it is studied that matters," notes Harold Perkin.* In the following reading, G. Kitson Clark, an elder statesman among British historians, points out the need for high critical standards, not only among learned scholars but among general readers as well.†

A framework of unquestionable fact covers, after some sort, a large area of human affairs. Unless for some philosophical reason all knowledge is uncertain, the knowledge of these facts is certain. It has never covered the whole field of human affairs, and as you go further back into history the spaces in the lattice work get larger. Though the main members of the framework are by definition unquestionable it must always be a matter of dispute and judgment how far it extends, and there are also in the

*History: An Introduction for the Intending Student (**London, 1970**) p. 11.

†In this connection, it may be worth noting Marc Bloch's impassioned plea written at a time of crisis a generation ago. "It is a scandal that in our own age, which is more than ever exposed to the poisons of fraud and false rumour, the critical method is so completely absent from our school programmes . . . . [H]istory may reckon among its most certain glories that, by this elaboration of its technique, it has pioneered for mankind a new path to truth and, hence, to justice." Marc Bloch, The Historian's Craft (**New York, 1953**), pp. 136-137.

[8] Reprinted from G. Kitson Clark, "The Scholarly Attitude" in *The Critical Historian* (London, 1967), pp. 125-127, 127-128, with the permission of Heinemann Educational Books Ltd., London.

history of any period disputable facts, likely guesses and probable hypotheses about facts which are not sustained by it.

The nature of human motive can never be guaranteed by the framework of fact, nor probably can the results of human action or of events, since it is not possible to know with certainty what would have happened if the facts had not been as they were. Nor is it possible to be sure that you know, or at least you know completely the causes of things. For this reason the framework of fact will never by itself supply the interpretation of history, though any interpretation that disregards the framework of fact can itself be disregarded.

Into the consideration of anything which lies beyond the framework of fact the human element will intrude. This is obvious in relation to any question of interpretation, but it is also true of any question of disputed fact. It will be necessary to take into account the extent and limitations of the powers of human beings to observe, to form inferences from what they observe, to remember, to record, to present what they have recorded in a newspaper or history book. But not only will the powers of human beings to observe, infer and record be in question, but also the ways in which they do these things will be controlled by their wills, by their passions, by their interests and by the very fact that they are human beings.

All this will produce uncertainty, but there will be degrees of uncertainty. The question with what degree of uncertainty a fact should be accepted will provide problems to be resolved by the use of trained judgment and the teaching of an experience of the problems which history presents. That judgment and experience will without doubt suggest that much of what human beings accept as part of their picture of the past is spurious, or doubtful, or unknowable. But they will also suggest descriptions and explanations of historical events which, though tentative and hypothetical, are probably a better guide to reality, and a surer basis for action, than what is proposed by the confidence of ignorance.

Unfortunately it is not normally possible for the ordinary user of history to press home himself the questions which ought to be asked of evidence into which the human element has introduced this element of uncertainty, or to resolve the problems which history presents. He may not have the skill and experience to do these things; he will probably not have the leisure; he will almost certainly not have command of the necessary material. Yet it is of considerable importance that he should understand the rudiments of historical criticism. He is after all the consumer. It is for his use that history and journalism is written. If he demands a high critical standard in what is written for him he will in the end get it. If he objects that questions have not been asked of the evidence which should have been asked, in due course those who are in a position to ask such questions will make it their business to do so.

In order to press home his legitimate requirements it is however necessary for the ordinary reader to learn more than he normally knows today about the techniques of scholarship even if he is not going to use them. For instance it is important that more ordinary unprofessional readers should understand the significance of footnotes than now seem to do so. Footnotes are not as many people seem to think the mere exuberance of pedantry, and they ought not to be, as they sometimes are, the tiresome reflections of an exhibitionist desire to parade erudition, or the result of an incurable diffuseness of mind. They should indicate, and when they are properly constructed they do indicate, the necessary links between the work of the historian and the evidence upon which it is based.

* * *

Scholarly writing demands scholarly reading and scholarly readers. Scholarly readers will demand a higher standard of scholarship in what is written for them, and higher standards of scholarship probably means a nearer approach to truth on matters which may be of considerable importance to mankind. But more important than any grasp of scholarly technique is the lesson of the habit of scholarly hesitation, the habit of the mind which teaches the great difficulty, even the impossibility, of arriving at the truth about many of the facts relating to events in the past. It is a habit of mind which leads to the rejection of much, and possibly the assured acceptance of little, but it can be used to dissolve for ever some of the legends, the dogmatic statements, the facile explanations which have troubled mankind.

Therefore the lesson of historical criticism as applied to the facts of history is to a large extent a lesson in how to doubt what perhaps might have been accepted previously without question. But it teaches doubt not scepticism, an uncertainty about what is to be accepted as truth not a belief that anything might be true or that everything may be false or that knowledge is impossible. The exercise of historical criticism does not teach blind doubt, doubt that does not discriminate between the degrees of certainty and probability, but rather trained or skilled doubt, that has learnt from man's experience to make this discrimination.

To learn how to doubt should therefore be one of the important rewards of an historical education.

FIVE

DO HISTORIANS TELL US WHAT ACTUALLY HAPPENED?

People are often disturbed by the failure of historians to produce unbiased interpretations of the past. Scarcely a year passes without an exposé of a writer's wrong-doing. Within the last decade or so commentators in Great Britain, Canada and the United States have accused history of being a "betrayer," "teaching prejudice" and contributing to "international misunderstanding."[1] Historians, apparently, have been pronounced guilty of not telling the truth about the past.

There appears to be clear evidence to support the charge. Nationalistic viewpoints among historians are not difficult to document. The story of the Armada in a Spanish history book, for ex-

---

[1] E. H. Dance, *History the Betrayer: A Study in Bias* (London, 1960),
G. McDiarmid and D. Pratt, *Teaching Prejudice* (Toronto, 1971) and
Ray Allen Billington, *The Historian's Contribution to Anglo-American Misunderstanding* (New York, 1966).

ample, bears little similarity to the same event in a British book.[2] Catholic and Protestant historians have tended to give contradictory opinions about the role of Luther in the history of the Christian Church. Nor do the bitter differences among historians over issues which the layman cannot understand inspire confidence in the public.

In his own defence the historian points to the great difficulty of being certain about the past. Knowing about events, or even entire civilizations, is by no means as clear cut as the layman imagines. As we have noted in the previous chapter, there are many incidents and peoples about which documentation is very skimpy. On other topics, however, the evidence exists by the ton and teams of scholars working for a life-time cannot read and reflect on all of it. Whether the evidence be overly abundant or almost non-existent, if a history is to be written, then facts must be selected, generalizations made and opinions formed. All of these processes require decisions and actions based more on human judgment than scientific methodology. Since the historian is an artist using his personal skills to recreate the past as he sees it, it is not surprising that honest disagreement should exist among scholars or that "the truth," as D. J. Goodspeed puts it, "— the infinitely complex, incomprehensible, multitudinous truth — is blurred or is comprehended only in outline or vaguely, as a shape seen through a mist."[3]

In more recent years, especially since the end of the Second World War, scholars have tried to limit the excesses that have characterized some historical writings in the past. The dangers of allowing a personal standard of moral conduct to guide one's pen, or writing history from a nationalistic point of view, are well known. Historians try to place in proper perspective pressures to organize the past to explain the present or to write history to justify contemporary conditions. Contemporary writers may not be able to isolate themselves from these problems but at least they will not stumble into an unmarked quagmire.

In the last resort, questions about the truth of history are closely related to one's conception of the subject and the form in which it should be written. If it is regarded as a catalogue of events capable of scientific verification, the problem of veracity is of a different order than if history is seen as a humanistic impression of the past. Whatever one's view of the subject, however, there are standards and canons of scholarship that cannot be ignored. The answer to a question about what actually happened may be found not in the past itself but in the questions the historian brings to his evidence, the scholarly integrity with which he handles that evidence, and

[2] J. Trueman, The Anatomy of History (Toronto, 1967) pp. 45-47.

[3] D. J. Goodspeed, "The Calculus of History," The Dalhousie Review, 38 (Winter, 1959) p. 432.

the judgments he makes. Although his answers may be far from certain, in the long run the final result may be more mind-enlarging than any simplistic solution. Wisdom may come not from knowing but from reflecting on how the known is known.

1. Some writers have been so concerned with patriotism or good citizenship that their histories have shown their nation's heroes and achievements in the best light possible. Livy, in his story of the founding of Rome, gave short shrift to the culture of the enemies of his state and extolled the virtues of Roman generals. The widespread use of nationally oriented histories in the present century has been seen as a major feature in the growth of a blinkered nationalism.* If readers always encounter interpretations stressing their own nation's point of view, the argument goes, they are more likely to take an unsympathetic or even belligerent stance on questions related to their nation's dealings with other peoples. In the early 1960s a team of American and British scholars investigated this thesis. The title of their final report, The Historian's Contribution to Anglo-American Misunderstanding *(New York, 1966) left no doubt about the tenor of their findings. In a companion article R. A. Billington indicated how certain types of bias can deflect a writer from a judicious interpretation of the past.†*

Fortunately the fiery nationalism that marred American history textbooks a half-century ago has largely disappeared, but enough remains to alter the viewpoint of future statesmen and hinder the international cooperation essential to peace in a contracting world. This is the conclusion of a team of British and American historians who have just completed a survey of the secondary school textbooks most widely used in the history courses of the two nations today.

Nationalistic bias, they find, exists as it did in the nineteenth century, but in a less blatant form. Gone is the day, happily, when an author could write that "it is impossible for the imagination to conceive of characters more selfish, profligate, and vile, than the line of English kings." Gone is the era when English schoolboys were taught that George Washington was a black-hearted villain who engineered an unjustified revolution for

---

*"Each people tends to recall and record the things which are congenial to itself, and to forget or ignore those which are favourable to foreigners." E. H. Dance, History the Betrayer: A Study in Bias (London, 1960), p. 21.

†It may be worth noting Max Beloff's perceptive comment that "one must be grateful to Professor Billington and his colleagues for the work they have done, but their version of Anglo-American history is just as subjective as mine or that of anyone else." "Subjective Objections," The Listener, 75 (February 17, 1966), p. 252.

[1] Reprinted from Ray Allen Billington, "History Is a Dangerous Subject," *Saturday Review*, January 15, 1966, pp. 59-61 with the permission of the author and the publisher. Copyright 1966 Saturday Review, Inc.

personal aggrandizement. Modern youths on both sides of the Atlantic are too sophisticated to accept such patently one-sided untruths.

Yet nationalistic bias persists, and in somewhat more dangerous form than the monstrous distortions of a past generation. Today's bias is more subtle, more persuasive, and far less easy to detect, partly because it often mirrors subconscious prejudices of which the textbook author himself is unaware. Today's textbooks plant in the minds of their readers a belief in the overall superiority of their own countries, not simply an exaggerated image of the virtues of past leaders. The misconceptions accepted unquestioningly by the students of this generation may warp their judgment no less seriously than the misstatements forced on Franklin D. Roosevelt at an earlier time.

The team of five British and American historians reached the conclusion that proper care and training can produce objective judgments suitable to the taste of both nations. But they also found that remarkably few textbook authors in either the United States or Great Britain have achieved that degree of objectivity. Every single volume surveyed contains some indications of national bias; only seven of the twenty-two English books and only two or three of the fourteen American could be graded as even relatively free from prejudice. If these discouraging results can be drawn from the reading of texts used in two countries that have been traditionally friendly and usually allied in world conflict, what would be revealed by a study of German and American textbooks, or of those used in the United States and Russia? Clearly national bias is a besetting sin of today's authors, and equally clearly it should be eliminated in the interest of world harmony.

Many are guilty of what might be called "bias by inertia." They have shown a regrettable disinclination to keep abreast of the findings of modern historical scholarship, relying instead on discredited legends and outworn viewpoints that more often than not perpetuate the nationalistic prejudices of a bygone day. Thus current research students picture George III as a sincere and moderately competent ruler bent on achieving administrative reforms amidst an impossible political situation. Yet a disgracefully large number of authors (some in England) still paint him as a power-hungry monarch, buying votes and manipulating ministers to achieve absolutism. Historians know that most of the acts for which he is blamed by textbook writers were the common practice of his day, on both sides of the Atlantic; "bribery" is a word that must be defined within the context of its times to become meaningful. Yet the findings of recent scholarship have seeped down to only a few authors of secondary school books.

*　　*　　*

If text writers on both sides of the Atlantic can be charged with foisting disproven myths on their readers, they also stand indicted for manipulating facts in a manner designed — consciously or unconsciously — to glorify their own nations at the expense of others. An almost universal sin among them is what can be labeled "bias by omission." Every historian has as a principal duty the selection of facts and interpretations that will most accurately portray the event he is describing. When an author chooses *only* information that will reflect credit on his personal heroes, he is violating the canons of sound historical writing no less than the writer who openly distorts the truth.

Such is the practice of a disgracefully large number of authors in both England and the United States. American writers time and time again recite the impressive record of General George Washington's military victories during the Revolutionary War, while barely mentioning his defeats. Readers emerge from such accounts with the impression that the patriots (itself a biased word) lost only the Battle of Bunker Hill, and that because they ran out of powder. English writers dwell with equal affection on the triumphs of their generals, leaving the student bewildered that such a series of victories could have lost a war.

The War of 1812 offers textbook writers an even more tempting paradeground for one-sided distortions that tell less than half the truth. Every text read by junior high school students in the United States describes in some detail the victory of the *Constitution* over the *Guerrière,* but only one mentions the triumph of the *Shannon* over the *Chesapeake,* and then apparently only as an excuse to repeat the command of the American commander: "Don't give up the ship." Every British textbook that mentions the sea battles of the War of 1812 dwells on the victory of the *Shannon* over the *Chesapeake,* omitting any mention whatsoever of the *Constitution's* conquest of the *Guerrière.* Not a single junior high school textbook used in the United States fails to describe the burning of Washington by British troops during the war, and not one tells of the American burning of the Canadian city of York that led to England's retaliation. This is not objective history, and certainly conjures up visions of bloodstirring triumphs in the youth of each nation that are not sustained by the facts.

The most flagrant example of bias by omission can be found in the treatment — or lack of treatment — of the War of 1812 in English textbooks. Admittedly, this was not a major conflict in Britain's long history. Yet this war set the stage for the future as did few conflicts of the nineteenth century; from it stemmed a series of agreements that underlay the long period of cooperative friendship between Britain and the United States; to it can be traced the century-long era of internal development that allowed America to emerge as a major power. These are crucial developments, and well worth the telling to English audiences at a time when world events are driving the two nations ever more closely together. Yet in several British texts no mention whatsoever is made of the war; in the remainder it usually appears as a minor distraction engineered by former rebels bent on hampering Britain's major effort against Napoleon. To say of this conflict *only* that Wellington was handicapped because "the best of his veterans had been sent to fight in a war that had broken out between Britain and the United States of America" (as does one book), or that "this led to a short, ignominious war (1812-1814) between England and the United States, which as a neutral country objected to Britain's claim to board and search her ships" (as does another), is to surrender to national bias almost as flagrant as that of a flag-waving superpatriot.

If a subjective selection of materials to be included reveals the nationalistic bias of nearly all textbook writers, so does the sense of group superiority that permeates the writing of many of them. They write unabashedly as Americans or Englishmen, standing squarely with feet planted in Boston or Washington or London. The result is distortion, often subconscious, but nonetheless dangerous. To write sound history an author must make every effort to view the total picture, not only the half nearest him. He must strive to see events through the eyes of both George Grenville and Samuel Adams; he must sound the prejudices of George Washington no less than those of George III. Only then will he fully understand the national problems and viewpoints that determine history's events. Admittedly this is a difficult task, but it is not impossible. Intelligent reading of the sources and secondary works originating in *all* nations concerned with any one event, and constant awareness of the inherited prejudices that are part of every national culture, allows the writing of unbiased history, as a few textbooks prove. Eternal vigilance is the price of good history, no less than of liberty.

Instead a subconscious sense of group superiority leads textbook authors to glorify their own nation at the expense of all others, and blinds them to the motives and purposes of rival powers. British writers especially are inclined to use "our armies" or "our people," encouraging the schoolboy to associate himself with a superior in-group that is sharply distinguished from an inferior out-group. Many mirror belief in English superiority when they consistently cast their leaders in the role of heroes and repeatedly suggest the invincibility of their armies. One only exaggerates this tendency by declaring that the British regulars during the Revolution "could be relied upon to beat the irregular levies of rebels whenever they fought on anything like equal terms." This may be a subconscious manifestation of national bias, but it is no less destructive of international understanding.

2. When a historian organizes his data and begins to interpret the past, he may find himself unconsciously thinking of the problems of his own day rather than those of the period he is studying. Some nineteenth-century historians, for example, investigating the development of parliamentary institutions, tended to look so diligently in the past for evidence of that growth that events were distorted and individuals given greater significance than they deserved. Sir Herbert Butterfield, in a famous book published forty years ago,

[2] Reprinted from Herbert Butterfield, *The Whig Interpretation of History,* 1931, pp. 3-8 with the permission of G. Bell & Sons Ltd., London.

stated a very strong case that many historians had looked at history through highly coloured spectacles, that their ideals had formed their framework of their past and that their value systems had proved the touchstones by which other peoples were judged. The title of his book, The Whig Interpretation of History, *is used throughout the English-speaking world to indicate an attitude of mind. Professor Copp in an article in the next chapter, shows how Butterfield's concept can be applied to Canadian history.*

It is astonishing to what an extent the historian has been Protestant, progressive, and whig, and the very model of the nineteenth century gentleman. Long after he became a determinist he retained his godly rôle as the dispenser of moral judgments, and like the disciples of Calvin he gave up none of his right to moral indignation. Even when he himself has been unsympathetic to the movements of his own generation, as in the case of Hallam, who bitterly opposed the Great Reform Bill and trembled to think of the revolutionary ways into which the country was moving, something in his constitution still makes him lean to what might be called the whig interpretation of history, and he refuses historical understanding to men whose attitude in the face of change and innovation was analogous to his own. It might be argued that our general version of the historical story still bears the impress that was given to it by the great patriarchs of history-writing, so many of whom seem to have been whigs and gentlemen when they have not been Americans: and perhaps it is from these that our textbook historians have inherited the top hat and the pontifical manner, and the grace with which they hand out a consolation prize to the man who, 'though a reactionary, was irreproachable in his private life.' But whether we take the contest of Luther against the popes, or that of Philip II and Elizabeth, or that of the Huguenots with Catherine de' Medici; whether we take Charles I versus his parliaments or the younger Pitt versus Charles James Fox, it appears that the historian tends in the first place to adopt the whig or Protestant view of the subject, and very quickly busies himself with dividing the world into the friends and enemies of progress. It is true that this tendency is corrected to some extent by the more concentrated labours of historical specialists, but it is remarkable that in all the examples given above, as well as in many others, the result of detailed historical research has been to correct very materially what had been an accepted Protestant or whig interpretation. Further, this whig tendency is so deep-rooted that even when piece-meal research has corrected the story in detail, we are slow in re-valuing the whole and reorganising the broad outlines of the theme in the light of these discoveries; and what M. Romier has deplored in the historians of the Huguenots might fairly be imputed to those in other fields of history; that is, the tendency to patch the new research into the old story even when the research in detail has altered the bearings of the whole subject. We cling to a certain organisation of historical knowledge which amounts to a whig interpretation of history, and all our deference to research brings us only to admit that this needs qualifications in detail. But exceptions in detail do not prevent us from mapping out the large story on the same pattern all the time; these exceptions are lost indeed in that combined process of organisation and abridgment by which we reach our general survey of general history; and so it is over large periods and in reference to the great transitions in European history that the whig view holds hardest and holds longest; it is here that we see the results of a serious discrepancy between the historical specialist and what might be called the general historian.

The truth is that there is a tendency for all history to veer over into whig history, and this is not sufficiently explained if we merely ascribe it to the prevalence and persistence of a traditional interpretation. There is a magnet forever pulling at our minds, unless we have found the way to counteract it; and it may be said that if we are merely honest, if we are not also carefully self-critical, we tend easily to be deflected by a first fundamental fallacy. And though this may even apply in a subtle way to the detailed work of the historical specialist, it comes into action with increasing effect the moment any given subject has left the hands of the student in research; for the more we are discussing and not merely enquiring, the more we are making inferences instead of researches, then the more whig our history becomes if we have not severely repressed our original error; indeed all history must tend to become more whig in proportion as it becomes more abridged. Further, it cannot be said that all faults of bias may be balanced by work that is deliberately written with the opposite bias; for we do not gain true history by merely adding the speech of the prosecution to the speech for the defence; and though there have been Tory — as there have been many Catholic — partisan histories, it is still true that there is no corresponding tendency for the subject itself to lean in this direction; the dice cannot be secretly loaded by virtue of the same kind of original unconscious fallacy. For this reason it has been easy to believe that Clio herself is on the side of the whigs.

3. Some historians have despaired of ever coming close to the truth. The issues are too many: the evidence too voluminous. Such a vital part is played by the observer himself, the argument goes, that history becomes a series of personal statements formed by and in the historian's mind. Everyman His Own Historian, *(New York, 1935), written by the author of the following reading, became a doctrine for many writers. By examining three questions, what is the historical fact, where is the historical fact, and when is the historical fact, Carl Becker shows the close relationship of truth in the past*

[3] From Carl L. Becker, "What Are the Historical Facts?"
from the *Western Political Quarterly*, Vol. VIII, No. 3, (Sept. 1955)
pp. 327-340. Reprinted by permission of the University of Utah,
copyright holder.

to the personality of the historian. Professor Becker (1873-1945) taught for many years at Cornell University and wrote, among other distinguished works, The Heavenly City of the Eighteenth-Century Philosophers *(New Haven, 1932).*

What ... is the historical fact? Far be it from me to define so illusive and intangible a thing! But provisionally I will say this: the historian may be interested in anything that has to do with the life of man in the past — any act or event, any emotion which men have expressed, any idea, true or false, which they have entertained. Very well, the historian is interested in some event of this sort. Yet he cannot deal directly with this event itself, since the event itself has disappeared. What he can deal with directly is a *statement about the event.* He deals in short not with the event, but with a statement which affirms *the fact that the event occurred.* When we really get down to the hard facts, what the historian is always dealing with is an *affirmation* — an affirmation of the fact that something is true. There is thus a distinction of capital importance to be made: the distinction between the ephemeral event which disappears, and the affirmation about the event which persists. For all practical purposes it is this affirmation about the event that constitutes for us the historical fact. If so the historical fact is not the past event, but a symbol which enables us to recreate it imaginatively. Of a symbol it is hardly worthwhile to say that it is cold or hard. It is dangerous to say even that it is true or false. The safest thing to say about a symbol is that it is more or less appropriate.

This brings me to the second question — Where is the historical fact? I will say at once, however brash it sounds, that the historical fact is in someone's mind or it is nowhere. To illustrate this statement I will take an event familiar to all. "Abraham Lincoln was assassinated in Ford's Theater in Washington on the 14th of April, 1865." That *was* an actual event, occurrence, fact at the moment of happening. But speaking now, in the year 1926, we say it *is* an historical fact. We don't say that it *was* an historical fact, for that would imply that it no longer is one. We say that it *was* an actual event, but *is now* an historical fact. The actual occurrence and the historical fact, however closely connected, are two different things. Very well, if the assassination of Lincoln is an historical fact, where is this fact now? Lincoln is not being assassinated now in Ford's Theater, or anywhere else (except perhaps in propagandist literature!). The actual occurrence, the event, has passed, is gone forever, never to be repeated, never to be again experienced or witnessed by any living person. Yet this is precisely the sort of thing the historian is concerned with — events, acts, thoughts, emotions that have forever vanished as actual occurrences. How can the historian deal with vanished realities? He can deal with them because these vanished realities give place to pale reflections, impalpable images or ideas of themselves, and these pale reflections, and impalpable images which cannot be touched or handled are all that is left of the actual occurrence. These are therefore what the historian deals with. These are his "material." He has to be satisfied with these, for the very good reason that he has nothing else. Well then, where are they — these pale reflections and impalpable images of the actual? Where are these facts? They are, as I said before, in his mind, or in somebody's mind, or they are nowhere.

*   *   *

Now for the third question — When is the historical fact? If you agree with what has been said (which is extremely doubtful) the answer seems simple enough. If the historical fact is present, imaginatively, in someone's mind, then it is now, a part of the present. But the word present is a slippery word, and the thing itself is worse than the word. The present is an indefinable point in time, gone before you can think it; the image or idea which I have now present in mind slips instantly into the past. But images or ideas of past events are often, perhaps always, inseparable from images or ideas of the future. Take an illustration. I awake this morning, and among the things my memory drags in to enlighten or distress me is a vague notion that there was something I needed particularly to remember but cannot — a common experience surely. What is it that I needed to remember I cannot recall; but I can recall that I made a note of it in order to jog my memory. So I consult my little pocket memorandum book — a little Private Record Office which I carry about, filled with historical sources. I take out my memorandum book in order to do a little historical research; and there I find (Vol. I, p. 20) the dead historical fact — "Pay Smith's coal bill today: $1,016." The image of the memorandum book now drops out of mind, and is replaced by another image — an image of what? Why an image, an idea, a picture (call it what you will) made up of three things more or less inseparable. First the image of myself ordering coal from Smith last summer; second, the image of myself holding the idea in mind that I must pay the bill; third, the image of myself going down to Smith's office at four o'clock to pay it. The image is partly of things done in the past, and partly of things to be done in the future; but it is more or less all one image now present in mind.

4. D. J. Goodspeed, a Canadian historian now teaching at Brock University who specializes in military history,* points to some of the great difficulties in establishing the truth about the past. The meanings of the facts upon which we rely are elusive and the thoughts of men imponderable. It is scarcely surprising, therefore, that he concludes that "all roads lead ultimately to the Perilous Wood where all men lose their way."

*Professor Goodspeed's published works include The Conspirators: A Study of the Coup d'Etat (Toronto, 1962), Ludendorff: Genius of World War I (Toronto, 1966) and The Road Past Vimy: The Canadian Corps 1914-1918 (Toronto, 1969).

[4] Reprinted by permission from D. J. Goodspeed, "The Calculus of History," in Dalhousie Review, 38, (4) Winter 1959, pp. 426-428.

Even a little thought soon shows that it is easier to say what history does not attempt to do than to be positive about what it does. And it is very obvious that, whatever else the aim of history may be, it cannot be complete cognition. That, in the nature of things, is unattainable for the historian. In the first place his subject matter is too vast and too complex, and in the second, the relationships between phenomena are in time, and time, if not infinite, must certainly be regarded as such for the purposes of history.

The historian then must select events and compress time. Not even the most factual history of the most trivial occurrence can hope to be complete. The simplest historical event, the tiniest battle, is in its ramifications factually beyond our comprehension. Some aspects of it indeed we may grasp — the count in dead and wounded, what the commanders or certain prominent figures did, the final positions and conditions of the armies (although even here we are soon out of the factual and into the speculative when we speak of condition), but the detail — that is to say, the event itself — escapes us.

Even more serious a handicap is the fact that all historical phenomena are *sui generis*. They are fixed in point of time and are non-repeatable. Thus, anything in the nature of a controlled experiment becomes impossible. To do it justice the event would have to be re-lived, and that is an attempt beyond our powers. Modern science, like a lantern in a fog, can push back only a little way the encompassing circle of our ignorance. The techniques of chemistry and of criticism may expose the Donation of Constantine, as the techniques of geology may explode the delightful hoax of the Piltdown Man, but this is merely negative assistance. More positively, the motion-picture camera may take us on a warm summer morning to the streets of Marseilles and may show us what happened that day to Barthou, the foreign minister of France, and to King Alexander of Yugoslavia. We may thus vicariously see the sudden dart forward of the assassin, the firing of the fatal shots, the grimaces of pain on the faces of the victims, the cutting down of the murderer under the sabres of the mounted guard. As we watch the film we feel that here at last we are approaching complete factual cognition.

But all of this is, in reality, a double illusion. We deceive ourselves if we believe that it brings us appreciably nearer to the truth. Such a record does not reveal to us either the physical event itself or the meaning or force of the event. We do not see the dew-drops on the hedges of the Marseilles streets; we do not smell the sea; there are a thousand aspects of the occurrence that are denied us. And since they are denied us, we call them inconsequential. But they are not therefore necessarily so. Was it not, perhaps, some childhood memory, some recollection of sunlight on the snow, that caused the nameless boy who should have been the murderer of Alexander II of Russia to turn away that morning beside the banks of the Catherine Canal and not throw his bomb? The terrorists in that case were wise to insure against such possibilities, to see to it that there was also a Rysakov and a Grinivetski to push the work forward to its completion. Yet in each case history deals only with the dead matter; the substance of life eludes us. The murdered king and the dying minister in the carriage are facts, and upon these our imagination, starved of reality, seizes. What the Tsar Alexander said as he lay bleeding in the snow we eagerly record, but of what he felt, of what he thought, what memories or what regrets came flooding into his pain-clouded mind we can only guess.

And is not this also the case in our own lives? Which of us, by taking thought, can explain the failure of first love, or the motivation of decisions, or the incalculable results of actions? We are all in a sense amateur historians. We try to piece together the remembered segments of our lives and make a pattern out of them. And all of us, just like the professionals, fail in this. We find, if we look attentively enough, if pride, or fear, or some arrogance of the intellect does not intervene, that there are patterns overlaid on patterns. As we peer into the profundities of any event, the sunlight, and refraction, and the inadequacy of our own eyes, but most of all the terrible depth of the water, prevents us from seeing the bottom. It is not in practice true that any road will take you to the end of the world. It would be more fair to say that all roads lead ultimately to the Perilous Wood where all men lose their way.

5. One of the commonest demands made of both historians and history teachers is that they should be "objective." In the following extract Marcel Trudel, Professor of History at the University of Ottawa, attempts to define this difficult word and show how the need for objectivity affects the work of the historian. (See Appendix for translation of this article.)

On comprend d'abord que l'objectivité n'existe qu'en rapport avec l'objet, c'est-à-dire que l'objet doit conserver toute son intégrité: l'histoire reste donc objective pour autant qu'elle reste elle-même dans l'absolu de son être. C'est ensuite par extension que l'on peut dire d'un historien qu'il est objectif, s'il respecte l'intégrité de son objet. L'objectivité, dans ses exigences absolues, demande donc que le passé, entrevu par l'historien, grâce à un témoin intermédiaire, garde son intégrité absolue. Or, dans les conditions actuelles, il est impossible qu'on lui conserve son intégrité absolue, il est impossible que la Nouvelle-France se présente à nous aussi exactement que si nous étions les employés supérieurs de la Compagnie des Cent-Associés, et c'est pourquoi, les historisants, découragés ou sceptiques, nous recommanderont d'éditer tout simplement le texte de la charte de cette Compagnie et celui de ses états de compte, au lieu de tenter de

[5] Reprinted by permission from Marcel Trudel, "L'Objectivité en Histoire," in *Revue D'Histoire de L'Amérique Française*, 5(3), December 1951, pp. 316-318.

la faire revivre, au lieu de l'expliquer et de la juger: ce ne serait plus de l'histoire. Et pourtant l'histoire a sa raison d'être, elle reste toujours à faire et l'historien, à qui l'on impose l'objectivité absolue, demeure toujours perplexe devant son objet.

Il faut donc reconnaître qu'une exigence qui empêche l'objet de se manifester, n'est plus légitime; qu'une objectivité absolue n'est plus objective parce qu'elle détruit l'objet lui-même. Il faut donc admettre d'abord que l'histoire sera écrite par l'intermédiaire d'un témoin. Mais quand on écrit l'histoire, il faut faire appel à de très nombreux témoins et parfois les témoins que la postérité nous a conservés peuvent se présenter à nous en grand nombre, facilement et comme d'eux-mêmes: qui fera le choix entre tous ces témoins? Rien d'autre, personne d'autre que l'historien: rien d'autre parce que nous ne sommes plus ici dans un laboratoire, personne d'autre parce que personne ne peut mieux travailler dans ce domaine que l'historien rompu à la besogne. Ainsi, on atténue une seconde fois l'objectivité absolue: on reconnaît que l'historien peut légitimement se placer entre nous et les témoins du passé.

Ce deuxième intermédiaire entre nous et le passé, cet historien est bien une personne humaine, un homme en chair et en os: quelle sera la position de cet homme en face du passé? Fénelon a écrit: "Le bon historien n'est d'aucun temps ni d'aucun pays"; on s'est autorisé de ce mot pour revendiquer l'objectivité absolue, et pourtant Fénelon, pour bien se faire comprendre, avait aussitôt ajouté que le bon historien ne doit prendre parti ni pour l'un ni pour l'autre. Comme il ne s'agit pas ici de répondre à Fénelon, mais à ceux qui abusent de lui, nous prenons quand même le mot tel qu'on l'explique d'ordinaire: si l'on tient compte que l'historien est un homme bien vivant (et il ne peut en être autrement), ce mot, tel qu'on l'interprète, rend l'histoire impossible ou vaine. Si l'historien écrit l'histoire, il ne peut être autrement que de son temps, il ne peut installer son observatoire ailleurs que dans son temps: comment pourrait-il se situer dans un avenir qu'il ne peut connaître ou dans un passé qu'il cherche précisément à connaître; chassez-le de son temps et la position que vous lui donnez, en plus d'être aussi localisée que celle que vous lui reprochez, aura le désavantage d'être bien plus dangereuse. Peut-il être autrement que de son pays? Prenons, à titre d'exemple, un historien du Canada français. C'est lui, avant tout autre, qui doit écrire l'histoire du Canada français, car, mieux que tout autre, il la connaît parce qu'il en vit intimement; il sera du Canada français, à condition évidemment qu'il se place au-dessus (ce qui ne veut pas dire au dehors); il respectera l'intégrité de son objet, le Canada français; il écrira même l'histoire générale du Canada en fonction de cet objet: procéder autrement, ce serait vraiment manquer d'objectivité, puisque ce serait anéantir l'objet lui-même. Ceux qui s'opposent à l'histoire du Canada français se trouvent ainsi les plus grands destructeurs de l'objectivité. Ils nous disent que cette histoire devrait désormais s'intégrer, se confondre dans l'histoire générale du Canada, mais on ne voit pas pourquois cette histoire serait plus objective, car on pourrait alléguer, à bon droit, que l'histoire générale du Canada n'a alors aucune raison de ne pas se confondre à son tour dans l'histoire pan-américaine; et si l'on voulait nous restreindre à l'histoire panaméricaine, on pourrait encore alléguer que cette histoire panaméricaine doit se perdre tout normalement dans la grande histoire européenne et ainsi, de l'histoire européenne à l'histoire mondiale, on en arrive, en recherchant l'objectivité absolue, à ne plus avoir d'objet ou plutôt, l'historien demeure toujours aussi perplexe que tantôt devant son objet. A la lumière du principe de l'objectivité, rien ne nous oblige à laisser de côté l'histoire du Canada français, sous prétexte qu'il existe depuis quatre-vingts ans une entente aussi artificielle que celle de la Confédération. L'historien sera de son temps et de son pays: ce sera pour lui une excellente disposition pour respecter l'intégrité de son objet, pour être objectif. Remarquons, en passant, que nous ne parlons pas d'impartialité: l'objectivité ne comporte que l'intégrité, l'impartialité fait partie de la *méthode* et non de la nature même de l'objet.

6. According to earlier readings in this chapter, historians are influenced by problems of their own day and age. J. H. Hexter, an American expert on British sixteenth- and seventeenth-century history at Yale University, accepts the premise but subjects the conclusion to engaging criticism by examining his own "day" and its effect upon his own work.

As I write, portentous and momentous things are no doubt being done in Peiping, Teheran, Bonn, and Jakarta. But these things are no part of my day; they are outside of my experience, and though one or two of them may faintly impinge on my consciousness tomorrow via the headlines in the morning paper, that is probably as far as they will get. At best they are likely to remain fluttering fragments on the fringe of my experience, not well-ordered parts of it. I must insist emphatically that the history I write is, as the present-minded say, intimately connected with my own day and inextricably linked with my own experience; but I must insist with even stronger emphasis that my day is not someone else's day, or the ideal Day of Contemporary Man; it is just the way I happen to dispose of twenty-four hours. By the same token the experience that is inextricably linked to any history I may happen to write is not the ideal Experience of Twentieth-Century Man in World Chaos, but just the way I happen to put in my time over the series of my days.

Now it may seem immodest or perhaps simply fantastic to take days spent as are mine — days so little attuned to the great harmonies, discords and issues of the present — and hold them up for contemplation. Yet I

[6] Reprinted from J. H. Hexter, "The Historian and His Day," in *Reappraisals in History* (London, 1961), pp. 7, 8-9, 10-12 with the permission of the author and the publisher, Longman Group Limited.

will dare to suggest that in this historian's own humdrum days there is one peculiarity that merits thought. The peculiarity lies in the curious relation that days so squandered seem to establish between the present and a rather remote sector of the past. I do not pretend that I am wholly unconcerned by the larger public issues and catastrophes of the present; nor am I without opinions on a large number of contemporary issues. On some of them I am vigorously dogmatic as, indeed, are most of the historians I know. Yet my knowledge about such issues, although occasionally fairly extensive, tends to be haphazard, vague, unsystematic and disorderly. And the brute fact of the matter is that even if I had the inclination, I do not have the time to straighten that knowledge out except at the cost of alterations in the ordering of my days that I am not in the least inclined to undertake.

*　　*　　*

The austere rule we live under as historians has some curious consequences. In my case one of the consequences is that my knowledge of the period around the sixteenth century in Europe is of a rather different order than my knowledge about current happenings. Those preponderant segments of my own day spent in the discussion, investigation and contemplation of that remote era may not be profitably spent but at least they are spent in an orderly, systematic, purposeful way. The contrast can be pointed up by a few details. I have never read the Social Security Act, but I have read the Elizabethan Poor Law in all its successive versions and moreover I have made some study of its application. I have never read the work of a single existentialist but I have read Calvin's *Institutes of the Christian Religion* from cover to cover. I know practically nothing for sure about the relation of the institutions of higher education in America to the social structure, but I know a fair bit about the relation between the two in France, England and the Netherlands in the fifteenth and sixteenth centuries. I have never studied the Economic Reports to the President that would enable me to appraise the state of the American nation in the 1950s, but I have studied closely the *Discourse of the Commonwealth of England* and derived from it some reasonably coherent notions about the condition of England in the 1550s. Now the consequence of all this is inevitable. Instead of the passions, prejudices, assumptions and preposessions, the events, crises and tensions of the present dominating my view of the past, *it is the other way about.* The passions, prejudices, assumptions and prepossessions, the events, crises and tensions of early modern Europe to a very considerable extent lend precision to my rather haphazard notions about the present. I make sense of present-day welfare-state policy by thinking of it in connection with the "commonwealth" policies of Elizabeth. I do the like with respect to the contemporary struggle for power and conflict of ideologies by throwing on them such light as I find in the Catholic-Calvinist struggle of the sixteenth century.

*　　*　　*

In the controversy that provided the starting point of this rambling essay, the essential question is sometimes posed with respect to the relation of the historian to his own *day*. In other instances it is posed with respect to his relation to his own *time*. Having discovered how idiosyncratic was the day of one historian we may inquire whether his time is also peculiar. The answer is, "Yes, his time *is* a bit odd." And here it is possible to take a welcome leave of the first person singular. For, although my day is peculiar to me, my time, as a historian, is like the time of other historians.

For our purposes the crucial fact about the ordinary time of all men, even of historians in their personal as against their professional capacity, is that in no man's time is he *really* sure what is going to happen next. This is true, obviously, not only of men of the present time but also of all men of all past times. Of course there are large routine areas of existence in which we can make pretty good guesses; and if this were not so, life would be unbearable. Thus, my guess, five evenings a week in term time, that I will be getting up the following morning to teach classes at my place of employment provides me with a useful operating rule; yet it has been wrong occasionally, and will be wrong again. With respect to many matters more important, all is uncertain. Will there be war or peace next year? Will my children turn out well or ill? Will I be alive or dead thirty years hence? three years hence? tomorrow?

The saddest words of tongue or pen may be, "It might have been." The most human are, "If I had only known." But it is precisely characteristic of the historian that he does know. He is really sure what is going to happen next, not in his time as a pilgrim here below, but in his own time as a historian. The public servant Conyers Read, for example, when he worked high in the councils of the Office of Strategic Services did not know what the outcome of the maneuvers he helped plan would be. But for all the years from 1568 during which he painstakingly investigated the public career of Francis Walsingham, the eminent Tudor historian Conyers Read knew that the Spanish Armada would come against England and that the diplomatic maneuvers of Mr. Secretary Walsingham would assist in its defeat. Somewhat inaccurately we might say that while man's time ordinarily is oriented to the future, the historian's time is oriented to the past. It might be better to say that while men are ordinarily trying to connect the present with a future that is to be, the historian connects his present with a future that has already been.

The professional historian does not have a monopoly of his peculiar time, or rather, as Carl Becker once put it, every man is on occasion his own historian. But the historian alone lives systematically in the historian's own time. And from what we have been saying it is clear that this time has a unique dimension. Each man in his own time tries to discover the motives and the causes of the actions of those people he has to deal with; and the historian does the like with varying degrees of success. But, as other men do not and cannot, the historian knows something of the results of the acts of those he deals with: this is the unique dimension of the historian's time. If, in saying that the historian cannot escape his own time, the present-minded meant this peculiarly historical time — which they do not — they would be on solid ground. For the circumstances are rare indeed in which the historian has no notion whatever of the outcome of the events with which he is dealing. The very fact that he is a historian and that he has interested himself in a particular set of events fairly assures that at the outset he will have some knowledge of what happened afterward.

This knowledge makes it impossible for the historian to do merely what the history-minded say he should do — consider the past in its own terms, and envisage events as the men who lived through them did. Surely he should try to do that; just as certainly he must do more than that simply because he knows about those events what none of the men contemporary with them knew; he knows what their consequences were. To see the events surrounding the obscure monk Luther as Leo X saw them — as another "monks' quarrel" and a possible danger to the perquisites of the Curia — may help us understand the peculiar inefficacy of Papal policy at the time; but that does not preclude the historian from seeing the same events as the decisive step towards the final breach of the religious unity of Western Civilization. We may be quite sure however that nobody at the time, not even Luther himself, saw those events that way. The historian who resolutely refused to use the insight that his own peculiar time gave him would not be superior to his fellows; he would be merely foolish, betraying a singular failure to grasp what history is. For history is a becoming, an ongoing, and it is to be understood not only in terms of what comes before but also of what comes after.

7.   *Historians over the years have disagreed with one another about whether they ought or ought not to make moral judgments. Professor J. J. Gwyn, a member of the History Department at the University of Ottawa, notes that such men as Leopold von Rankë rejected the proposition that historians should judge the past whereas Lord Acton welcomed the prospect. Gwyn himself argues that although they cannot be avoided, the judgments made by the historian are necessarily tenuous and tentative. But, he adds, our knowledge of the historian's attitudes — subjective though they may be — should assist us to understand the past.*

Moral judgments are an essential part of our intellectual activity. They are part of our thought. They cannot artificially be removed from our daily conversation. No amount of conscious self-discipline can wholly eliminate them. Our ordinary speech would become fantastically distorted by

[7] Reprinted from Julian J. Gwyn, "Moral Judgments in History,"
    Revue de l'Université d'Ottawa, 34 (1964), pp. 227-228, 231-233 with
    the permission of the publisher.

any conscious effort to eliminate from it so basic an ingredient as everything remotely likely to convey value judgments. Therefore, to restrict an essential part of our intellectual activity, to suppress the natural inclination to make moral judgments is to destroy the possibility of all communication.

Now we explain and elucidate as historians in the same manner as we do in ordinary speech. We cannot separate the man and the historian. In ordinary life one tends naturally to look for goodness and justice in a man; and one feels an irresistible urge to define a man's character. An historian has the same urge when looking at historical figures. It is a natural, a healthy urge, so long as it is kept within bounds, and should not be artificially suppressed. E. H. Carr, Fellow of Trinity College, Cambridge, recently noted that :

Historical interpretations always involve moral judgments — or, if you prefer a more neutral sounding term, value judgments.[17]

The historian retains moral assumptions no matter how scrupulously dispassionate he may attempt to be. These assumptions influence his interpretation. His selection and arrangement of evidence, his choice of words, and the emphasis he puts on them are all subject to cultural traits and personal experiences. In other words, where moral judgments are concerned the historian is [and] must be subjective.

But the conclusion that moral judgments are unavoidable should not create undue consternation. It has rightly been suggested that they perform at least two very useful functions. In the first place, they tell us a great deal about the historian's mind. The more we know of the historian, the better fitted we are to interpret his works. "Before you study the history, study the historian. . . . Before you study the historian, study his historical and social environment."[18] By knowing the historian's attitude towards moral judgments we will be better equipped to estimate the value of his works. Thus indirectly the historian's moral judgments help to spread historical knowledge. Secondly, no truly excellent piece of historical writing can be executed without real interest and firm conviction. The most elementary teachings of psychology deny that the human intellect can function vitally in an emotionless and aimless void. The historian who hopes to become an entirely frigid being, devoid of all human passions and prejudices is in desperate danger of becoming feeble-minded. He must possess the ability to understand the living.[19] He must be naturally inclined to observe the men, the things, or the events around him lest he be described as a useful antiquarian. He must perceive the vibrance of human life about him. As the very controversial American historian, Harry Elmer Barnes, once wrote :

[17] Edward Hallett Carr, *What is History?* London, 1962, p. 73.

[18] *Ibid.*, p. 38.

[19] Marc Bloch called this "the master quality of the historian." *The Historian's Craft*, Manchester, 1954, p. 43.

Human life is, in reality, a vital and dynamic affair and can only be discovered, recreated and interpreted by a person as vital as the data which he uses.[20]

*   *   *

There is, however, a . . . fundamental limitation imposed on the historian when faced with [the] prospect of making moral judgments. Whereas the historian can achieve a very high degree of certainty when making ordinary historical judgments, he can never marshall sufficient irrefutable evidence to make an absolute moral judgment. When the historian perceives a man acting in the past, it is a thinking man with whom he deals, and some would add a man with a soul and a conscience. When the historian looks at such a man he is seeking his soul, he is attempting to detect the experiences of the soul, he is aiming at the seat of the personality. Yet as soon as this is recognized, it must also be admitted that a definitive conclusion is beyond the historian's grasp. The historian can never quite attain an internal knowledge of historical personages. He cannot pierce the most inward recess of a man; ". . . he can never quite carry his inquiries to that innermost region where the final play of motive and point of responsibility can be decided".[32] At best he can get a mere glimpse of a man's soul. He can never penetrate a man's conscience. He can never estimate a man's moral responsibility. Thus on the basis of Stern's human condition or Acton's universal moral law, it could be argued that Hitler performed certain acts which could be described as antihumanitarian or morally evil. Yet one can never know to what extent he was responsible for his actions. If he was a mad-man as some historians assert, there would be no moral guilt. Thus a clear distinction would have to be made between the historian's moral judgment of an act and the moral responsibility of the one performing the act.

This whole argument can be put differently. History can be described as the re-enactment of the events of the past in the historian's mind. Moreover, as Carr has rightly observed :

History cannot be written unless the historian can achieve some kind of contact with the mind of those about whom he is writing.[33]

Yet our knowledge of history, our contact with the minds of the past is severely restricted because of a serious shortage of evidence about the events of the past. This means that much remains unknown for all time. Included in that word "much" is a knowledge of the moral responsibility of men's actions, for this requires a degree of knowledge of the events of the past which cannot be perceived by the historian even under the most ideal circumstances. David Knowles, a Benedictine monk and since 1954

[20] Barnes, *A History of Historical Writing,* 2nd Revised Edition, N.Y., 1962, p. 272.

[32] Butterfield, *History and Human Relations,* London, 1951, p. 116.

[33] Carr, *op. cit.,* p. 19.

Regius Professor of Modern History at Cambridge, understands this perfectly. In his inaugural lecture he said :

The degree of ignorance, the degree of malice, the degree of weakness, the degree of guilt must always elude us.[34]

Thus a moral judgment seems no more absolute than an expression of taste or emotion.

What then are our conclusions? The first is that moral judgments are unavoidable. Secondly, moral judgments actually serve useful purposes. Thirdly, there can be no agreement about the moral standard that should govern moral judgments. Finally, among the various limitations imposed on the historian's moral judgments, the most important is his inability to know the degree of moral responsibility of those whom he judges.

[34] David Knowles, *The Historian and Character*, Cambridge, 1955, p. 18.

8. If historians are unable to tell us the "truth" about the past, they can at least help us to understand a complex situation and to subject theories to the test of good sense. In the final reading in this chapter, David Thomson outlines the nature of that understanding, the training necessary to acquire it and its value to the young reader. Dr. Thomson, an authority on modern French history, is the author of Europe Since Napoleon *(London, 1957) and other works.*

Historical understanding, [the historian's] most precious equipment, is compounded of an accumulated knowledge which warns him against what is anachronistic or improbable; of mature judgment derived from investigation of how, in the past, a tangled skein of events could produce certain unexpected consequences; and of sufficient experience and sophistication for him to have a "hunch" about the relative significance of immeasurable forces. Though there is no unfailing prescription by which a man may acquire historical understanding, it is apparent from his work whether he has or has not acquired it. It is akin to that flair of creative imagination already mentioned, and conjoins the historian as technician and craftsman with the historian as creative writer. Without it he may be a happy antiquarian or a busy dryasdust; with it he has no guarantee of producing great historical writing, though he is likely to gain a livelier satisfaction from his work and to be a shrewder and wiser human being. The task of the teacher of history is to transmit something of this—at least some appreciation of this capacity—to his pupils. It will be the surest antidote to the seductions of historical system-making, the mystifications of ideology and the distortions of propaganda.

[8] Reprinted from David Thomson, "The Historical Attitude: The Point of It All" in *The Aims of History* (London, 1969) pp. 103-105, 107, with the permission of the publishers, Thames and Hudson Ltd., London.

It is exercise of this very capacity of historical understanding which has given rise to the great vitality of historical study in our times, and which has produced such rich diversity as well as a rapid expansion of contemporary and world history. Corresponding in many ways to the equally great growth of scientific understanding of man and nature, it is one of the twin pillars of modern culture. The sense of being in one great continuum in time, no less than in space, is the outcome of our century's remarkable devotion to historical studies.

Even in this devotion western civilization, at least, is being historical and traditional. Its main religions are historical religions, and the scriptures of Jews and Christians alike are history books. We believe, almost instinctively, that one good way to begin to understand something, whether it be the policy of President de Gaulle or the Suez crisis of 1956, is to examine its historical origins and evolution. To know and to understand how a situation arose is felt to be the first step towards appreciating why it arose; and that, in turn, is a prerequisite to dealing intelligently with the situation. This pragmatic, realistic approach to situations—however complex or critical they may be—has become so natural and 'obvious' to us (and perhaps so closely attuned to the empirical and experimental methods of natural science) that we experience a sense of shock when somebody holds to a quite different attitude. A situation may be denounced, *a priori* and on dogmatic or ideological grounds, as so unacceptable that no time or energy need be spent on trying to understand how or why it has arisen: the only thing to be done is to change it. Hitler was not in the least interested in how or why the Jews came to be in Germany: he simply moved to exterminate them. That such an attitude seemed to sophisticated minds merely barbaric or fantastic was an advantage to Hitler, because it meant that his future victims regarded Nazism as incredible until it was upon them.

Likewise the manner in which Soviet historians are induced, despite immense learning and much worthy scholarship, to rewrite accounts of the Bolshevik Revolution or assessments of its leaders from time to time, in contradiction to previous accounts but in conformity with the latest party line or the dictates of the prevailing party boss, seems incredible to western intellectuals. The degradation of spirit and intellect imposed by a régime which itself claims to rest on historical materialism will remain a thicker iron curtain between east and west than any mere policies or economic plans. The marvel is that some of the victims of the system contrive, none the less, to write history with integrity and genuine scholarship.

The moral of such degradation is that study of history must be independent of creed or régime or orthodoxy of any kind. The autonomy of historical investigation—that is, its pursuit and achievement for the sake of the truth alone and not in order to serve or support or defend any system of thought or of politics— is indispensable for its vitality. In this respect the existence of a vigorous and flourishing historiography is a symptom, and evidence, of a free society and a free culture. To fear the truth even about the past is a mark of true despotism.

The historical attitude, by definition, is hostile to system-making. This need not . . . lead to the nihilistic view that the past is a tale of sound and fury, signifying nothing. But it does mean constant emphasis on the uniqueness of situations, the individuality of men, the novelty of each new historical situation that arises. It does not deny the regularities or trends for which men look in history, but it distrusts attempts to build up these regularities into laws or systems, and to weave of these discernible trends some pattern which is then extended to lengthy periods of time or to most peoples. The concern of the historian must be to find precisely how far such regularities can be convincingly traced, and just where they cease to be applicable or plausible; and also to find other different or even contradictory regularities which may cut across or modify the first. Simplist answers to complex questions may not always be wrong: but they should not be accepted as right or adequate until other reasonable answers have also been investigated. Wisdom comes from discovering the complexities behind simplicities, and a power of discernment which is sometimes called good sense.

Contrary to popular belief that good sense is innate, it can be and needs to be cultivated. Herein lies the educational purpose of historical teaching, in which it best complements scientific studies. Cultivated good sense, a sensitivity to realities nurtured by the historical attitude, can be especially valuable amid the perplexities of current affairs.

*   *   *

The case for a form of "instant history", at least in the sense of assessing new situations with as much sense of realities as the historical attitude can cultivate, is therefore strong. The mental habits and attitudes encouraged by historical study and understanding can contribute to a more rational grasp of the dilemmas confronting statesmen; and so, one may hope, to more effective measures for dealing with them. This does not mean that wisdom lies in seeking remote roots of current problems—the fallacy of excessive historicism. Wisdom comes from powers of discernment between situations, problems of conflicts which have deep roots and those which may be more contingent and novel: and then capacity to analyse each kind with a sense of how things happen in history.

In the last resort, of course, it looks like common sense. Certainly it means a healthy refusal to be fudged. When Mark Twain was told that rumours were circulating that he had died, he suggested that they were, in all likelihood, greatly exaggerated. He had the right idea.

SIX

HOW HAVE HISTORIANS TOLD THE STORY OF CANADA?

The story of history is written to a very great degree in international terms. A heritage from the classical historians, medieval chroniclers and early rationalists is acknowledged by writers in all countries in the western world. The nineteenth-century literary experience and the development of new techniques in the present century is one shared by Germany, France, Great Britain, the United States and many other nations. The literature on such problems as objectivity and interpretation, causation and explanation and the nature of historical truth is written in many languages. A trend towards a professionalization of the discipline occurred roughly at the same time in Europe and America and many historians consider themselves members of an international community of scholars.

Nevertheless a shared experience is not necessarily an identical one. Some nations have been able to devote more resources to support writers and scholars. Historical writing in one country may have taken a particular twist through the influence of a powerful school of historians or even the work of a single great historian. In an age of specialization, some nations have concentrated on the development of particular techniques. Thus communities of scholars in one country may be noted for their pioneer work in the use of sources, in another for their innovative experimentation with concepts from kindred disciplines and, in a third, for their stress upon literary style and grace. Of even greater significance has been the pressure of national concerns which have affected, or even determined, no matter how strenuously some scholars have resisted, the issues and topics selected for study by historians.

Outside influences have been strong in the writing of Canadian history. Nineteenth-century writers brought with them ideas and concepts developed in other countries. The professionalization of history in Canadian universities followed patterns established elsewhere. Modes of historical writing and the application of new techniques in examining data and sources tended to conform to practices in those foreign countries in which many Canadian historians completed their professional training. Many historiographical models pioneered elsewhere were later applied to Canadian history. The very framework in which our nation's experience was cast was often patterned in a foreign design.

Yet our history was never totally colonialized. Despite the attraction and power of the international traffic in historical concepts and models, Canadian historians from an early date began to develop their own themes. So diverse were settlements that the force of regionalism was always strong. The peculiar relationship of Canada to Britain and the United States was subjected to special examination. In more recent decades, population patterns, economic developments and the influence of certain urban centres have been closely studied. Although never a large group by the standards of other countries, Canadian historians have produced a series of high quality images and patterns of the nation's past.

One of the characteristics of Canadian historiography has been the separate and parallel growth of English- and French-Canadian versions of our past. Historians in Quebec have played an important part in the intellectual development of the province and their themes are closely related to French-Canadian national aspirations. In English-speaking Canada, on the other hand, largely because academic professionalization appeared much earlier than in Quebec, historians seemed to follow more closely the patterns established within the international community of scholars; their written histories, therefore, tended to be more varied in scope and theme. These basic divisions among Canadian historians, and the intellectual and cultural conditions which foster them, continue to affect contemporary intellectual, and educational, inquiry.

1. At the time of the one hundredth anniversary of Confederation, Canadians became far more introspective than they had been before that time. In Universities, scholars of literature and history seemed to assume leadership of a new movement to study the Canadian heritage. At the meeting of the Canadian Historical Association in June 1967, Dr. Richard M. Saunders noted a special obligation of historians to the nation.

One hundred years ago the passing of the British North America Act set the seal of final accomplishment upon the long and difficult negotiations of the Fathers of Confederation. Then was the new nation of Canada brought to birth. Four years later in 1871, with the joining of British Columbia, the new nation reached in truth *A Mari Usque Ad Mare.* What was this nation whose shores are washed by the waters of three oceans? What, indeed, is a nation?

A nation is above all a community of people living together over such a period of time that common interests and experiences, common feelings and sympathies, loves and fears all merge into a body of mutual understanding and desired association. It is fundamentally a state of mind and feeling, one that is more felt than described, more lived than written about. Without this living together the concept of a nation could scarcely arise, without it the national feeling which is the lifeblood of the nation would never flow. Without a continued living together the concept and the feeling would die. Yet this means, surely, that time and the common experiences that accumulate over a long period of time are the real basis upon which a nation rests; but time, and the story of a people living together in time, are the substance of history. A nation is, therefore, more than anything else a venture in history.

In consequence, those who treat of its history, its historians, have necessarily a special relationship, indeed, a special obligation to the nation in which they study and teach, live and have their being. They are by virtue of their profession the discoverers, the recorders, and the keepers of the national experience, of the record of the living together, of the memories that are the ultimate source of national feeling and identity. "History is", as Allan Nevins has so aptly said, "the sextant and compass of state which, tossed by wind and current, would be lost in confusion if they could not fix their position . . ."[1] In fact, what the historian writes and says, what he records and teaches, will inevitably have a profound effect upon the thinking and feeling of the generations on the march, for it is a well-known truth that one cannot write or teach history without making history. Whether the historian wants it so or not he is cast in the role of guide and mentor to the nation.

---

[1] A. Nevins, *Gateway to History* (New York, 1938), p. 3.

---

[1] Reprinted from Richard M. Saunders, "The Historian and the Nation," *Canadian Historical Association Annual Report, 1967,* pp. 1-3 with the permission of the author.

The names of those historians who have openly and eagerly accepted this role in the past are amongst the most distinguished in many nations: Lord Macaulay in England, Jules Michelet in France, George Bancroft in the United States. To them and to countless others it has seemed not merely a duty or an obligation but an inspired purpose to serve the nation. So it was to him who in Canada wrote, "Que les Canadiens soient fidèles à eux-mêmes; qu'ils soient sages et persévérants . . . ."[2]

François-Xavier Garneau wrote these lines nearly thirty years before Confederation. He was thinking not of the yet unconceived Dominion but of *la nation canadienne,* that community which had already lived two centuries on the banks of the St. Lawrence and which he was prepared to serve as historian-guide. That he did so with success needs no demonstration here and now. One has only to scan the pages written by his successors throughout the years, from the Abbé Ferland, Thomas Chapais, and Canon Groulx on to his present emulators. If today there is a vigorous, self-conscious, up-pressing *nation canadienne* within the Canada that stretches from sea to sea it owes much, very much, to the persistent and successful leadership of its *historiens nationaux.* They have done for the French *nation* in Canada what their spiritual forefather, Jules Michelet, did for France; they have articulated the concept of a nation.

The nation, however, whose centenary we are celebrating this year is something more than *la nation canadienne* that was defined and has been so ably defended by Garneau and his successors; something greater, indeed, than any of the components that have gone to make it up. When under the historic name of Canada the founding peoples agreed to come together for the creation of a new state they were laying the foundations of a country whose continent-wide extent was soon to encompass a wealth of resources and varieties of dwelling space quite beyond those possessed by any of the original members of the Confederation. To this richness and diversity of lands and resources was quickly to be added an equally rich variety of peoples, many peoples, who would learn to live together in this broad new land. Canada was to be truly more than a new state, it was to be a new nation. The many peoples who came to inhabit this varied country would by successfully living together, generation after generation, become all together, Canadians.

The consciousness of what it means to live together in any community, in any nation, will be passed on to each succeeding generation in many different ways, but there can be no doubt that one of the most critical ways is through the schools. The importance of the educational system of any nation to that nation's common life and especially to its people's understanding of their own nation and their place in it needs no proof more than the historical record of what has been done here and elsewhere. The case for Canada in this regard was stated some forty years ago by the Honorary President of this Association, the Right Honourable Vincent Massey, one-time member of the History Department of the University of Toronto, who wrote in 1926:

[2] F.-X. Garneau, *Histoire du Canada* (8th ed., Montreal, 1946), IX, 151.

In a country with so scattered a population as ours and a vast frontier exposed to alien influences the task of creating a truly national feeling must inevitably be arduous, but this is the undertaking to which our educational systems must address themselves for by true education alone will the problem be solved. To our schools we must look for the Good Canadian.[3]

Within the Canadian schools the teachers of no subject have been more conscious of this need and purpose than those of history.

[3] V. Massey in C. N. Cochrane and W. S. Wallace, *This Canada of Ours* (National Council of Education, 1926), p. 11.

2. An unmistakable feature of the Canadian experience has been the powerful pull of local forces. Scattered across the northern rim of the United States, the Canadian people have often tended to identify with the region rather than the nation. For many of them the focus for cultural and social development has been their own province. An appreciation of these local ties is essential to an understanding of Canadian history especially in those long centuries before inventions in communications reduced the significance of both distances and individuals. Dr. G. F. G. Stanley, the author of the following reading, is currently Professor of Canadian Studies at Mount Allison University. His writings include The Birth of Western Canada *(Toronto, 1936),* Louis Riel *(Toronto, 1963) and* New France: The Last Phase 1744-1760 *(Toronto, 1968).*

It is not difficult to recognize the parentage of Canadian regionalism. History and geography. But if the former was a tolerant parent, the latter was never an indulgent foster mother to that political adoptee which we call Canada. She gave it no continuous belt of arable land stretching from east to west to bind Canadians together. Instead she interposed various barriers to unity, mountains, rivers, rocks and trees which divide the country into clearly marked geographical regions, namely the Maritimes; Central Canada or the St. Lawrence-Great Lakes valley; the Canadian or Pre-Cambrian Shield; the Prairies; and the Pacific Slope; to which may, perhaps, be added another, barely yet appreciated economically or historically, the Mackenzie River Basin. Each of these regions has its "natural" frontiers; each of these regions, too, has its characteristic economic activity—fishing, manufacturing, mining, farming, and lumbering.

Our early history did much to reinforce the impact of geography. Our first settlers came from a common Fatherland, France; but they settled, some along the Atlantic seaboard, and others in the St. Lawrence valley. They developed along different lines economically and politically. The Atlantic region may have been looked upon as an integral part of New France, and La Vallière as subordinate to Frontenac; but in reality Acadia

[2] Reprinted from George F. G. Stanley, "Regionalism in Canadian History," in *Ontario History* 51(3), Summer 1959, pp. 164-167, with the permission of the Ontario Historical Society and the author.

was an entity separate from Canada, and the Acadian psychologically distinct from the Québecois. The accessibility of Acadia by water and its inaccessibility from Canada by land, were very real factors in Acadian life and history.

The expulsion of the Acadians during the Seven Years War and their replacement by Americans both before and after the Revolution, added to the regional sense of separate identity. The coming of the Scots and Irish made little difference. They simply took on the Maritime way of thinking. They might have their own religious and political quarrels, but they conducted their affairs with dignity and drew self-righteous comparisons between themselves and those turbulent, disloyal French of Lower Canada, and those self-assertive misfits in Upper Canada. They might speak their prayers with soft Gaelic accents or nasal Yankee tones, but they all thanked God that they were not as the Canadians were. And if, eventually, the Canadians were able, with Imperial approval and Imperial assistance, to drag the suspicious Maritimers within their political ambit, they never succeeded in making Canadians out of them. For the sea, the Notre Dame mountains, and the Maine salient were still there, and the ghost of Joseph Howe was never laid by "better terms".

Geographically and economically one, the St. Lawrence valley and its tributaries has become two distinct culture regions. And for this the American Revolution is largely responsible. For Guy Carleton in 1774, the future of Canada was to be that of a French-speaking colony; but in 1783-4 the Revolution provided Canada with an unexpected influx of English-speaking settlers, the Loyalists, the displaced persons of America. The French Canadians were anxious to preserve their cultural identity; so, too, were the Loyalists. And the differences between the two groups, separated from one another by language, system of law and land tenure, religion, and historical memories, was recognized by the Imperial enactment which brought about the establishment in 1791 of the two separate colonies, Lower and Upper Canada, an arrangement which was considerably facilitated by the fact that the Loyalists had, for the most part, settled in the unoccupied lands to the south-west of the Ottawa river.

Fighting a constant battle against the Imperial and later the colonial governments, the French Canadians succeeded in maintaining certain political and religious rights which made it possible for them to preserve the basic elements of their culture to a far larger degree than did those of their kindred who settled in Louisiana or who were attracted during the nineteenth century to the flesh pots of New England. The French fact in Canada is a fact and not a fiction. It has withstood the cession of 1763, the political union of 1840, and the federation of 1867; it has resisted efforts at assimilation in the eighteenth century, political ostracism in the nineteenth, and heavy non-French immigration in the twentieth. The cradle, the school and the church have been its bulwarks. The solidarity of French Canada as a political entity and as a cultural concept is an essential thread in the fabric of Canadian history.

Upper Canada, unlike Lower Canada, was something of a melting pot. Composed of Loyalist Americans, non-Loyalist Americans, Englishmen, Scotsmen, Irishmen, Germans and others, it developed under the guiding hands of geography, religion, economic and political self interest, a distinct outlook of its own. One may, of course, point to the political arguments, to the denominational rivalries, and to the armed rising of 1837 as evidence of the lack of cohesion of Upper Canadians. But when confronted with the rest of British America, and particularly with French Canada, Upper Canadians were as bigoted in their Protestantism as the Lower Canadians in their Catholicism, and as strong in their British loyalism as they suspected the French Canadians to be in their disloyalty. And there were always the memories of American military aggression in 1775 and in 1812, and the repeated threats of war and annexation to cement the cracks in the facade of unity. Today this sense of community based upon Loyalism and Orange fanaticism is weakening. But the Ontarian, always identifying the interest of Canada as a whole with that of his own region, is proud of his wealth, his numbers, his dominant role in Canadian politics, his fidelity to the Crown and his democracy. If he cannot see himself as a "provincial" or distinguish his own peculiar ethic, if he can only ascribe to irrational jealousy the jibes and criticisms of Canadians of other regions, that is simply because the beam in his own eye has never obscured the mote in those of his opponents.

The prairies too, have had a history of their own, as distinct and as regionalist as those of the Maritimes, of Quebec, and of Ontario. Until 1870 the western territories were the preserve of the fur-bearing animals and the Indians and the battleground of competing fur trading interests. One colony only was attempted, and that was inspired by a Scottish earl, assisted by an English fur company, and settled by dispossessed Highland crofters. Not until the territory had been acquired by Canada from the reluctant Hudson's Bay Company with the benign blessing of the British Government and against the determined resistance of the local settlers, were the plains opened to immigrants. And in they poured, from Ontario first, and then from Great Britain, from eastern and central Europe, and from the United States. This was the "frontier", the last and best west, the home of free land and great hopes, of the drought and the grasshopper. The prairie region never possessed the racial homogeneity of Quebec, or of the Maritimes, or even that of Ontario, but it did possess social homogeneity among its people. Even more important from the standpoint of regional history, it found a strong bond of unity in economic self-interest. For the prairies were, par excellence, the land of the staple, wheat, and the free trade antagonist of protectionist Ontario.

Still further west, on the green slopes of the Pacific was yet another geographical and historical region. A British colony, isolated from the other British colonies of the continental mainland, British Columbia drew many of its settlers and nearly all of its social and cultural traditions from England. And these have remained strong in spite of the infiltration of ideas and products from the United States, and the presence of the inscrutable Oriental market gardener. The old rawness, the lustiness of the gold mining days is conveniently forgotten or romanticised in the figures of Matthew Begbie and "Cariboo" Cameron. If there are still obvious vulgarities which accord ill with the genteel English tradition, they can be set aside as importations from south of the line, or from over the Rocky Mountains. In any event the mountain ranges are broad and high, the seas are ever lapping the shores of the province, and the climate is the last refuge of the tired and retired businessman and army officer.

Regionalism, like nationalism is an organic thing. It lives, grows, thrives, and sometimes dies. In Canada regionalism was born with the arrival of our first settlers. It has developed steadily throughout history. Today it is a lusty, vital reality in Canadian life. The one dominant theme underlying all our political, constitutional, economic, and even cultural development, has been the interplay, or struggle, between the regional and the national idea, between unity and diversity. There can be no understanding Canadian history without an appreciation of the strength of this fact. Need we do more than recall the names of Howe, Mowat, Riel, Mercier, Bourassa, Crerar, Forke, Wood, the "Ginger Group," or more recently those of Ferguson, Hepburn, Pattullo, Aberhart, Angus Macdonald, or Maurice Duplessis?

The regions of Canada are a fact. So, too, is Canada. But Canada's existence does not, and never has, depended solely upon the concept of national uniformity. The Canadian Confederation came into being not to crush but to reconcile regional diversities. It was not a spontaneous response to a strong popular demand. It was an achievement of the head rather than of the heart; the work of governments rather than of peoples. Union, not unity, was the result. That Canada ever came into existence at all is evidence of the community of fear inspired by the threatening United States; that it continued may be explained by the determination of Canadians of all regions to remain outside the American union; that it has grown in strength may be attributed in part at least to the deep spiritual experiences of one major economic depression and two European wars.

3. French-Canadian historians have played a special part in la survivance de la nation canadienne-française. *In a brilliant article, of which an extract is given here, Dr. Ramsay Cook describes that role and comments upon the changes introduced by successive generations of French-Canadian scholars. Dr. Cook, one of the most perceptive critics of Quebec affairs is the author of* The Politics of John W. Dafoe and the Free Press *(Toronto, 1963) and* Canada and the French-Canadian Question *(Toronto, 1966) among other works.*

[3] Reprinted from Ramsay Cook, "La Survivance French-Canadian Style," in *The Maple Leaf Forever: Essays on Nationalism and Politics in Canada*, 1971, pp. 114-116, 140 with the permission of The Macmillan Company of Canada Limited.

The historian in French Canada has always played a very special role. From François-Xavier Garneau in the 1840s to Michel Brunet in the 1960s, he has been something more than a mere keeper of the records of the past. Consciously or otherwise, his concern for the past has stemmed from a deep interest in the present and the future of the people about whom he writes. His story has been that of the survival of a small people struggling against heavy odds. He has written that story with the intention of convincing his people that, having survived in the past, they must continue to struggle in the present in order to guarantee survival in the future. The Abbé Lionel Groulx, perhaps the greatest French-Canadian nationalist historian, spoke for this tradition when he declared, *'Our Master, the Past, that is to say, the Past, master of the future.'*

Thus, the historian in French Canada has played a leading part in the definition of the ideology of nationalism. It is from history that the definition of French-Canadian society and values is drawn. The historian speaks of the society's past, in order to define its future, or, to put it another way, to give it that sense of mission which is a necessary part of every nationalism. Discussing the role of history and the historian in the development of modern nationalist consciousness, a French political scientist has written that 'There is no nationalism which does not attach itself to certain profound values of heritage and tradition. This affirmation remains true even for those who insist on affirming most audaciously their revolutionary character; if they repudiate the image of a certain past, it is almost always to oppose to it, or to substitute for it, the image of another past.' Perhaps it was nationalist historians that Sir Lewis Namier had in mind when he remarked that 'the historians imagine the past and remember the future.' It would be difficult to imagine a group of historians who better exemplified both of these statements than the group of men who, over the past century or so, have acted as the keepers of the French-Canadian historical consciousness.

The century between the publication of Garneau's *Histoire du Canada,* the first volume of which appeared in 1845, and Abbé Lionel Groulx's *Histoire du Canada-français* may be described as the years of the traditionalists. These are years when French-Canadian society was changing at an increasingly rapid tempo from a predominantly rural and static society to an urban and mobile one. Yet despite these changes most historians, and other nationalist intellectuals, insisted on clinging firmly to the values of the past — to the mystique of what Professor Brunet has called 'ruralism, anti-statism and messianism'. It is true that Groulx was to some extent conscious of these changes, and even tried to come to terms with them, but on the whole he manifested a sense of unease, fearing that the loss of the old virtues would lead to the disappearance of French Canada's uniqueness. It is only since the 1950s and the emergence of a new generation of historians that the values of the new, urban, and industrial society have been accepted, understood, and in some measure assimilated into the quest for survival. The traditionalists and the moderns, as they may be called, are united in their desire to assure *la survivance de la nation cana-*

dienne-française. Where they differ is about the means of survival, and therefore they also differ in their interpretation of the past.

*   *   *

Historical writing is too deeply woven into the fabric of French-Canadian nationalism ever to be completely wrenched free. Every new technique, every new approach to the study of the past has readily been assimilated and used by the nationalist historians who believe, with sincere conviction, that the importance of studying the past is largely in the lessons it offers the present. This attitude is well expressed by Professor Frégault:

> *Ah, if history was only a game that deployed erudition without relation to the present! But then it would be necessary, under another name, to find a discipline which would fill the same office; it would be necessary to create a science which would measure the pressures of the past on the present and determine their nature; it would be necessary to invent history.*

The great French historian of the nineteenth century, Ernest Renan, once again argued that 'Forgetfulness, I would even say historical error, are factors essential to the creation of a nation, and therefore the progress of historical studies is often a danger for nationalism.' The contention is far from accurate in the case of French-Canadian historical studies, for it remains no less true today than it was in the time of Garneau that historical writing and nationalist ideology remain inextricably linked. As long as there are French-Canadian nationalists, there will be nationalist history for, as George Orwell once remarked, 'every nationalist is haunted by the belief that the past can be changed.' He might have added that nationalists hope that, by changing the past, they can also alter the present and guarantee the future.

4. In a famous article published originally in the Canadian His-
*torical Review, Dr. J. M. S. Careless critically analyzed certain
"schools" among Canadian historians. In the late nineteenth century
and early twentieth century, for example, historical writing was noted
for its fidelity to British institutions or for its attempts to catalogue
the steps in Canada's rise to nationhood. Forty years ago historians
on the Canadian side of the border became interested in various aspects of the "frontier thesis" or "environmentalist school" popular-
ized in the United States by Frederick Jackson Turner. More recently, however, scholars began to formulate a view of Canadian history
based on water routes, staples and metropolitanism. The names usually associated with this so-called "Laurentian School" are H. A.
Innis and D. G. Creighton. Accepting some and rejecting other features of the "frontier thesis," the Laurentian framework is an import-*

[4] Reprinted from J. M. S. Careless, "Frontierism, Metropolitanism and Canadian History," *The Canadian Historical Review*, 35(1), March 1954, pp. 14-16, 17-18, 18-19, 20-21, with the permission of the author and of the publisher, University of Toronto Press.

ant contribution to Canadian self-knowledge. Dr. Careless, a colleague of Professor Creighton for many years at the University of Toronto, is well known for his own writings which include the prize winning two-volume study of Brown of the Globe *(Toronto, 1959 and 1963).*

[Professor Creighton's] approach, in fact, has been said to establish a "Laurentian School" of Canadian historiography, since it largely rests on the idea that the long St. Lawrence water route and its connections across the continent became the basis of an extensive communications system around which Canada itself took shape. The commercial empire of the St. Lawrence, the broad domain of Montreal, first flung a Canadian fur trade across the continent, then competed vigorously with New York and the American seaboard through canal and railway enterprises for control of the trade of the mid-western heartlands of America, and finally built a new economic dominion across the northwestern plains to the Pacific that was, in fact, the Dominion of Canada. It followed that the existence of a separate Canada was not just a fortuitous result of the American Revolution, of French determination to survive, nor of Loyalist emotional resolves to "stay British" — despite the hard facts of the environment — nor again of the mere continuance of the imperial tie. It was also rooted in powerful factors of geography and commerce that underlay the whole Canadian development.

This, in a sense, was environmentalism, since the St. Lawrence was as real a feature of the North American environment as the North American forest, and a good deal more permanent. Environmentalists had stressed before that the main natural lines of North American geography ran north and south, linking the regions of Canada more effectively with their United States counterparts below the border than with their Canadian neighbours to east and west. But the St. Lawrence, the Great Lakes, the Saskatchewan, and the Fraser traced lines across the continent that were quite as natural; and, as the writings of Professors Innis and Creighton indicated, they made possible the east-to-west linking of Canadian regions from the earliest days of the fur trade, as communications spread by the lakes and river valleys from sea to sea. Perhaps we could even call this the Waterways School, especially since it made clear that the environment did not stop short at the Atlantic edge of North America. For the St. Lawrence system that funnelled traffic from the continental interior out to the sea was closely connected with British finance and markets across the waters in an east-west trading network that thus reached halfway around the world.[28]

[28] The growing emphasis on "maritime factors" in Canadian and indeed North American history was a major development of the 1940's that extended and greatly recast environmentalist thinking, or—as it might also be put—marked the transition to a newer, wider interpretation of Canadian history. Perhaps the growing recognition of "extra-continental" forces could be linked to the impact of the Second World War, which sharply checked isolationist tendencies in Canadian thought, as the outside world was borne in upon it: a different result from that of the First World War, already noted, which enhanced a rather inward-

Yet the Laurentian interpretation did not mean just a new emphasis on material environmentalism, since it also revealed that this huge communications and transport system could transfer immigrants, ideas, and impulses in one direct channel from Britain deep into the heart of the continent. As a result, the Ontario frontier of the earlier nineteenth century might actually be in closer contact with the sea and the mind of Europe than were the mid-western regions of the United States, more isolated behind the Appalachian barrier in a Mississippi Valley world of their own.

The Laurentian School, however, tended to go even further, and to reverse the earlier environmentalist position in this respect: it looked not from the forest-born frontiers for its perspective of Canadian history but from developing eastern centres of commerce and industry. Indeed, it primarily studied the effects of the East on the West, and largely regarded business men and conservative urban political elements as agents of national expansion who might well be more far-sighted in their outlook than were their agrarian opponents. Here then was a metropolitan rather than a frontier viewpoint. Moreover, this Laurentian view could be effectively linked with the monumental studies of H. A. Innis on the organization of the staple products trade of broad North American areas through costly and complex transport systems controlled in large urban centres.[29]

---

looking nationalism. The significance of broad strategic factors, many of imperial or at least extra-continental origin, was newly observed in Canadian history, largely owing to the rise of a "military" school, if the name be permitted, in which the rather neglected military and naval side of Canadian development were dealt with by such historians as C. P. Stacey, G. S. Graham, and G. N. Tucker. On the primarily economic side, H. A. Innis' *The Cod Fisheries* (Toronto, 1940) was of critical importance in showing the Atlantic not as a dividing waste of waters but as a linking network of waterways that served an international and intercontinental economy. As Dr. J. T. Shotwell said in its preface, "it extends the frontiers of North America over a vast area that we have never thought of before as constituting a part—and a fundamental part— of the continent." In more general terms than just the economic, G. W. Brown had answered the question of whether the Americas had a common history by asserting that they had, as integral parts of an Atlantic world ("Have the Americas a Common History? A Canadian View," *Canadian Historical Review*, XXIII, no. 2, 1942). And J. B. Brebner, in closing and climaxing the great Carnegie series of studies in Canadian-American relations with his *North Atlantic Triangle* (Toronto, 1945), had found, strikingly enough, that his original plan to "set forth the interplay between Canada and the United States" had had to be extended to take in transatlantic influences stemming from Britain— and thus his significant title. His book was of double importance. Not only did it markedly reveal the transfer of forces and culture across the Atlantic lake and around the great triangle of Britain, the United States, and Canada; it also indicated that a massive set of studies on Canadian-American relations, whose very inception in the early thirties expressed the then-current concern with North American environmentalism, had ended in the forties in a new awareness of forces that reached far beyond the continental limits. Certainly a new approach to Canadian and North American historiography was taking shape.

[29] See, as well as works of Professor Innis already cited, *Problems of Staple Production in Canada* (Toronto, 1933); *Settlement and the Mining Frontier* (Canadian Frontiers of Settlement, IX, part 2, Toronto, 1936); "Transportation as a Factor in Canadian Economic History," *Proceedings of the Canadian Political Science Association*, 1931; and "Significant Factors in Canadian Economic Development," *Canadian Historical Review*, XVIII, no. 4, 1937.

The result was virtually to establish "metropolitanism" in Canadian historiography, the study of the role of metropolitan forces in this country, a vitalizing approach that may yet undergo considerable development.

*   *   *

London and New York are of course the classic examples of modern metropolitanism. But the metropolitan relationship is a chain, almost a feudal chain of vassalage, wherein one city may stand tributary to a bigger centre and yet be the metropolis of a sizable region of its own. Thus, for example, Winnipeg is Montreal's subsidiary but is the metropolis of a large area of the prairie West. The Toronto metropolis is a subsidiary of both New York and Montreal, while Canada's main metropolitan centre, Montreal, has traditionally been bound to London. These facts are not new in themselves; but when it is remembered that the metropolitan pattern includes not only economic ties but social and cultural associations also, then many effective lines of inquiry may present themselves. For example, one might suggest that the survival of British customs sometimes noted in the English-speaking ruling class of Montreal, or Toronto's split personality, whereby it strives both to be a minor New York and to maintain its "British" character, may be comprehended through the weighing of various metropolitan connections and influences in these cities' history.

*   *   *

Returning to the frontier itself, one might say that it is developed by a metropolitan centre of dominance which supplies its capital, organizes its communications and transport, and markets its products. The frontier's culture, too, originally stems from a metropolitan community; at root, learning and ideas radiate from there — and thus is Turner answered. True, there may be frontier religious movements, but these begin with preachers going out to the frontier and end in the focusing of the sect on the city.[33] The economic and cultural metropolitan processes go hand in hand, as newspapers, books, and men of education spread from the centre. Frontiers may often supply grievances for political movements. Urban centres as often supply the intellectual leadership; so that frontier demands take form at the hands of urban journalists and professional men.

It may be seen when this analysis is carried through that the frontier, far from being essentially independent and self-reliant, is in the largest sense a dependent. It constantly requires metropolitan aid and control, though by the same token it may come to resent and resist it. Frontier protest movements are a natural accompaniment of the extension of metropolitan power into new areas.

*   *   *

Metropolitanism can be seen operating even more clearly in Canadian history where there are no frontiers of actual settlement to block the view, so to speak, and by their undoubted colour and liveliness rather steal the centre of the stage. In the Canadian fur trade, from earliest French times

[33] See S. D. Clark, *Church and Sect in Canada* (Toronto, 1949), especially 90-173.

on, the role of the dominant organizing metropolis is plain: Montreal and Quebec the metropolitan centres for the posts of the whole fur-trading West, Paris and later London the metropolis for these Canadian towns. On the Canadian lumbering and mining frontiers, in our present northern expansion, the directing, extending, organizing, and exploiting functions of metropolitan interests are evident once more. In fact, metropolitanism has shown itself even more clearly in Canadian development than in American precisely because we have had far less fertile acreage for agricultural settlement than has the United States. Hence the agrarian frontier of the sort that Turner described has played proportionately less part in our history. This, then, is a distinctive attribute of Canada's own version of the North American story.

*   *   *

Historically speaking, the functioning of metropolitanism may do more to explain the course of Canadian history than concepts of frontierism borrowed from the United States and set forth before the significance of the modern metropolis was clear. For example, the greater conservatism of Canada as compared to the United States may be read as a mark of the much stronger influence exercised in this country by conservative-minded eastern urban centres — which were certainly far removed from any impulses of forest democracy. Moreover, the stronger influence of British ideas and institutions — and even of colonialism — must have been fostered in Canada by its long and close focusing on the British metropolis itself. Finally, the fact that Canada has pioneered not so much in democracy as in the large-scale combination of public and private interests to overcome the problems raised by a difficult environment, again suggests the greater power throughout Canadian history of the forces seeking to organize communication systems and extend commerce. One might well say that the building of the C.P.R. so far ahead of settlement, and Macdonald's policies of economic nationalism in general, were plain manifestations of the power of metropolitan influences in Canadian politics. And many other instances might also be brought to mind.[35]

[35] It has been said by J. B. Brebner that "the most substantial Canadian nationalism in time of peace has been economic nationalism" ("Canadianism," *Canadian Historical Association Report*, 1940, 8), and others, such as W. S. MacNutt, have echoed that view (see his letter to the editors of the *Canadian Historical Review*, XXXIV, no. 1, 1953, 108). Since economic nationalism is pre-eminently the result of metropolitan forces, it might appear that the way to the "national" heart of Canadian development, if that is a desirable goal, lies not through the frontiers of field and forest, where the environmentalists sought it, but rather through the metropolitan approach.

5. *In a reading in the previous chapter, Sir Herbert Butterfield described how it was possible to look at history through coloured spectacles. Professor J. T. Copp has applied a similar concept to*

[5] Reprinted from Terry Copp, "The Whig Interpretation of Canadian History," *Canadian Dimension*, 6(1), April-May 1969, pp. 23-24, with the permission of the publisher, *Canadian Dimension*.

Canadian historians and concludes that many of the accepted versions of our past are "Whig dominated." He ends his article by suggesting that there is only one constant in history — change — and that preconceived interpretative patterns of any variety tend to diminish the significance of that all important feature.

Butterfield defined Whiggery in the context of British historical writing as " . . . the tendency in many historians to write on the side of Protestants and Whigs, to praise revolutions provided they have been successful, to emphasize certain principles of progress in the past and to produce a story which is the ratification if not the glorification of the present."

It is a simple matter to adapt Butterfield's elaboration of this definition and come up with a description of whiggery in Canadian history.

It is part and parcel of the whig interpretation of history that it studies the past with reference to the present. Through this sysem of immediate reference to the present day, historical personages can easily and irresistably be classed into men who furthered progress through compromise and men who tried to hinder it. Working through this system the whig historian can draw lines through certain events, some such line as that which leads from Robert Baldwin and L. H. Lafontaine and a long succession of whigs to Canadian independence and bi-cultural nationality. The total result of this method is to produce a scheme of general history which is bound to converge beautifully upon the present — all demonstrating throughout the ages the workings of an obvious principle of progress of which Quebec and the Liberals have been perennial allies, while the west, the maritimes, minority parties and tories have perpetually formed obstruction.[1]

Canadian whiggery did not always converge upon "independence and bi-cultural nationality;" the latter value is an aspiration of the 1960s. Before the First World War, events converged beautifully on the virtues of evolutionary, internal self-government and partnership in the British Empire. After O. D. Skelton, W. P. M. Kennedy, J. S. Ewart and a host of others had done their work, we enshrined Dominion status and Laurier's wistful paternalism towards French Canada as ultimate values. Laurier, Skelton told us, never made a decision without first asking what its effect would be on national unity. National unity, it turned out, could be achieved if French Canada, which possessed only emotions, not opinions, could be persuaded to remain quiescent in the face of economic depression, capitalist exploitation and the contempt of English Canada for its linguistic existence outside the boundaries of Quebec.

During the 1930s the orthodoxies of political whiggery were made to seem irrelevant by the crisis of the Great Depression. Historians responded by examining the economic basis of Canada's existence. In the brilliant

[1] With apologies to Ken McNaught, "Canadian Foreign Policy and the Whig Interpretation." C.H.A.R. 1957, p. 44 (who has already apologized to Butterfield, *Ibid.*, p. 11, 12.)

monographs of H. A. Innis and the baroque prose of Donald Creighton, Canadians were offered a new insight into their existence. Canada, it turned out, was not primarily the product of British institutions and political compromisers. It was the child of geography, of the St. Lawrence and the vast Canadian Shield. Its history was determined by economic forces, its class structure arranged by the individual's relationship to the exploitation of the staple products which were the country's resource base and only area of comparative advantage. The real heroes of Canadian history were the merchants of Montreal who fought to strengthen the east-west transportation axis against the unprogressive farmers of Upper and Lower Canada.

For Donald Creighton and more recently for Fernand Ouellet, liberalism, nationalism, and the ideological impact of the two fundamentally opposed religious principles of voluntarism and authoritarianism, not to mention the social democracy of the frontier experience, do not exist as factors shaping the Canadian character. As J. K. McConica pointed out

> *The discovery of the economic approach was a liberation, but has perhaps, in turn, proved to be a kind of covert whiggery . . . once again the emphasis is on the national achievement, now seen to have had an earlier history in the creation of a trading empire in the St. Lawrence system. But the basic political and social issues are lost from view in favour of a refurbished "great man" theory and an adapted environmentalist view. In fact this view raises the spectre of lost economic advantages, perpetually abdicated to preserve the nation, without suggesting why this effort should be made. No more than the imperialist interpretation does the economic view discover a rationale of the Canadian achievement.*

The "covert whiggery" of the economic determinists has been kinder to tories and conversely more critical of liberals who believed in liberalism. But it has banished the west, the maritimes and minority parties, as well as French Canada, from participation in the essential tasks of nation building.

Whiggery continues to dominate popular Canadian history. Edgar McInnis's *Canada, A Political and Social History,* the most widely-used survey text book, tells us that our history's

> *. . . essential drama does not lie in armed struggles in which the nation's destiny is at stake, or in political conflicts in which irreconcilable and contending forces press their quarrel to a decisive issue. It lies rather in the slow and tenacious advance from one step to another along the road to nationhood, the patient evolution of successive compromises in politics and government, the determined conquest of the physical obstacles to national economic development . . .*

J. A. Lower, in the recently published *Canada: An Outline History,* describes the period 1760-1791 as "The Formative Years," and labels 1843-

1867 as "The Struggle for Confederation;" we then live through "The Age of Laurier." Joseph Schull subtitled his biography of Laurier *The First Canadian.* Dale Thomson presented us with *Louis St. Laurent: Canadian.* This leaves us Tories, you socialists and the peripheral east and west in something of an identity crisis! Traditional whiggery is far from dead.

Of even greater concern to those impressed with the need for sensitive social and ideological enquiries, based upon a recognition of regional differences as well as on long overdue studies in labour history, urbanization, immigration and business history, is the possibility of the emergence of a new whig *ligne de force.* The present crisis presented by Quebec's awakening to the meaning of the positive state may be leading us to rewrite our history to culminate in the glorious future of the B and B report.

There are already signs of this. No historian of the younger generation is more influential than Ramsay Cook. It is paradoxical that the man whose superb biography of J. W. Dafoe provided a model of the kind of history we require to understand the nature of Canadian diversity and conflict should be known to the public as the author of a book which argues that

Canada and the French Canadian question is really the Canadian question . . . we must find institutions that will give full expression to the cultural duality of the Canadian nation-state.

Now as a description of the realities of power in Canadian society, this is a respectable, though debatable, point of view. But if historically it is to lead to the popularization of the "Compact Theory of Confederation,"[2] and to the view that Quebec was willing to participate in building a nation from sea to sea but was confined to the "Quebec Reservation" by Anglo-Protestant bigotry (manifested in the hanging of Riel, successive defeats on "school questions" and the tyrannical imposition of conscription), then we are in the process of choosing a new whiggery.

[2] Cook, as editor of Confederation, vol. III of the CANADIAN HISTORICAL READINGS SERIES, selected G. F. G. Stanley's article propounding the "two nations" concept as the only article on the interpretation of Confederation.

6. In recent years a growing number of Canadian scholars have expressed discontent with what may be called establishment theories about the nation's past. They have looked, in particular, for alternative economic interpretations of our history. Professor Kenneth McNaught, whose books include A Prophet in Politics: A Biography of J. S. Woodsworth *(Toronto, 1959) and* History of Canada *(London, 1970), illustrates in the following article how the concept of American dominance may be used as a framework for Canadian history.*

[6] Reprinted from Kenneth McNaught, "The Permanent Colony," *Canadian Forum* 49(587), January 1970, pp. 227-228 with the permission of the publisher.

We have not yet, mercifully, achieved a consensus view of Canadian history. For a while in the 'forties and 'fifties a number of anglophone historians thought they were moulding such an interpretation based upon the idea of a long, almost excessively patient and nearly inevitable progress from colony to nation. But 'sixties revealed much that was both inadequate and misleading about such a view — just as that decade challenged even more violently the consensus view within American historiography.

In Canada, Quebec's increasingly unquiet revolution has demonstrated that the liberal-conservative anglophone story of steady growth to political independence, economic competence and national unity was a kind of non-self-fulfilling prophecy rather than penetrating historical analysis. It was a version of our history which could be sustained only by assuming that the angular historical manifestations of racial friction, colonial-mindedness and economic dependency had all more or less passed away with the ultimate defeat of the integrated Empire-Commonwealth, the successful weathering of the second conscription crisis and our emergence as a "leading industrial state." Without recognizing the dangerous extent to which our 'maturity' and 'unity' were based upon the twin bases of anglo-saxon superiority and unlimited American investment, we religiously celebrated our new and influential independence. We had shared in the secret development of atomic energy, we were equal partners in NATO and in NORAD, we were righteous leaders in a multi-national Commonwealth of Nations and in international peace-keeping and we had produced another francophone prime minister who had threatened to build the St. Lawrence Seaway entirely in Canadian waters — thus forcing the mightiest nation in the world to co-operate with us and proving our talents in the field of racial conciliation. We had entered a new and glittering Laurier era.

Well, it is now clear that the bases of an anglophone consensus history were being disastrously undermined at the very time that we were celebrating unity and the final success of the good old east-west economy. Instead of listening to the heart-warming assurances of Uncle Louis and Lester B. we should have been reading *Cité Libre* and Frank Underhill. Especially Professor Underhill who told us clearly enough that "in 1940 we passed from the British century of our history to the American century. We became dependent upon the United States for our security. We have, therefore, no choice but to follow American leadership." Of course this did not bother Mr. Underhill, although he did warn that our American century would be a tough one. It didn't bother him — or his new and somewhat surprised friends in Canadian Liberalism — because they all believed that fighting against the inevitable is futile. They believed, too, that the best way we could use our independence was in close, voluntary co-operation with the United States. Only thus could we derive the full economic benefits of superior American technology and investment. And, in any event, we should act upon our recognition that the best in American culture was the best in the West — was, in fact, the complement of an essential American military defence against an illiberal and brutalizing communism.

It was this kind of reasoning that led most anglophone Canadians (save for a nervous twitching of their political subconscious in the Diefenbaker elections) to accept a new colonialism. Like the colonialism of our British era, our relationship to the American empire is based upon a perception of personal interest by the Canadian anglophone economic elite. And as in our previous colonialism the life-styles and social values of the imperial power tend to become the success criteria of the colonial elite. But it is now evident, also, that the comparison of our British and American colonial periods does not end with the facts of economic-military integration and of social emulation.

In both colonial periods resistance to "foreign domination" is to be found spearheaded by French Canadians, more-or-less vigorously supported by the political Left in English-speaking Canada, and occasionally endorsed by establishment politicians who sense the cyclical mood of their constituents and do not wish to be too obviously at variance with it. The most essential point about recurring Canadian resistance to domination from abroad is that it is based firstly upon a cumulative desire for the survival of basic identities — regional, cultural, provincial and even, on occasion, national. The second most important characteristic of such resistance is that it holds suspect the nature and purposes of the dominating imperial power. This was true of the attitude to imperial Britain expressed by French Canadians, the Progressives and the CCF. It is equally true of their successors who now look with dismay at the new imperial power — an empire even more violently discordant in its own homeland and at least as ruthless in exercising its power abroad as was Britain in South Africa or India.

But here a comparison between our British and American colonial relationships leads to a fundamental and ominous point of difference. We released ourselves from the British relationship with comparative ease, despite a lot of political clamour which was useful principally to Mackenzie King. This was possible largely because Britain was losing her power much more rapidly than most Canadians at the time realized and because we were able to tie ourselves economically and militarily to the "countervailing power" of the United States. Any attempt to shake free of the American empire will be almost infinitely more hazardous. And it will be hazardous for more reasons than appear at first glance.

Not only is the United States at the peak of its power (one may hopefully assume) but also the nature of its domination of Canada is both more subtle and more complete than was Britain's at any time in the twentieth century. In the case of our British colonial relationship, political, military and economic dominance were present from the beginning. Political dominance slipped away almost automatically with the erosion of Britain's economic and military power. This can scarcely be the case with our American colonial relationship. In the American case political domination has followed economic and military dominance. And it has followed in a way that is normally so subtle that it is frequently indiscernible. Only occasionally is it felt necessary that a general or a State Department spokesman should openly point out the error of our ways.

Like American reformers in the Progressive era, most Liberal and Conservative Canadians feel that they still have the political power to impose mastery over drift — to legislate regulation of business while leaving business to create ever larger corporate structures whose control of public appointments and public policy became virtually complete. Like the American reformers however, many Canadians are now awakening to the fact that if you permit great 'private' corporations to own your economy you also grant to them the control of public policy. You grant to them the right to use your resources to protect the 'right' of multinational corporations to operate and regulate their own world-wide market system. You grant to them the right to impose upon the areas within their writ their own technological values and their own definitions of liberalism and freedom. American reformers discovered too late that they had been hoodwinked by regulatory reforms which were merely provisions by which a corporate elite could use the power of the state to rationalize its market operations. As they take to the streets, or flee to Canada, in opposition to the corporate-military values of their kept government, they almost scream their warning to those who inhabit the provinces of the informal American empire.

And we live in the most important of those provinces. Just as we were the "senior Dominion" of the Empire-Commonwealth, so now we are the most reliable of the American provinces. As a Dominion we gratified ourselves by saying "no" to proposals for formal integration, and finally we broke the relationship altogether — but only when our economic elite no longer needed money from British investment houses. Now we find ourselves within an even more powerful empire and the recipient of four times as much investment from our metropolitan centre as is bestowed upon any other country. Occasionally we say "no" to requests for *formal* commitments, as in Vietnam. But we are clearly nowhere near breaking the colonial relationship. Because our economic elite (including a number of trade union leaders) find it to their advantage to co-operate with multinational corporations, the most strenuous opposition to serious countervailing measures comes from inside the colony itself. As it did also in the days of Sir John A.

As in our former colonial experience, it is the French Canadian and the anglophone Left that perceive what is necessary if their various versions of survival and the good society are to retain meaning. Each recognizes that it is not enough to say that American corporations in Canada act like good citizens — for this merely means that they convey to us whatever modicum of their technological expertise they find convenient, while exercising a vast, if indirect political influence, the precise nature of which remains to be documented. Each recognizes, too, that however beneficial the technological fall-out it more often than not inhibits the central purpose of a liberal society which is self-fulfillment — in both the individual and collective sense. Self-fulfilment (let alone the good society), as the humane sector of American society has discovered, is not possible within even the metropolitan country as long as it is dominated by politically irresponsible corporations. Much less are the essential liberal goals attainable in a wholly dependent colony.

It is because of these obvious considerations that the Left in Canada (both English and French-speaking) has given a nationalist and a *nationaliste* tone to its demands for public ownership of those debatable 'key' sectors of the economy and for stringent regulation of foreign investment. And it is the Left's growing awareness of the nature of the multi-national corporate agents of the American empire that lead to doubts about the absolute need of the Canadian economy for unlimited foreign investment when already the dividends flowing south are greater than the annual rate of foreign investment.

In the circumstances it is scarcely surprising that the tentative anglophone consensus history of Canada failed to survive the 'fifties. It now appears that a consensus version of our history would have to be built upon the assumption that Canadians have always really wanted to be colonials — whereas, in fact, it is only our elites that have enjoyed the colonial condition. That kind of consensus history would do as much, or greater violence to the facts than does American consensus history.

7. In 1967 and 1968 L. F. S. Upton and J. M. Bliss debated the nature of the English-Canadian experience in North America. The discussion was provoked by Upton's article in the Queen's Quarterly *in which he stated that English-language history, unlike the version in Quebec, has failed to provide English speaking Canadians with any sense of belonging to a nation.*

He begins his article by comparing the situation today with that in the nineteenth century.

The plain truth is that, if English Canadians do not think of themselves as a nation, but rather of Canada as a nation, it is not that they have more expansive minds than Quebecers; it is rather that they have been brought up on an English language history which has failed to provide them with any definite idea of who they are, whence they came, or whither they are going. No history has ever been presented to English Canadians that can convince British Columbians, for example, that their destiny is justly tied to that of Newfoundland, or Albertans that they must stand or fall together with Ontario. By contrast, French Canada has developed a compact historical justification which is a complete rationale for its existence as a separate entity in North America.

It is trite to say that Canada has two histories; it is necessary to say that these two histories are never taught Canadians. The difficulty does not lie simply in the selection of fact, although it is notorious that there are two "invisible men" in our history: for the English it is the French Canadian who receives scant attention; for the French, the English scarce obtrude on the scene. But underlying this obvious difference is a mutual

[7] Reprinted from L. F. S. Upton, "In Search of Canadian History," *Queen's Quarterly*, 74(4), Winter 1967, pp. 674-675, 678-679, 682, with the permission of the author.

lack of comprehension over the very art of history itself. While French Canadians look to fulfilment for their nation, the English Canadian bumps along from topic to topic, unsure of his path, ignorant of his goal.

The amateur historians who wrote in the English language in the nineteenth century provided a story with a moral, a justification for being, not Canadian, but English Canadian. Their history was based on three certainties: the superiority of the English to the French Canadian; the superiority of the English Canadian to the United States American; and the superiority of the English Canadian by virtue of his first class membership in the British Empire. Unpleasant as much of this historical writing now appears, children brought up on its teachings grew to manhood proud of their origins, content with the present, and confident of the future.

Professor Upton argues that these three certainties are firmly etched in nineteenth century histories. More recent developments, however, have removed the underpinnings from these foundations. New interpretations shattered the image and all the desperate strivings of modern writers have not reassembled a sense of English-Canadian pride.

Many things have changed in this century. The pride of the English Canadian in not being French is now held to be shameful. Anti-Americanism is still with us, but the omnipresence of the United States is proof positive of the success of republicanism, and classroom presentations of a cautionary tale are futile. The British Empire has passed on. That it did so was no fault of the English Canadians, and its passing has left a gap, a break in the sense of purpose, that has not been made good.

The three certainties of English Canadian history received their first hard blow before the end of the nineteenth century. The man who wielded the club was Goldwin Smith, that "perverse expatriate Englishman" (in a phrase of W. L. Morton's), a journalist-historian with a knack for popularizing his ideas. Frustrated in his search for a Canadian nationality by those colonials who denounced the mere thought as treasonable to the Empire, Smith eventually fitted his adopted home into the framework of an Anglo-Saxondom to come. The arguments he penned in *Canada and the Canadian Question* cut right across the conventional lines of thought, and emphasized the closeness of Canada to the United States: "The continent is an economic whole, and . . . to run a customs line athwart it and try to sever its members from each other is to wage a desperate war against nature. Each several province of the dominion is by nature wedded to a commercial partner on the south, though a perverse policy struggles to divorce them."[9] By emphasizing the unity of North America, Goldwin Smith knocked the Humpty Dumpty of Anglo-Canadian history off the wall.

The king's horses and the king's men have tried to put it all back together again. Their part has been played by the professional historians of this

[9] Goldwin Smith, *Canada and the Canadian Question*, Toronto, 1891, 284.

century who have replaced the amateurs of an earlier age. These new men have taken up frontierism, metropolitanism, the fur trade, the St. Lawrence, the northern imperative, the mosaic. They have argued with each other over abstract forces, ineluctable pulls, inevitable conjunctions. They have not put Humpty Dumpty together again; they have not even cleaned up the pieces; they have not provided even as useful a basis for history as the three certainties of a century ago. As a result, the three old irrelevancies are still the stuff of Canadian school histories in the English language.

Professor Upton concludes by contrasting the disorder and disillusionment among English-speaking Canadians with the sense of purpose exhibited by French Canadians.

While English Canadian history was being desiccated with economics, French Canadian history was enriched with passion, immediacy and purpose. Survival was not a question of hanging on because there was no alternative; it was a means to an end. Subsequent historians have questioned Groulx's bias, decried it as a disservice to a community in mid-century America, but they have not wished to break out from within its grand design. A spiritual mission can be easily secularized and remain a mission. It makes for a very different Canadian history from that described by Chester Martin as a "tough and intractable business" where little "falls into neat patterns against the background of the universe" leaving "blind and baffled courage" the principal resource of past generations.[18]

English Canadians may be tempted to think that the French Canadian is somehow peculiar in having developed a national history with its own integrity and purpose. Yet it is the English Canadian, with all his vagueness and imprecision, who is the odd man out on this continent. There are striking similarities between the development of French Canadian historiography and that of the United States: both peoples have responded to North America as founding races, reacting to its physical isolation from Europe by developing a sense of mission to justify their existence. The oldest theme in United States history is that of the Covenant: the early settlers of New England were men of sufficient moral stature to make an agreement with God to found His city in the wilderness. Their mission was to find a state of grace and innocence removed from the corruptions of the world.[19] No matter that these men really came for fish, the ideas woven around them have proved infinitely adaptable as the United States has grown, giving a unity of purpose, a sense of distinctiveness, to its history. Only in the past decade has the English Canadian begun to feel the isolation that turned fishermen and fur traders into the founders of purposeful states. The English Canadian, whose history rests on the three certainties of a hundred years ago, is still blind and baffled; let us hope he is still courageous.

[18] Chester Martin, *The Foundations of Canadian Nationhood,* Toronto, 1955, 514.

[19] David Noble, *Historians against History,* Minneapolis, 1965, *passim.*

118

8. Almost a year later, J. M. Bliss' rejoinder to the previous reading appeared in the same periodical. First of all, he chides Professor Upton for unfairly attacking textbooks currently used in schools. Secondly, he asserts that many French-speaking historians were frankly propagandist in tone, a quality not prized among modern historians. In the following sections he offers an alternative explanation of the English-Canadian identity and relates the whole debate to profound disagreements over the nature of the historian's craft.

Whatever English Canadian identity historians may be able to scrape together from their researches, it cannot be defined in terms of a "mission", as Mr. Upton so clearly hopes it can. The concept of "mission" is obviously teleological and for substantiation requires the insight of the moral philosopher, metaphysician, or theologian rather than the restricted inductive powers of the historian who is bound to empirical evidence. Perhaps English Canada did make a Covenant with the Lord or was assigned a Manifest Destiny by Heaven. One wonders how the usual methods of historical research can be adapted to the discovery and analysis of such a literally unnatural development.

Would it be satisfactory if we could at least find evidence that English Canadians have thought they had a mission or a purpose in North America? What would count as sufficient evidence for such a conclusion? How many English Canadians thinking alike over what period of time are required to establish a generalization valid for a whole society throughout its history? At one time or another many different groups of English Canadians have thought they had a mission in North America. But to extrapolate from specific, limited currents of thought to a set of propositions about the total English Canadian experience would be just as absurd and naively dishonest as to claim that in the mid-1960s English Canada is devoted to Queen Elizabeth (some of us, no matter how few, are English Canadians and are not devoted to Queen Elizabeth; therefore we invalidate the proposition). In any case, the kinds of statements that groups of English Canadians have made about the purpose of their community, such as the three "certainties" of the nineteenth century, now seem to be, as Professor Upton realizes, partly ludicrous, partly false, and at least quite irrelevant to what is now a different historical situation. Even if English Canadians did have an identity in the past they have quite rightly abandoned it in the present.

Is it not time for someone to blow the whistle on this whole tedious game of trying to define an English Canadian or even a Canadian identity. Probably the most honest statement that can be made about the English Canadian identity — and it is a descriptive statement about identity — is that there has never been a very significant degree of identification among English Canadians. They have been and are divided by geography,

[8] Reprinted from J. M. Bliss, "Searching for Canadian History," *Queen's Quarterly*, 75(3), Autumn 1968, pp. 501-503, 504-505, 506-507, 508, with the permission of the author.

class, religion, age, sexual practices, cultural tastes, and — if English-*speaking* Canadians are considered (another point that Mr. Upton never clarifies) — by ethnicity. The concept of identity entails commonality or similarity. But how much does a sixty-year-old, wealthy, sickly, Anglican, Torontonian, university-educated executive have in common with a twenty year old, poor, healthy, Roman Catholic, semi-literate logger on Vancouver Island? Or what do either of them have in common with the average practising Canadian historian, unlikely even to watch Hockey Night in Canada? Can it possibly be denied that by almost every criteria for measuring "identity" each of these people has more in common with his American, British, or Australian counterpart — yes, even his French Canadian counterpart — than he does with the others in this little sample? The mind boggles at the claim that a sense of national purpose, mission, or destiny establishes an elemental difference between Americans and Canadians of identical age, religious, and occupational groups — who also in this century share increasingly similar cultural pursuits.

Since Canada has survived as a separate political entity in North America for several hundreds of years, one might object that the fact of survival alone proves that there is a broad identity among Canadians. We are united by our historical determination to survive.

*　　*　　*

Compelling reasons do exist for English Canadians, and French Canadians, to stand or fall together. In the 1960s many of us obviously desire that there should continue to exist a North American community in which young men are not conscripted, the problems of urban society have not yet become insurmountable, and violence is not the ordinary means of handling civil rights issues. These are the considerations that confirm my own Canadian nationalism; but it is difficult to see how they can be said to give me either a sense of mission or a uniquely English Canadian identity. I have no quarrel with other English Canadians who desire Canadian survival for quite different reasons from mine. Indeed, I welcome them as allies. But I can also foresee future circumstances which would compel me to break this alliance and advocate union with the United States. If American society were to restore itself and become committed to the same social and political values that many of us as English Canadians share, while French Canada were to adopt social and political values that many of us find intolerable, why should we not repeat Goldwin Smith's arguments for a wider, more fulfilling English-speaking community in North America? Probably this contingency will not develop. My only point is that it is not inconceivable and there is no rigid and absolute commandment existing in human history decreeing that the relations of North American nationalities be never altered.

*　　*　　*

The disagreement between Professor Upton and myself is rooted in a profound difference of opinion about the role of historians and the function of nationalism in a society. As an historian I will not don the homespun of the nationalist or the surplice of the moral prophet. My only duty as an historian is to make an honest attempt to find out something about what happened in the past, to try to tell it as it was, and to repudiate other historians who say "no matter" about how it did happen. I must also resist and protest the presumption of integral nationalists — English Canadian, French Canadian, or Plain Canadian — who tell me that I have "sadly failed" in my duty to my society because I have not enlisted in their ideological army.

Few expressions of the human consciousness are as dangerous as the integral nationalism of the nineteenth and twentieth centuries. After nazism and fascism, and now after Vietnam, the consequences of the attitude of mind that is willing to disregard empiricism and plurality in favour of homogeneity, efficiency and national purpose are too starkly obvious to be disregarded. English Canada is not poorer in spirit for sharing little of this temperament and rejecting the certainties that it provided for us when we did abide by its categories. The old certainties of Anglo-Saxondom were directly responsible for the development in Canada of racism, restrictive immigration policies, censorship and blue laws, and an overall leaning to chauvinism that have incalculably lowered the quality of Canadian life. In French Canada the certainties of the French Canadian mission may have encouraged *la survivance,* but they have also sustained racism, censorship, chauvinism, political corruption, and economic backwardness. It is at least debatable whether less national consciousness and more pragmatic adjustments to the real world would not have been of far greater service historically to the flowering of French Canada in North America. Many of us wonder today whether the secularized missionary zeal of contemporary nationalists is not leading Quebec dangerously close to social, political, and economic disruption. If English Canadians in turn were now to abandon their commitment to a pluralist, rationalist society in favour of a resurgence of mission, purpose, and collective assertiveness the consequences for Canada would be dissolution and disaster.

*   *   *

Which historian, then, representing which community, is "the odd man out" on this continent? Is it the English Canadian historian whose "vagueness and imprecision" is in fact a cautious respect for the complexity of historical experience, shared by many of his colleagues in French Canada and virtually all of his colleagues in the United States? Or is it the nationalist historian, emotionally committed to specious and dangerous certainties, careless of facts and documentation, desperately eager to implant his own values in the consciousness of society? Insofar as Professor Upton supports a nationalist approach to history — an approach which survives on this continent only in a few universities in Quebec and at increasingly fewer meetings of the Canadian Historical Association — he is assuming a traditionalist posture which withstands neither logical analysis nor the simple moral imperative of the historian's responsibility to the past.

SEVEN

CRITICAL COMMENT

History in school is influenced by two powerful masters, the discipline and the state, who seem on occasions to pull in different directions. One master may demand greater uniformity while the other recommends a variety in approach. Public curriculum committees may require the subject to assume duties within the educational system that scholars are reluctant to support. Some historians, on the other hand, seem unwilling to recognize the state's claim that the school must serve social purposes which take priority over intellectual objectives. Although the extent of their disagreements ought not to be exaggerated, it is quite evident from a survey of the periodical literature that historians and some other scholars have criticized provincial policies and practices quite severely.

Almost every aspect of history teaching has been attacked. Sending textbooks scuttling for cover is a seasonal occupation among critics. Others bemoan the inclusion of history in social science courses or bewail the continuation of different versions of the past in English- and French-speaking provinces. Although there seems to be general agreement that Canadian Studies courses deserve a large share of school time, an ardent minority is fearful of national- istic feelings and worried lest world civilizations be ignored. A similar agreement does not exist, however, on the relationship of a history program to the teaching of contemporary affairs, some scholars arguing against the proposition and others just as vehe- mently for it.

Naturally enough the critics have been much less vocal on the subject of their own responsibilities than they have been on the duties of others. Very little comment has been made in Canada about the role of historians in reforming the school curriculum. Some scholars, it is true, have argued that teachers need assistance in the design of new types of programs. In this connection, the Canada Studies Foundation is the most serious attempt ever made to form curriculum teams of scholars and teachers on a national rather than provincial basis.[1] Generally speaking, however, historians in Canada have not gone as far as those in other coun- tries in the investigation of such problems as the relationship of course and materials to the learning process of the child. A scholar, even when he assumes the role of a hostile critic, does not neces- sarily offer an acceptable alternative.

Nevertheless, the school system needs its critics. Hampered by administrative details and blinkered by official policies, educational authorities require comments from outside observers. Systems often become so large that they tend to stifle inner renewal: the force for change must come from other sources. In this chapter, these sources include academic historians, researchers and Royal Com- missioners. Such critics serve the schools best when they highlight first principles and scorn arrogances, self-satisfaction and plain, old-fashioned wrongheadedness.

[1] "The Foundation assists in the development of, and encourages cooperation between, project teams of educators located in different parts of Canada. These regional teams are composed of people from different levels and interests in education — that is, of university professors representing different disciplines, experts in learning theory and practice, administrators and classroom teachers." *Canada Studies Foundation: Annual Report, March 31, 1971*, p. 6.

1. Scholars have often experienced difficulty in understanding or agreeing with what provincial departments of education may be at- tempting to accomplish. On occasion, they have virtually thrown up their hands in disgust and condemned political control of the nation's schools. Dr. Hilda Neatby's So Little for the Mind *(Toronto, 1953) and Frank MacKinnon's* The Politics of Education *(Toronto, 1960)*

[1] Reprinted from Lewis Hertzmann, "The Sad Demise of History : Social Studies in the Alberta Schools," *Dalhousie Review*, 43 (1963), pp. 515-517, 517-518, 519-520 with the permission of the publisher.

are two examples of open disapproval with public systems. In a similar vein, Dr. Lewis Hertzmann, now Professor of History at York University, takes issue with what he regards as the failure of the Alberta curriculum builders to understand the nature of history. Although it should be stressed that the Alberta curriculum has been changed in recent years, the sorts of criticisms made by Professor Hertzmann are still current among historians.*

Perhaps much of the unfruitful controversy in Alberta on the teaching of history and social studies derives from the failure of some people to understand the nature of historical studies, and indeed social sciences, at this juncture of the twentieth century. It should be clearly understood that historians are immediately concerned with the work not only of social scientists, but of scholars in all areas, as well as with the literature of all countries and eras. Although our professional educators will often not admit the fact, or perhaps do not know it, history has been healthfully aerated for over half a century by contact with all the social sciences, by anthropology no less than economics, psychology, and other branches of knowledge. Of course, it is beyond the capacity of any single man to have all the knowledge he should have to be a historian of any given period. But surely, too, it is beyond the capacity of any person to teach all that is known of any period. The conception of social studies as imagined in the Alberta curriculum is beyond the wisdom and knowledge of an Arnold Toynbee to devise; it is beyond the capacity of a Socrates to teach. But to be coherent as a study, history must remain history, not social studies.

Each of the social sciences, let it be remembered, has its own useful technical vocabulary, set of assumptions, and technical modes of operation. All make sense within their respective disciplines. But to mix them haphazardly, as has been done in the Alberta programme, is to invite incoherence and chaos.

I have a number of specific criticisms of the unit arrangement of the Alberta curriculum, of the confusion of the so-called "understandings", "skills", and "attitudes" in terms of which it is set up, of the poor literacy of the curriculum, and of the lack of balance in the whole.

For one thing, each course in social studies has an exaggerated Canadian orientation that is offensive to the historian and social scientist. On page 14 we actually find the Grade X course on Mesopotamia, Greece, and Rome called "Ancient Origins of Canadian Civilization". To speak of "Canadian civilization" in this manner is to reveal ignorance of the very idea of civilization, and to leave us open to justified reproaches of arrogant nationalism.

It is curious, moreover, that each social studies course intended to approach the experience of mankind in the broadest and most general way, in effect is fragmented each year into five or six, often little related, blocs,

*See also Blair Neatby, "The Curriculum Committee that Never Was," The Canadian Journal of History and Social Science, 5(3), June 1970, pp. 59-64.

an arrangement that surely does not aid understanding. In bewildering sequence the Grade X student is faced with units on geography, trade, demography, democracy, the family, and the church. There is little progress of thought, and the barest framework of place or time. The arrangement is no better in other grades.

Skills and attitudes are the natural results of good education and good teaching, and not the by-product of lists in a departmental publication. I am not prepared to comment on teaching methods in the schools, but I doubt that the desired results are obtained by following lists of "expressional activities" such as "asking and answering questions", "drill activities" ("practising the Social Studies skills"), and "leadership activities" ("accepting responsibility for having good work and work done on time"). All such virtues, and many more, are desirable. They are the product of character, intelligence, and environment, as well as of education. The school is demanding the impossible by requiring students to show acquired attitudes of a specified character within the framework of courses. The school, in demanding these attitudes, is undertaking an indefensible task of indoctrination, indeed of invading the inmost soul. Thus a student in Grade X, unit 5, must show *concern* "for the family's permanency in performing its social function successfully." He must *desire determinedly* "to achieve and maintain worthy home membership on his own part." In unit 2 of the following year, while studying "the effect of science on our economic life", the student must show *sympathetic interest* "in the problems of labour in a highly industrialized society." Thus the student is not so much being educated as indoctrinated according to a long list of norms acceptable to the Department of Education, but not necessarily acceptable to all families, students, political parties, religions, philosophies, or the social sciences that allegedly are being taught.

*   *   *

The so-called "understandings", and the more numerous related "tentative conclusions"/"guides to understanding", are for scholars the most disturbing part of the Alberta curriculum. Many of them are debatable, at best, and by no means capable of simple acceptance by an informed and thoughtful individual. Some of them are quite false. Others are misleading. In the indoctrination unit on democracy (Grade X, unit 4) there is a most distressing confusion between primitive and modern democracy, a confusion that does a disservice to the understanding of both. For example, the section on Greek democracy makes no reference to the place of slavery, or to other variants from our society. "Understanding 5" is the appalling comment that "the end of the Dark Ages was marked by the emergence among the Teutonic peoples of the ideas of individual freedom and representative government." To correct the ignorance contained in that "understanding" alone would require a lengthy essay, indeed a course in itself. But the Alberta curriculum bristles with such dangerous misinformation on every page. Then, having been misinformed on early democracy, the student is given the task of applying his newly learned concepts to the modern world: to the societies of Eskimos and North American

Indians, the Ottoman Empire, Tsarist Russia, and Nazi Germany among others (page 42)! The task is, of course, impossible for teacher and student.

*   *   *

The exaggerated Canadian nationalism exemplified in the titles of all the present social studies courses in Alberta has already been commented on. It is deplorable. The emphasis on so-called immediate history is not going to achieve desired ends. On the other hand, studying people and their problems in other societies and times will by itself extend the horizon of students and help them find their own road to understanding and wisdom. *Wisdom* seems to be a word not much found in the professional educators' vocabulary. As for current events, students need only read the newspaper and listen to the CBC in time readily available to them outside of school hours. The importance of following current events, of reading the editorial columns of newspapers, of reading journals such as the *Atlantic Monthly,* of going to the theatre and to concerts—the importance of all these activities, and others, is obvious. Schools can do much to prepare students for a way of life in which all these activities are a part. But the schools must realize their limitations. Their most important contribution to individuals and society lies positively in teaching well the disciplines within their control. Among these is history. The schools have it within their power to arouse the interest of students in history, or to kill it. At present it is clear that social studies courses have generally failed to arouse students' enthusiasm and interest in Alberta, and certainly they have left students unprepared for further work in relevant subjects.

2. *The Liberal government that won a narrow victory in 1960 in Quebec decided to conduct an inquiry into the state of education in that province. The Parent Commission, after exhaustive study, made a large number of suggestions for change, some of which concerned the teaching of history. In these comments, the Commissioners offered not only general criticisms but also proposals for curriculum change. Their suggestion that history should not be used for nationalistic purposes was not well received in certain intellectual circles in Quebec.**

The teaching of history in the Province of Quebec has been the object of many criticisms. One of the main problems is the separation between the Protestant element, mainly English speaking, and the Catholic element, in majority French speaking. If history is a science aiming at an objective interpretation, it is difficult to understand why it is taught from two ex-

*Ramsay Cook, The Maple Leaf Forever : Essays on Nationalism and Politics in Canada, (Toronto 1971), p. 227.

[2] Reprinted from "History" in *Report of the Royal Commission of Inquiry on Education in the Province of Quebec,* 1965, Part Two, Volume III, pp. 140-141, 142-143 with permission of the Quebec Official Publisher. Paragraph numbers and marginal headings have been removed.

tremely different perspectives, as is actually the case. At the level of the programmes of general history, such a great difference is hardly justified: ancient history, the history of the Middle Ages, of Europe and of the World, of the American continents, of the United States—all of these should be the same for the French- and English-speaking students of Quebec. As for the history of Canada, it is understandable that the French students study in greater detail the French regime, and the English students the events since 1760. But both groups have everything to gain from a good knowledge of the whole history of Canada, and the main lines of the programme could be the same for all. In the same way it is natural for the Catholics and Protestants in as far as the role of the Catholic Church or the Protestant Churches is concerned, to put greater emphasis on Bishop Laval or Bishop Mountain respectively. However, the facts and the fundamental historical documents could be the same and a sincere desire to understand the mentality and the intentions of the different historical figures should always underlie the history course.

The syllabus in the elementary and secondary schools of the Catholic sector recommend a teaching of the history of Canada directed towards an apology of national and religious goals. This teaching must "reveal to the child the action of Divine Providence", and show that "nations do not possess true happiness" unless they are "faithful to the law of God". It must point out "the purity of our French-Canadian origins, the religious, moral, heroic and idealistic character of our ancestors . . . the visible protection of Divine Providence in the survival of our nationality"[5]. The Handbook for Teachers of the Protestant schools, among the principal aims assigned to the teaching of history, mentions only one concerning a national education: "To develop a healthy nationalism while promoting an attitude of tolerance for other races, religions, political ideas and nationalities"[6]. The programme of the English-Catholic schools sees history as making the students appreciate "our rights and our responsibilities as Canadians" and as developing "loyalty and national pride . . . rooted in historical reality"[7]. The textbooks used in the French-Catholic sector accentuate even more, especially at the elementary level, the sentimentality and the national and religious morality towards which the official programme aims. On the English side, the Catholic schools and the Protestant schools use in part the same textbooks for the history of Canada.

*   *   *

For history to be taught as a science, taking into consideration the full meaning of relativity in the study of human behaviour, it is necessary to review the conception of the whole, at the level of the preparation of the programmes. It is important to dissociate history from patriotic justification; the first aim in the teaching of history is not the development of a civic, patriotic or religious conscience. This confusion can only be harmful to

[5] *Programme d'études des écoles élémentaires*, 1959, pages 481-482.
[6] *Handbook for Teachers*, 1957, page 105.
[7] *Course of Study for the Elementary Grades* (I-VII) — English-Language Catholic Schools, 1963, page 145.

history, to patriotism and to religion. The teaching of history aims to develop the human mind by the objective and honest study of the past, based on documents.

The programmes, the textbooks and the texts to be studied should give a large place to the various aspects of civilization: economic conditions, the history of art, the history of the social classes, the history of ideas and of social behaviour patterns, and the evolution of cultures. Of course it is necessary to continue to make use of chronology, political history, battles, wars, conquests; these are the definite and fixed points and the chronological skeleton has an unquestionable educational utility. But it should only be the skeleton for a greatly enriched, diversified study of history, based on the development and the progress of societies rather than on the listing of their quarrels.

Besides the history of Canada, which in the French-Catholic schools is taught mainly in terms of the Province of Quebec, the syllabus seems to give too great or even too exclusive a place to the history of France. A balanced programme should also cover the history of modern Canada, of England, of the United States. Also attention should be given to the development of the other European civilizations, as well as to the rich and ancient civilizations of Asia, and the recent evolution of the African countries should be studied. However, this should be directed to a study of the major currents of civilization and art rather than the listing of wars and dynasties. In the last years of the course, there should be a concentration on the contemporary history of civilization; in the case of Canada, the concentration should be on the nineteenth and twentieth centuries, on the study of civil and parliamentary institutions, on the conquest of democratic rights, all within the North American context.

It is urgent to submit the textbooks in use to a committee of historians, who will examine them from the point of view of accuracy. It would seem necessary to see to the preparation of new textbooks for the teaching of Canadian history; they should be adapted to the age of the students for whom they are prepared; it is for this reason the psychologists and educators should collaborate with the historians in the preparation of these textbooks. These text books should, at least on the secondary level, include copious documentary material and maps for analysis, as well as pictures of an historical interest. For the more advanced students, collections of historical documents are still the best starting point for a history lesson. As for textbooks for the general history of civilizations, from prehistoric times until today, they will present the most important movements, using reproductions of works of art, maps showing the main developments of civilization, tables of chronological concordance of events, etc; French textbooks, English textbooks or Belgian textbooks are centred too much around the history of France, England or Belgium. Textbooks for the history of civilizations could be prepared by an international committee. As for ancient history, French and English textbooks are very good.

In history, as in other subjects, progressive methods will be more fruitful if the teacher has been shown how to use them. If history is to be fully educational, if the student must learn to be objective, to make conjectures based on sound intuitions and inductions, to read documents critically and comparatively, it will be necessary to train the teachers in the methods of personal and group work. To awaken and satisfy his curiosity, films, photographs, pictures, visits to museums, historical sites, archives, and volumes of all sorts should serve to complement the lesson. The methods and the didactic material should first be carefully experimented with and then passed on to the specialists in the training of teachers. The teachers should be informed of the material available and the proper way to use it. Under competent guidance, school television could show students anywhere in the province various historical sites.

3. *Many general readers expect their school textbooks to give a balanced and judicious version of the past. Provincial adoption Committees go to great pains to ensure that no group that they consider politically significant in the community is offended by the contents of a school book. Nevertheless it is clear that history books in the past have given a particular interpretation of history.*

It is not difficult to find examples. George M. Wrong's Britain's History, *authorized in 1929 in Ontario, ended a chapter devoted to the praising of the British Empire with the statement that the "deep convictions and emotions" of the scattered British people "banish any wavering in the resolve to maintain its unity."* Dr. F. H. Armstrong, *an expert on the early history of Ontario, has shown how popular views of William Lyon Mackenzie have been influenced by misleading accounts written in some of the province's textbooks.† While it is true, as the Royal Commission on Bilingualism and Biculturalism pointed out in 1968, that "history teachers may present an interpretation not found in the textbook, and examination marks may reward students who disagree with the textbook version," the same Commission was forced to add that "observation . . . suggests that this rarely happens."‡*

What interpretations, we may ask, do modern textbooks contain? Dr. Gerald Walsh has attempted to answer that question by a careful examination of textbooks in every province of the country. He not only concludes that a number of distinct groupings can be distinguished but also states that students in various sections of the country tend to be taught different versions of the past.

*George M. Wrong, Britain's History (Toronto, 1929) pp. 379-387.

†Frederick H. Armstrong, "William Lyon Mackenzie : the persistent hero," Journal of Canadian Studies, 6(3), August 1971, pp. 32-34.

‡Report of the Royal Commission on Bilingualism and Biculturalism (Ottawa, 1968) Volume 2, p. 274.

[3] Reprinted from Gerald Walsh, "A Survey of Philosophies of History in Canadian High Schools", *Canadian Journal of History and Social Science,* 2(3), 1966-1967, pp. 8-9, 10, 12-13, 13-14 with the permission of the publisher.

The interpretations in the programmes fall into three main groups: the Catholic histories; histories of progress; and "histories of limited interpretation". Whereas the Catholic and "progress" histories are organized around a single unifying theme, the histories of the last sort are not.

The Catholic Interpretation. The Catholic interpretation finds its clearest expression in the programme of the French Catholic schools of Quebec. It is a view of history in which the coming of Christ to earth is central—the capital event of history. Before the birth of Christ, all human life is represented as lacking in a moral dimension. This can only be made good by the life and teachings of Christ. Men can only be whole, as it were, after Christ's work on earth is done. The pre-Christian civilizations are thus cast in a strange light, attaining great heights in many ways, yet always necessarily lacking in the Christian understanding of the relationship of man to God, and man to man. From this central idea, it follows that history is the progressive realization of the Christian ideal through the agency of the Catholic Church, and its highest expression in the civilization of medieval Europe. The modern period is regarded as a time of decline in which the sense of community and faith is eroded by the rise of individualism, skepticism, secularism and materialism. The contemporary scene is dominated by the struggle between the forces of materialism as expressed in Marxism and the communist powers, and the Church of Rome representing man's true spiritual nature, a struggle in which the masses are represented as being distracted and misled by the materialistic attractions of modern industrial society.

The historical treatment of those who are regarded as enemies of the Church, and, therefore, by definition, of the best interests of mankind, is less than fair. Voltaire and the *philosophes,* freemasons, freethinkers, and communists are brought to the bar of judgment, and, without evidence being offered on either side, are condemned *ex cathedra.*

Voltaire, says the textbook,

was the most complete incarnation of the eighteenth century. To French corruption and frivolity, he added the hateful fanaticism that he had gone to learn in England, in the school of the deists of that country . . . For nearly a century, he led the campaign (against the Church) with a spirit of irreligious proselytism the rancour of which is disconcerting, and he was, according to the expression of a great modern poet, the missionary of the devil to the men of his time. He is scarcely read now, but his spirit has remained as the evil genius of the modern world, and still to-day the Christian cannot look at his hideous mask without a feeling of fear and horror.[4]

At the same time, the lives of popes, saints and saintly kings are given prominence and receive sympathetic treatment. Thus, this history is more in the nature of a morality play than a rational attempt to discover some

[4] Gérard Filteau, *Le Monde Moderne, Les Amériques et Le Canada* (Quebec: Centre de Psychologie et de Pédagogie, 1957), p. 250.

truths about the past. The interpretation is unbalanced in two other respects. Firstly, there is the tendency of the narrative to cross and re-cross the line between sacred and secular history without making any distinction between them, so that miracles and elements of religious dogma are included as historical facts.

*   *   *

The "Progress" Histories. Prescribed textbooks for world history programmes are of Canadian, United States, or British origin. All the texts which embody the interpretation of history as progress are from the United States, and none of the others interprets history in this way. The association of American historians with this view of history is not new. Some thirty-five years ago Butterfield remarked that historians of this persuasion "seem to have been whigs and gentlemen when they have not been Americans."[7]

*   *   *

Two influences have shaped the "progress" histories—their Whiggishness and the necessities of abridgment. As treatment has become more generalized, historical development has taken on more the quality of an unbroken linear progression, which moves forward without substantial let or hindrance. The treatment of man's progress from primitive savagery to present civilization is so compressed and generalized that change comes to have an almost inevitable character. This is not only due to the interpretation of particular periods or episodes. It springs more from the compression whereby the study of the process of change, the tracing of infinitely complex transitions whereby one state of affairs changed into another, is so grossly over-simplified as to make a qualitative difference in the history. It gives a misleading impression of a smooth and ineluctable onward and upward movement of events which belies the reality it purports to describe. And so change—or progress if we wish to call it that—appears as a lineal, evolutionary development, possessed of a certain quality of inevitability, when, in fact, as Butterfield has pointed out, it is more truly conceived of as a series of mutations, crooked and perverse in its ways.[20] In seeking to examine the way things happen, he asserts, the more we are driven from the simple to the complex.[21] These histories have moved in the opposite direction—towards increasing simplification in which the complexity and unpredictability of change disappears. Instead, things change smoothly and steadily in the direction of the present.

This oversimplification is one important factor in influencing the character of these histories. The second is the fact that they are organized on a Whig view of history. The former compounds and emphasizes the essential characteristics of the latter, which has been defined as "the study of the past with direct and perpetual reference to the present".[22] In the Whig

---

[7] Herbert Butterfield, *The Whig Interpretation of History* (London: Bell and Sons, 1931), p. 4.

[20] Butterfield, *op. cit.,* p. 23.

[21] ibid., p. 21

[22] ibid., p. 11.

historian's view, the present is the absolute, and the past is seen as a series of stages in a line of evolution which culminates in the present. The past is the present writ small. Therefore, far from believing that "the chief aim of the historian is the elucidation of the unlikenesses between past and present,"[23] the Whig historian seeks to find similarities, and to trace lines of development from the past to the present. In holding this view and organizing his account in terms of it, he has been criticized on several scores: in the first place, he finds roots or "anticipations" of the present in the past, which, when closely examined, prove to be misleading analogies; secondly, he traces too direct a line of development between the past and present; thirdly, he abstracts things from their historical context and judges them apart from it; fourthly, he is thereby able to produce a scheme of general history which converges upon the present and demonstrates throughout the ages the workings of an obvious principle of progress, of which Whigs and progressives have been allies while tories and reactionaries have been its enemies; fifthly, in all this, his study is faulty since he does not attempt to make the past his present and understand it in its own terms; he therefore misunderstands the whole nature of historical change which comes not from the successes of progressives over reactionaries, but as the clash and interplay of the ideas and actions of both, and often in a direction which neither side either desired or envisaged.

The results of simplification and abridgment on a basic Whig interpretation of history are to be seen in the school "progress" histories. The search for the present in the past results in strange anachronisms and a general unhistorical tone: Hammurabi is said to be "undemocratic," and Henry II of England is an "autocratic medieval king". The "people" are shown as struggling for their rights as long ago as the thirteenth century. The course of progress is shown in the gradual triumph of the common man over autocrats, absolute kings, aristocrats and oligarchs; and in the triumph of reason and science over superstition and obscurantism. There is little possibility for any true understanding of the past. On the contrary, the tendency is to view the past and its people with some condescension from the lofty heights of our place at the end of the line of evolution, and to judge their way of life in terms of our own. Ironically, these histories of progress end with a static view of things. They construe the present not in terms of further progress, but in most cases as the search for security.

*　　*　　*

Histories of Limited Interpretation. These are the histories written by professional historians in eastern Canada and used in the programmes of Ontario and Prince Edward Island. This category also includes the books of C. F. Strong which are used in Saskatchewan and British Columbia.

The name given to them here is intended to make the distinction between them and the first two categories of history, both of which are organized around a single principle.

---

[23] ibid., p. 10.

These histories are surveys, and necessarily suffer from the disadvantages that accompany abridgement. Yet they are superior to the other two kinds of history in two important respects: they are more accurate, and, they offer a more balanced interpretation.

They are more accurate because the authors have incorporated in their texts the more recent findings of historical scholarship. They are also more accurate in the sense that they are more factual in content and more rigorous in generalization.

They offer a more balanced interpretation in the sense that they are not distorted as are the "progress" histories or the Catholic histories by strong preconceptions which have influenced the selection and ordering of data. In contrast to the "progress" histories, they make some attempt to study the past in its own terms, so that the student is able to gain some idea of life in the past, to understand the issues of the past, and to gain some idea of the way in which change occurred. They avoid a present-minded view of historical development and portray and document change as a complex process of transition. In contrast to the French Catholic interpretation which is distorted by the undue emphasis given to the Church and to religion, they provide a more balanced view of the interplay of social, economic, political and intellectual factors.

Whereas the other two kinds of history are essentially *credos,* designed to provide the student with a view of the past that will help to make him a good Catholic or a good democratic citizen, these are designed to help develop an informed person with some kind of real historical understanding. It is easy to exaggerate the extent to which these histories embody historical truth. They are necessarily limited by the exigencies of abridgement and simplification for use by students. Their intent, however, is not to support a preconceived point of view, but to try to get at the truth about the past. They are more circumspect in their judgments and more cautious in their generalizations. They discern patterns and trends, but no overarching pattern or trend which applies to the whole of the past. Finally, they present their views tentatively. It is only in these histories that one is told that these are interpretations expressing the views of particular historians, and that other interpretations do exist. Furthermore, students are given some insight into the fact that the traces of the past from which the historian derives his information are often fragmentary.

4.   In recent years, reservations have been expressed about the treatment of certain groups in school textbooks. At the request of the Ontario Human Rights Commission two scholars at the Ontario Institute for Studies in Education, Dr. Garnet McDiarmid and Dr. David Pratt, examined over two hundred books authorized by that

[4] Reprinted from Garnet McDiarmid and David Pratt, *Teaching Prejudice : A Content Analysis of Social Studies Textbooks Authorized for Use in Ontario* (Toronto, 1971) pp. 83-85 with the permission of The Ontario Institute of Studies in Education. Copyright OISE, Toronto, 1971.

province in 1967 and 1968. Using carefully controlled techniques, they assessed the significance of evaluative assertions, pictorial stereotypes and treatment of critical issues in these officially approved texts. The results were startling. For example, in the following extract, the authors report, with certain interesting exceptions, unsatisfactory or poor treatment of certain key issues connected with minority groups.

[The table reproduced below] summarizes our findings on the eleven critical issues. Given the methodological limitations of the present study, the two issues which relate to French Canadians can be considered to have been adequately treated in most texts. But the treatment of other French-English issues should be examined in future studies designed for that purpose. The treatment of one issue, concerning legislation against discrimination, is borderline. The treatment of the remaining eight issues is clearly unsatisfactory — in all but a few texts, they were either not mentioned at all or inadequately dealt with.

A number of texts in the samples were anthologies of source materials. Such books tended to receive high ratings on "validity" and low ratings on "balance" and "comprehensiveness," although in many instances explanatory paragraphs introducing or linking the source passages served to overcome this limitation.

Another limitation in many of the texts was their date of publication. Texts published in the 1950s were generally deficient in their treatment of

Table — Evaluation of Treatment of Eleven Critical Issues

Issue	Number of texts	Percentages*			
		omitted	poor	fair	good
Concept of race	34	68	12	9	12
Expulsion of Acadians	12	8	0	33	58
Conscription crisis	7	14	0	29	57
Extinction of the Beothuks	27	93	4	0	4
Canadian Indians today	23	78	22	0	0
Japanese Canadians in World War II	7	57	43	0	0
Legislation against discrimination	8	13	38	50	0
Negro during Reconstruction	11	45	27	9	18
Negro civil rights movement	9	46	22	33	0
Ireland, 1916-1921	17	53	29	12	6
Nazi persecutions	19	42	47	11	0

* Deviation from 100% total is due to rounding.

legislation against discrimination, much of which was not passed until the 1960s. The treatment of the Negro civil rights movement and the present status of the Canadian Indian were similarly deficient, probably because these issues were not of wide concern when the texts were written. This scarcely justifies such deficiencies, however. If a text's age adversely affects its treatment of important issues, it should be revised or withdrawn.

Part of the difficulty in satisfactorily dealing with issues such as those assessed in this study may lie in the very nature of the textbook. The need to cover a large section of the history and geography of a nation or a continent may leave little room for detailed treatment of specific issues. However, each of the protocols we developed was approximately a thousand words in length, and there is little doubt that any of the issues could have been satisfactorily presented in a quarter of that length in a text. It may be that there were scattered references we missed; certainly our research was constantly hampered by such nonsubstantive defects in textbooks as unhelpful tables of contents and inadequate indexes. But if our resources were hindered, what does this say for independent student activity?

Although the textbooks reviewed in our study of the treatment of critical issues present a gloomy picture, there are some bright spots on the educational scene. Some schools have introduced a measure of flexibility into their programs, offering courses on such topics as Indian and black studies alongside the more traditional ones. According to press reports, students at one school opted in large numbers for an Indian studies course precisely because they were "tired of the feathered, moccasined, peltgarbed, tomahawk waving, teepee-dwelling Indians they have encountered in their history textbooks."[10] Thus, despite the inadequacy of many textbooks, there is a possibility that students will study in school some of the issues related to their lives as members of both dominant and minority groups, even though they may have to turn to other resource materials to do so. The researchers do believe, however, that textbooks could perform a useful role in this regard. The principal question is whether they will in fact do so.

[10] "Indian Studies Program Popular with Students," *Kingston Whig-Standard,* 27 December 1969, p. 26.

---

5. *In 1965 the National History Project, inspired by its brilliant Director, Mr. A. B. Hodgetts, began an intensive examination of Canadian Studies in the nation's schools. Its final report, published as* What Culture? What Heritage? *attracted attention throughout Canada, the* Canadian Historical Review *taking the most unusual step of printing four reviews of the book.* The greater part of* What Culture? What Heritage? *is devoted to an assessment of the status of history in our schools. J. L. Granatstein in* The Canadian Forum *labelled the book "the most devastating attack on the teaching of Canadian history in primary and secondary schools."†*

*Vol. L., no. 3 (Sept. 1969), pp. 297-307.

†The Canadian Forum **48 (March 1969), p. 283.**

[5] Reprinted from A. B. Hodgetts, "The Course of Study" in *What Culture? What Heritage? : A Study of Civic Education in Canada* (Toronto, 1968), pp. 20, 21-22, 24-25 with the permission of The Ontario Institute for Studies in Education. Copyright OISE, Toronto, 1968.

Although we laugh at ourselves for doing so, and perhaps have convinced each other that today things are different, in actual fact we are continuing to teach a white, Anglo-Saxon, Protestant political and constitutional history of Canada. We are still teaching the history that preoccupied Chester Martin, George Wrong, R. M. Dawson, G. D. Glazebrook and and other academic historians during the 1920s and 1930s. The "new history," developed to counteract the criticism that this discipline has been too narrowly political and has failed to use the insights of the other social sciences, has not reached the Canadian studies classroom. Consequently, such things as protest and minority movements, class developments and issues, the influence of art, literature and ideas, education and religion, industrial growth and a great many other aspects of human endeavour that should be an integral part of history are virtually ignored in our schools.

Secondary schools cling more tenaciously to this outmoded course than do elementary schools, especially if there is a provincial examination hanging over the heads of their students. The narrow political and constitutional emphasis, therefore, is most apparent in the textbooks prescribed for such courses and in the ridiculous examinations we continue to set in Canadian history.[3] It was also apparent to the staff of the National History Project. Of the 422 secondary school classes we visited, 69 per cent were trapped within the confines of political, constitutional or military history.

* * *

Weakened by overemphasis on constitutional and political developments, Canadian history is rendered almost useless as a stimulating school subject by three other major deficiencies.

In the first place, no prescribed course of study in Canada and no textbook (and very few of the classes we observed) make any attempt to relate the events of the past to the problems and concerns of today. A number of academic historians in Canada, clinging to what must be regarded as a nineteenth-century philosophy, lend intellectual support to this neglect by denying that history should be used to explain the present. History, they say, should be studied for its own sake, for its inherent interest and cultural values. The sole function of the historian is "to reconstruct the past in all its unique detail as accurately as possible."

This narrow view of history, permeating the elementary and secondary schools . . . is doing inestimable harm in the Canadian history classroom.

[3] Consider, for instance, the provincial examinations in Alberta Social Studies 30, Saskatchewan Grade 12, Manitoba University Entrance Grade 11 (both the regular June and August supplemental examinations), Manitoba General Course Grade 11, and Nova Scotia Grade 12. In 1965 and 1966 there was a total of 132 Canadian history questions, many of them divided into several parts, on these externally set examinations. Without exception, every one of the 132 questions fell within a narrow, outmoded course of study. . . . It is interesting to note, also, that the textbooks used in all these courses were written by Edgar McInnis, Maurice Careless or George Brown. These historians are among those those who uphold the Whig tradition in Canada and whose interests are predominantly political and constitutional. Examinations of this kind, based on textbooks that are from twelve to twenty-five years old, make it almost impossible for even the best of teachers to escape from the confines of the "traditional" Canadian history course.

It is also diametrically opposed to the advice of all departments of education. Every one of them, without exception, emphasizes the need to make "constant references to the present." One of the main purposes in studying Canadian history, according to all departmental publications, is "to promote an understanding of how the present has grown out of the past." History merits consideration because "contemporary life is the perennial source of all problems which necessitate and justify the inclusion of history in the curricula of the schools." This viewpoint does not deny the intrinsic values of history; it does not deny that the events of the past are unique and particular; it does not claim that history repeats itself. It maintains only that if the world around us has grown out of the past and not suddenly appeared out of thin air, then history to be truly meaningful must be related to the present.

The ideas of most of the great modern historians and philosophers support the position taken by our departments of education. The predominant nineteenth-century school of thought that tried to elevate history into an exact and dispassionate science that would "neither judge the past, instruct the present nor influence the future" has been discredited long ago. There is general agreement today that the past and the present are inexorably interwoven in both the mind of the historian and in reality. Benedetto Croce expressed it this way: "It is evident that only an interest in the life of the present can move one to investigate past fact. Therefore, this past fact does not answer to a past interest, but to a present interest . . . .This has been said again and again in a hundred ways by historians and constitutes the reason for the success of the very trite saying that history is 'magister vitae.' "[4] Thus, university professors and teachers who persist in divorcing the past from the present are ignoring a fundamental principle of history. Their detailed chronicles of what happened, mere story-telling, may be interesting and have some aesthetic value but, as Carl Becker and other eminent historians have pointed out, "their social influence is nil."[5]

*   *   *

Another major deficiency in the content of Canadian history courses is the almost total absence of any conflicting or controversial material. Here, again, a fundamental principle arising from the very nature of history is being neglected. [Earlier] the observation was made that dissent is an essential element in any free society. This is true of the past as well as of the present. Practically every development in our history aroused opposing points of view and controversy. This essential fact is almost completely

[4] Benedetto Croce, *History: Its Theory and Practice*, trans. by Douglas Ainslee (New York: Harcourt, Brace, 1921), p. 12. Also, R. G. Collingwood, *The Idea of History* (New York: Oxford University Press, 1956), pp. 236 ff.; Allan Nevins, *The Gateway to History* (New York: Doubleday Anchor Books, 1962), p. 18; Harry Elmer Barnes, *A History of Historical Writing* (New York: Dover Publications, 1962), pp. 266 ff.; and Hans Meyerhoff, ed., *The Philosophy of History in Our Time* (Garden City, N.Y.: Doubleday Anchor Books, 1959), chapters by Henri Pirenne, Arnold J. Toynbee, Charles A. Beard.

[5] P. L. Snyder, ed., *Detachment and the Writing of History: Essays and Letters of Carl Becker* (Ithaca: Cornell University Press, 1958), pp. 141 ff. Also, Collingwood, *The Idea of History*, pp. 214 ff.

ignored in the classroom. Canadian history in our schools is a shadowy, subdued, unrealistic version of what actually happened — a bland consensus story, told without the controversy that is an inherent part of history. Furthermore, by brushing aside the alternative courses of action offered by conflicting opinions, it also assumes that every choice made in the past was the right one, that there could not possibly have been any other. Thus Canadian history becomes a too-nice, straightforward, linear, dry-as-dust account of uninterrupted political and economic progress.

This unrealistic approach to Canadian history is very evident in the textbooks, in the prescribed courses of study and in classroom practice. Eighty-nine per cent of the classes we observed unquestioningly followed the gray, consensus version of the textbook, oblivious to the controversy, the viewpoints and the alternatives of all those in history who would have done things differently. Thus, the Quebec Act, the Constitutional Act, the British North America Act, or any other of the "nice, neat little Acts of Parliament," as the girl from Saskatchewan described them, seem dead because the great debates that made them living issues of the past are smothered in the classroom. Similarly, other events and developments throughout our history become drab chronicles of an unreal, noncontroversial past.

The record of the past, of course, remains completely dead until it is brought to life by the historian. History is subjective and individual, conditioned by the background, the interests, the intellectual vision of the historian and by the contemporary climate of opinion in his society. These factors should introduce another kind of controversial material into any realistic history course. Conflict and opposing viewpoints are an inherent part of history, as we have pointed out in the preceding paragraphs, but the interpretation of the past by different historians and by successive generations is another essential element in the study of history. "The history of any event," as Carl Becker has said, "is never precisely the same thing to two different persons; and it is well known that every generation writes the same history in a new way and puts upon it a new construction. . . . This is why there is no more fascinating or illuminating phase of history than historiography — the history, that is, of what successive generations have imagined the past to be like."[7]

This "fascinating and illuminating phase" of history is totally excluded from our elementary and secondary schools. Not one of more than seventy authorized textbooks, and no official publication of any kind, makes the slightest reference to the fact that successive generations of Canadian historians have rewritten the story of our past, reflecting the problems and interests of their own times. So far as we have been able to ascertain, this approach to the study of history is also overlooked in teacher-training institutions and in most university history departments. As might be expected, therefore, we did not observe a single class throughout the whole of Canada that even mentioned, let alone used, these important aspects of

[7] Snyder, ed., *Essays and Letters of Carl Becker*, p. 221. Also, E. H. Carr, *What is History* (London: Pelican, 1964), p. 23; Barnes, *A History of Historical Writing*, p. 240.

Canadian history. This is a major defect in Canadian studies. A much deeper understanding of modern Quebec, for instance, can be secured by studying the changing aspirations and needs of French-Canadian society as expressed in the writings of historians such as Garneau, Abbé Ferland, Chapais, Canon Groulx, Frégault, Brunet and others.[8] Similarly, the developing attitudes, problems and interests of English Canada are more clearly revealed through the various interpretations placed upon the past by Kingsford, Parkin, Wrong, Martin, Skelton, Innis, Creighton, W. L. Morton and many more. By neglecting this kind of approach, our schools are missing out on one of the best ways to make Canadian history a more interesting and meaningful subject.

[8] See, for instance, Ramsay Cook, "French-Canadian Interpretations of Canadian History," *Journal of Canadian Studies*, II (May, 1967), 3-17, for an excellent brief account of how the changing needs and interests of French Canada are reflected in the different interpretations of its past by successive generations of historians.

6. In the last five years or so many provincial authorities have introduced courses in the social sciences. World Politics, Man in Society and World Religions now occupy a firm place in the Ontario curriculum, and similar courses are being added to the course of study in other provinces. This trend towards studies considered "relevant" to the modern world has occasionally been accompanied by, or even caused, a reduction in the number of students enrolled in history programs. Dr. John H. Trueman, Professor of History at McMaster University, has taken exception to this development. A distinguished textbook writer and medieval scholar, Dr. Trueman has been interested in educational affairs for many years.

Is the traditional approach to history in Canadian schools destined to be maintained? It would seem not. In the past few years two influences have begun to [appear]. First there is the increasing tendency to "stream" students into academic (university-bound) and commercial and technical (nonuniversity-bound) groups. This selective process has been most highly developed in Ontario, where in the last year alone some eighteen Colleges of Applied Arts and Technology have sprung up for graduates of the four-year stream. Naturally the secondary schools have introduced special new history courses for these students, courses which bear such grandiose titles as "Man in Society" or "World Politics." These courses aspire to incorporate the techniques and findings of sociology, political science, and economics.

*   *   *

However popular such a course [in World Politics] may be, it has had the effect of eroding history's position in the curriculum — so much so that

[6] Reprinted from John H. Trueman, "End of an Era : History in Canadian Secondary Schools," *The History Teacher* 2(1), November 1968, pp. 29-30, 31-32 with the permission of *The History Teacher*, University of Notre Dame.

in the five-year academic stream it has now become possible to avoid taking any history in Grades 11 and 12.

The second influence which is working havoc with the traditional history patterns has been the importation of newer curricular approaches to history. Jerome S. Bruner's *The Process of Education* (1960) was, in fact, the inspiration for a solid Canadian volume examining the entire Ontario elementary and secondary school curricula and bearing the apt title *Design for Learning* (Northrop Frye, ed., University of Toronto Press, 1962). Recently, too, the ideas and techniques of Edwin Fenton have been increasingly recommended to the graduates of various Canadian Colleges of Education. Unfortunately Canadians have lacked the considerable financial resources available for the extensive curriculum experiments in the United States, the sole exception being the Ontario Institute for Studies in Education founded in 1965 and affiliated with the University of Toronto. The compounding of this lack of resources and the dissatisfaction with traditional methods is producing an alarming situation in Ontario.

*   *   *

The alarming thing is that those in Ontario who now embrace the gospel of Bruner and Fenton with such fervor have, so far at least, not given any indication that they have heeded one of the most important lessons Bruner and his colleagues learned. "It is that the best minds in any particular discipline must be put to work on the task. . . . Only by the use of our best minds in devising curricula will we bring the fruits of scholarship and wisdom to the student just beginning his studies." The hit-and-miss approach that seems to be the current style in Ontario bodes ill for the traditional history, a history which, for all its faults, offered a coherent body of knowledge along with a reasonable broad coverage.

I have dwelt on Ontario's educational revolution at such length because it is the one with which I am most familiar, and also because it seems to me it may well herald what is likely to transpire in other provinces. Ontario — the richest province, the one with the most universities (fifteen), and one of the two with a five-year secondary school — is likely to be the pacesetter.

Recently when it fell to my lot to publicly deplore the fact that henceforth it will be quite possible for a student to graduate from the Ontario school system completely ignorant of any civilization but that of modern Western Europe (or its North American offshoots), an official of the Department of Education was quoted in the press as springing magnificently to the defence of the new options, which would, he said, indeed force a complete revision of the history courses. And rightly so. For in the projected new scheme of things the students would be given "a look at Russia in Grades 8, 9, and 10 to make sure it is covered" lest, in the freedom of electives, they completely miss modern history in Grade 12 and so would be deprived of any serious study of Communism.

Such an approach, if it is really being seriously considered, would seem to be a long step backward. It could be an approach very subject to the dangers of propagandizing, and if so, fully deserving of all the strictures leveled against such dangers in Professor Hilda Neatby's brilliant indictment of Canadian education, *So Little for the Mind* (1953).

Without suggesting any disagreement with the political and moral views of those who have planned the course, one would feel reassured if the first aim were to give the pupils a thorough mastery of the general character of the periods studied, adding, if necessary, a note to indicate that certain possible interpretations should be drawn to the attention of the pupils. In all honesty, however, pupils at this age might be told that other, if not antagonistic, interpretations are possible. . . . Whether or not they go to university, no doubt they will soon hear other interpretations, if only from communist propagandists.

Thus in 1968 the exalted place held by history in the Canadian secondary school curriculum so firmly and for so long seems seriously threatened. Whether or not the increasingly American look will destroy or transform the subject in Canada's high schools is difficult to say. We will have to leave the verdict to the future historians of Canadian education.

7. History in many Canadian schools appears to be vanishing. Students are electing, as Dr. Trueman reminds us in the previous reading in this chapter, options within the curriculum that conflict with history. In the following extract Professor John Eisenberg shows us how traditional supports for the discipline are being seriously eroded. In his last paragraph, however, he suggests that all is not yet lost.

From the time that history has ceased being a compulsory subject in schools, history teachers have been observed to wonder aloud whether the subject could survive the next decade. With the introduction of competitive courses and with the gradual decline of student interest, there are good grounds for concern. In a number of ways the problems facing history teachers are like those facing spats salesmen. There are, to be sure, very good reasons for using both products — spats to keep the feet warm and and shoes clean, history to teach man about himself and to develop imagination. Both should give pleasure to the user, unless spats are worn too tightly or history is treated too obsessively. And above all both spats and history have a certain class to them, going back to earlier associations. But in both cases the product is going out of style and there is no dedicated group of idealists in the public at large to save the product as was done with the whooping crane.

[7] Reprinted from J. A. Eisenberg, "Contemporary History Education : Factors Affecting Its Survival," *Canadian Journal of History and Social Science* 6(3), March-April 1971, pp. 19-23 with the permission of the publishers.

Like the spats industry, history education is neither self-sustaining nor self-perpetuating. If any subject or discipline is to survive in a healthy state in the school curriculum, it must receive consistent support from related constituencies. To thrive and prosper, history education must have a devoted and interested public, a trusting, sympathetic patron cognizant of the intrinsic worth of the subject and a dynamic source of creative ideas and materials. Unfortunately it presently has none of these in adequate measure.

Perhaps the most immediate problem confronting teachers is the general apathy of the students for history. With irksome regularity, students echoing their teachers and politicians, cry out for relevance in the subject matter studied. Though there is rarely agreement on what specifically is relevant, the widespread use of the term indicates a demand for a practical pay off in the present. Undoubtedly this attitude is related to what C. Vann Woodward called "the antihistorical bias in contemporary culture." It has been claimed that in recent years society has turned inward and has focused its attention on its own needs and desires for material gratification. Curiosity and interest in other societies and times have waned, except if knowledge can be made to serve our own practical ends. If this is so, it would then seem that historians and history teachers are operating in a generally unreceptive, even hostile environment.

Waiting for the anti-historical spirit to pass on would be considerably more pleasant if only the politicians were intellectually and practically more supportive. Understandably, government officials deciding on educational policy and administrators implementing these decisions must be sensitive to public opinion. In some instances their responses to general needs have been sensible. For example, in recent years broader choices of subjects and forms of education have been opened to students, thereby enabling them to tailor their programs to their needs, interests and abilities. But some decisions have clearly been unjustifiable. Most notably, moral and religious education have been banned from the curriculum for the time being at least, on what appear to be purely political grounds. As a result, the educational needs of students are not being served and their development is being hampered.

Ironically, a directive prohibiting moral education is itself moral (or immoral) in nature. It would appear that the politicians responsible for this regrettable decision do not realize that every educational program must in some basic way have a moral component. The very choice of a program or a method presupposes a value belief that it is good and the very implementation of the program *imposes* (or attempts to impose) these values. The prohibition of open and direct discussion of ethical and religious issues will not make education neutral. It may, however, create an atmosphere in which the students will quickly detect deviousness and lack of candour. Moreover it is equally regrettable that such a political decision would also serve to hamper one effective way of enlivening and sustaining history. As most teachers are aware history can at times be enlivened and even "made relevant" through considering the moral issues and topics of religious interest within history. Inhibiting this possibility can clearly be damaging. If so, overtly political acts which intrude directly into program can, and in effect do, adversely affect the state and function of history education.

One constituency from which teachers could reasonably expect help, is the community of practising historians. For, where else could one expect new ideas and new insights to come from? But this expected help is simply not forthcoming. There is a marked tendency among modern historians to stay within their own professional confines, far away from "popular" history. One has only to glance at some recent issues of such journals as *Daedalus, History and Theory* or *Past and Present,* or works like *Population in History* to see how specialized and professionalized the writing of history has become. Gone are the days when any imaginative and intelligent teacher could pick his way through most historical works without difficulty. Somehow, Mark Krug's call for history "in the grand old style" of Gibbon, Macaulay, or Michelet has gone unheeded by historians. Instead, greater attention is paid to principles of logic than to flights of imagination. As a result, arguments are more carefully constructed than before, and with a few exceptions, less exciting. To make history rigorous and scientific, statistical techniques are being employed more and more, as are complex mathematical models devised for economics, psychology and sociology. All this may be very useful in attracting economists or psychologists with a weakness for history, but it clearly will not cause a run on the history section in the local public library.

It must be admitted, however, that this trend in historical enquiry is understandable. Voltaire's wry comment that "for the past fourteen hundred years the only Gauls, apparently, have been kings, ministers and generals" strikes a familiar note for students of history. Through its obsession with so-called "great men" and with events on castle grounds and battlefields, grand old history presented a lopsided view of the past. Concern with the goals, thoughts, strategies, and personalities of select individuals so monopolized the historian's consciousness that the nature and workings of society and social life were totally ignored. Awareness of the narrowness of the focus of traditional history led to an awareness of the limitations of the techniques used. To rectify this shameful imbalance new modes of inquiry and procedure had to be introduced to history.

With the introduction of these new techniques, a few benefits have resulted. The most obvious benefit is that the results of historical research and the claims made by the technical historian are much more reliable than the earlier, more speculative claims. For the standards of evidence are higher and the force of the reasoning more compelling. Moreover, new insights into social structure, the family, industry, trade and many other areas have been gained. In effect, a fuller, more balanced view of the past has been made possible.

However the new history is not an unmixed blessing, since serious disadvantages for the history teacher have also resulted. Reading some of the technical works in history is becoming as difficult as reading a technical paper in the natural sciences. In becoming technical and professional, history has become exclusive. Oddly, among those who have been excluded are many history teachers. As graduate students in the university are being beguiled by statistics and technicalities in greater numbers, one can expect this process of exclusion to continue. Greater specialization is bound to result, leading to greater fragmentation of the subject, greater isolation of working historians from their natural audience and the cutting off from history education its major source of fresh materials. It would thus seem that the unity of environmental studies called for in the Hall-Dennis Report is a pipe dream.

Finally, the fourth constituency which has been ineffective in sustaining a dynamic system of history education is comprised essentially of professional educational theorists. Paradoxically, this group as much as any has been dedicated to helping and advising teachers through theoretical clarification. Among the general matters upon which they have focused their attention are the cognitive structures of a discipline, the concepts and generalizations used in learning a subject and the cognitive skills required in conducting inquiry. However, none of the notions which have crept into the jargon of educational theorists is really clear or applicable. In some selected sample lessons, students are asked loaded questions, and when they come up with the answers implicit in the line of questioning, it is triumphantly asserted that they have made "discoveries" all on their own. And when students have learned to play this contrived indirect form of parroting, it is asserted that they have acquired inquiry skills or know how to conduct historical inquiry.

But this is doubtful and will remain so until the basic notions used are clarified and distinguished. For as long as the notions of induction and discovery are confused with one another, as long as concepts and/or generalizations are crudely identified with the structure of a discipline and all generalizations are mistaken for empirical generalizations (as they are in almost every work dealing with historical inquiry) when in fact there are general rules, principles and laws which are not empirical in nature, indeed as long as teachers and students have no inkling of what a generalization is, and are unable to distinguish, nor correlate, facts and values we shall not have developed authentic and usable inquiry skills for history in students. To some degree teachers are to blame for tolerating and being party to the deplorable confusion which infects the fundamental theory of history and history education. But the major blame must be borne by the legions of "experts" who have created it.

The question which now arises is, 'What can be done?' One would like to believe that man can cure what man has corrupted. If only politicians would gain broader visions that enable them to see beyond dubious short-term political expediency, if only historians and educational theorists were to become more sensitive to the needs of the community they should be serving and more sensible in going about forming their theories, and if only the objectionable lapses of sensibility of our age would be rectified, then the problems of the history educator would be manageable. But it is unlikely that any of these changes will come about. This means that the options open to the history teacher are narrow, but they are not closed. Despite current trends there still remain imaginative and exciting forms of history of good standard. Some potentially stimulating programs may include materials on the third world, general contemporary world history with an emphasis on the sociological and economic aspects of society (for not all technical works are unfathomable or unusable), or even materials on contemporary social, political and moral issues. As a source of fresh ideas, one can still tap the more imaginative modern works such as those by Peter Laslett or the earlier works of Dorothy George. Of course, one need not restrict the sources to books. As teachers are aware, television, tapes, slides and pictures can help illustrate certain concepts with dramatic force. More difficult for the teacher is working out the theoretical framework for the topics under consideration. However it is preferable to avoid explicit mention of theory than to commit oneself to unwieldy, inapplicable, confused theory. As for politicians, there is little one can do to persuade them if their considerations are not solely educational. Even so, until the storm passes, we can only do what we know is essential in forming a full person, and above all, do it well.

8.   Many of the critics of conditions in Canadian schools are not teachers in those institutions. As if sensitive to the retort that negative comments are not particularly useful, a few scholars have tried to work closely with practising teachers to effect curriculum change. Dr. Trueman in an earlier reading in this chapter advocated the same kind of interaction that has been very fruitful in other disciplines.

Cooperation, however, forces rigorous examination of University practices, as Dr. Charles Sellers found when he attempted to participate in a colloquium in California. The difficulties he and his colleagues experienced in relating practice to theory may be instructive for us especially in view of the growth of curriculum projects on this side of the border. Dr. Sellers is a Professor of History at the University of California at Berkeley and an expert in nineteenth-century American history.

One way to illustrate the impending doom of historical learning in the schools is to recount my experience as a member of the Statewide Social Sciences Study Committee, which was appointed some three years ago by the California State Board of Education. The task of this 4SC, as it came to be called, was to draw up a new program for the social studies in the

[8] Reprinted from Charles G. Sellers, "Is History on the Way Out of the Schools and Do Historians Care?" *Social Education* 33, May 1969, pp. 509-510, 510-511, 512-513 with the permission of the author and the National Council for the Social Studies, Washington.

state's schools, kindergarten through the twelfth grade. Of the twenty members of the committee, the chairman was a professor of education; ten members were professors representing the disciplines of anthropology, economics, geography, history, political science, psychology (cognitive processes), sociology, and social psychology; three members were classroom teachers; and six members were curriculum specialists in the social studies from various California school districts.

History was by far the most strongly represented discipline. Where each of the other disciplines had only a single professorial champion, there were three professors of history, including the vice-chairman of the committee. Other historians—Douglass Adair, Robert Huttenback, Wilson Smith, and Gordon Wright—joined the historian members as a panel to advise the committee on historical matters. Moreover, the executive secretary of the committee and all three of the classroom-teacher members were history teachers with undergraduate majors and graduate work in history, one of them having been a member of my own graduate seminar.

*   *   *

Most disturbing of all was the difficulty we historians had in coming up with a rationale for history in the schools that was clear and convincing even to ourselves. In the face of the teachers' hard-headed insistence on precision in defining the objectives of the social studies curriculum, we became aware that our heartfelt declamations about "historical wisdom" and "a sense of the past" really didn't convey very much. For the first time in our lives we were compelled to work out painfully and slowly just what these vague generalities meant to us, to define for ourselves as well as for our fellow committeemen just what it was we hoped we had been accomplishing through the history courses we had been offering for years.

Very early in this process it began to dawn on us what the essential problem was. History as taught bore little relation to the objectives we had finally begun to define. Lulled by our sense of the real intellectual values flowing from the specialized historical work in our research, in our graduate seminars, and to some extent in our advanced courses for college history majors, we had remained complacently indifferent to the freshman and sophomore courses that afford the only opportunities for historical learning to the vast majority of students, and to the history courses in the schools that afford the only opportunity for historical learning to the vast majority of the population. Worse, when we had thought about these channels for historical learning at all, we had more or less unconsciously conceived of them in terms of their utility in preparing students for the advanced historical learning that most of them would never undertake.

Once we began to look at these courses, we perceived that they are taught as though the principal objective were to impart a comprehensive factual and chronological mastery of specified blocks of man's historical experience. Implicitly, we perceived, we had shaped these courses, insofar as we had any conscious purpose at all, on the assumption that knowledge is essential to historical thinking and that we were preparing students for the historical thinking that would presumably occur in more advanced courses. Whenever we were forced to recognize that most of these students would never go on to advanced courses, we had consoled ourselves with the assumption that if they acquired the necessary information, they might utilize it for some historical thinking on their own. We could even congratulate ourselves that we had sought to encourage this process by exposing the students through our lectures to our own distinguished generalizations and interpretations, and through readings to the generalizations and interpretations of other distinguished historians.

But now for the first time our teacher colleagues on the committee were forcing us to confront the question of how much historical thinking and learning had actually gone on among our students in these courses. "The notion that students must *first* be 'given' the facts and then, at some distant time in the future, they will 'think' about them," as one thoughtful observer has phrased what they were telling us, "is both a cover-up and a perversion of pedagogy." These outstanding teachers had learned through their own experience, first as students in our college history courses and then as teachers of history courses in the schools, that "students never seem to reach that magic point where they have enough facts to think." The whole theory, our teacher colleagues kept reminding us, was a perversion of the relationship between facts and thought. "One does not collect facts he does not need, hang on to them, and *then* stumble across the propitious moment to use them," as one educator has put the matter. "One is first perplexed by a problem and *then* makes use of facts to achieve a solution."[3]

* * *

But the recurrent dialogue on these matters in the California 4SC has gradually forced me to ask whether it is not the invincible complacency of college historians about their own teaching that is the root of the problem. "There is nothing wrong with secondary school education that a substantial change and improvement in college and university teaching would not help," a high school teacher has declared in the *AHA Newsletter.* Ira Marienhoff goes on to ask some questions that I have heard again and again from my teacher colleagues on the 4SC. "Where do secondary school teachers come from? Who have been their models?" College instruction in history "has been atrocious and may be getting worse," he insists, and it is this that has "made secondary school teachers what they are."[5]

* * *

It was in the context of considerations such as these that the professional historians on the 4SC were forced into the long overdue task of thinking through what we had been trying to do in our history courses, whether

[3] S. Samuel Shermis, "Six Myths Which Delude History Teachers," *Phi Delta Kappan* (Sept., 1967), pp. 9-12.

[5] Ira Marienhoff, "A High School Teacher Looks at College Teaching," *AHA Newsletter,* V (April, 1967), pp. 13-16.

we had been doing it successfully, and if successful, whether it was worth doing. We did finally manage to articulate what seemed at least to us the profound values of historical learning; but in the process we realized that history courses as commonly taught were poorly calculated to realize these values. Therefore we were forced to think about new ways of structuring courses as settings for historical learning.[9] Unfortunately we found it almost impossible to communicate our desires and intentions to our school teacher colleagues. So disillusioned were they with the courses we had offered them in college, and so frustrated were they by their years of failure to interest students in similar courses in the schools that they simply could not believe in a "new history" that would be educationally effective.

It was at this point that the contrast between the indifference of historians and the zeal for curricular improvement of social scientists proved most damaging. A "new history," we recognized, would require substantially different kinds of courses, different classroom strategies for learning, radically new kinds of materials to replace the conventional textbook, new ways of learning for prospective teachers, and massive programs to assist established teachers in mastering new approaches to historical learning. In all of these areas the active participation of historical scholars would be required. Most fundamentally, college historians in general would have to rethink their objectives and practices as teachers. They would have to involve themselves more directly in the training of teachers as teachers, and large numbers of them would have to work at developing new types of learning materials with the same seriousness that they worked at scholarly research.

[9] *Report of the History Advisory Panel to the Statewide Social Sciences Study Committee* (Sacramento: California State Department of Education, December, 1967).

EIGHT

NEW THEORIES

Curriculum change in Canada during the last fifteen years has been accelerated by pressures from two sources, the one external, the other internal. Canadian education is strongly influenced by what happens in foreign countries.[1] Since there have been lengthy discussions on the role of history in schools in both Britain and the United States, it is scarcely surprising that the results, whether in books or learned journals, should be read widely in this country. At the same time, those searching for educational solutions to the ills of a divided nation have reassessed the uses of history in the training of the young. In both international and national investigations, therefore, a wide variety of conclusions have been studied. A number of schools of thought within the literature can be identified, a few of which are illustrated in this chapter.

One of the most fruitful and controversial claims by curriculum theorists has been that the study of the discipline itself may offer

[1] Hugh A. Stevenson, "Crisis and Continuum: Public Education in the Sixties," in J. Donald Wilson et. al., (eds.) Canadian Education: A History (Toronto, 1970), p. 490.

useful guides for program design in schools. Answers provided by historians to such questions as the nature of facts or role of bias in history may be directly applicable to the curriculum. Modes of inquiry developed by the scholar may serve as models for students learning the subject. Many of the historian's materials may also be appropriate for the novice. A very large number of generously funded curriculum projects have accepted these maxims on faith and their published packages are full of references to discovery or inquiry, hypothesis formation and document analysis.[2]

The disagreements that exist between historians and philosophers over the nature of the subject have intruded, as might be expected, into curriculum theory. Those who argue on the one hand that history describes in the very best literary style, the unique, discrete and different, maintain that the subject should demonstrate these same qualities in school. Thus Mark Krug in reviewing ten years of project development in America calls for a return to "great, inspiring, and instructive narrative history on the order of Prescott, Parkman, Gibbon, Macaulay, Trevelyan, and Morison."[3] *Others, noting not only advances in sister disciplines but also the civic incompetence of many students trained in the traditional mould, have supported the introduction of techniques from the social sciences. Such moves have usually been accompanied by a stress upon the development of concepts and the formulation of generalizations. Byron G. Massialas and C. Benjamin Cox, for example, envision the classroom "as primarily committed to the identification of important problems and their systematic examination by means of theory and empirical evidence. The product of such investigation would be the statement of supported empirical or value generalizations."*[4]

At its most extreme this latter position is clearly "presentist." Since history as it has been taught for so long is failing to instruct students to cope with the problems of the day, the argument goes, history or social science courses should be radically altered in shape. Instead of studying the past for its own sake, students should examine those topics which are clearly relevant to the present day situation. In designing such a program of studies, Donald Oliver tells us, "the interests of the community, and of the student who will

[2] The most convenient guide to these Projects is to be found in Bob L. Taylor and Thomas L. Groom (eds.), *Social Studies Education Projects: an ASCD index* (Washington, 1971). There is no similar guide in Great Britain although J. D. Fines, *The Teaching of History in the United Kingdom: A Select Bibliography* (London, 1969) is useful. A number of Canadian projects either in progress or under consideration are described in *The Canada Studies Foundation: Annual Report March 31, 1971*, pp. 7-14.

[3] Mark M. Krug, *History and the Social Sciences: New Approaches to the Teaching of Social Studies* (Waltham, 1967) p. ix.

[4] Byron G. Massialas and C. Benjamin Cox, *Inquiry in Social Studies* (New York, 1966), p. 90.

*live within the community, become the most essential factors."⁵
Despite the condemnation of this outlook by professional historians
(Geoffrey Elton, for example, holding the view that "to study the
past for the light it throws on the present" is a "cardinal error"⁶)
it has exercised a powerful effect upon modern curriculum theory.*

*But we should not be surprised that the range of proposals for
changes in the teaching of history is very wide. The interchange
between philosophy and psychology in recent years has been extraordinarily productive. Society's demands upon the school have
changed rapidly over the last decade or so. In addition, there is as
little likelihood of uniformity of approach among teachers of history
as there is among professional historians. In both camps some
emphasize technique or new comparative approaches and others
assert the importance of national studies written in the classic narrative style. Such diversity of theories in many disciplines and from
often contradictory sources represents a severe challenge — and
an inspiration — to the modern teacher.*

⁵ Donald W. Oliver and James P. Shaver, *Teaching Public Issues in the
High School* (Boston, 1966), pp. 7-8.
⁶ G. R. Elton, *The Practice of History* (New York, 1967), p. 48.

*1. W. H. Burston, Head of the History Department at the Uni-
versity of London's Institute of Education, published the* Principles
of History Teaching *in 1963. In his book he suggested that there
were three teaching problems closely related to theories about the
nature of history: what facts are, how facts are grouped and how the
syllabus should be arranged. In the following extract he considers
the second of these questions and makes an important connection between meaningful learning and historical thinking. Mr. Burston has
long been active in the Historical Association in Great Britain and
is a contributory editor of* Handbook for History Teachers *(London,
1962) and of* Studies in the Nature and Teaching of History *(London, 1967).*

How should facts be grouped for exposition to a class? All subjects are
concerned not merely to communicate facts, but also to explain them and
to show some logical and intelligible relationship between them. Thus,
when the chemistry teacher demonstrates that zinc and hydrochloric acid
produce hydrogen, he does more than produce three isolated substances—
he shows a relationship between them. This will naturally govern the
manner in which he groups them to present to a class—he will, for instance, deal first with the metal and the acid, and then only with the
product of the reaction, hydrogen. This will be so even if he seeks only

[1] Reprinted from W. H. Burston, "The Nature of the Teaching Problem,"
in *Principles of History Teaching* (London, 1963) pp. 6-8 with the
permission of the author and the publishers, Methuen & Co. Ltd.,
London.

to show an isolated casual sequence such as this one. If he wishes to show any general law concerning the interaction of metals and acids, then a larger grouping of many such sequences is implied, including other metals and other acids. If he wishes to show other methods of making hydrogen then a different grouping is needed, but none the less a grouping in which the facts are coherently and intelligibly shown to be connected. Still another arrangement is needed if his purpose is to study the different properties of the particular metal zinc.

Two further questions arise from this example. Either of the three groupings of facts outlined above is an intelligible grouping of facts in which they are shown to be related in some way. In this, they differ from a group of unrelated facts, like the well-known test of powers of observation, in which some twenty unrelated articles are placed on a tray, and the candidate required to remember as many of them as he can. But although the examples from chemistry which we quoted all show a grouping in which *some* relationship between facts is shown, it is not necessarily the particular relationship which it is the special business of chemistry to demonstrate. My point is that chemistry is concerned to show not *any* relationship between substances, but a *particular type* of relationship. All the questions cited above are intelligent questions, but it may be argued that the first, and its answer, is a real introduction to the chemist's characteristic method of thinking, to the special discipline of his subject. For in this example, the chemist is first generalizing about zinc, secondly explaining its behaviour in relation with one acid in terms of a general law, but thirdly, and most important, turning to a more inclusive class of substances—all metals, rather than all pieces of zinc, and explaining their behaviour in terms of a more general and all pervading law. Whether this is or is not the most characteristic feature of a chemist's way of thinking is not the main point. The main point is the general one that, in order to teach we have to group facts in an intelligible fashion, but in order to teach a *subject,* it is not sufficient to group facts in any fashion which is intelligible: they must be grouped in the fashion which accords with the special discipline of that subject. If we do this, we are introducing our pupils to the subject, to its discipline, to its distinctive manner of thinking: if we do not, we may communicate facts but we are teaching little more than general knowledge.

The point may be clearer if we revert for a moment to teaching and learning as general problems. If we try to memorize a disconnected set of facts, and if they are presented to us in this way by a teacher, then we can describe our learning as blind and mechanical, because there is no meaning to be attached to the group of facts which we learn. Secondly, we may bring to our aid a memorizing device such as the analogy of the positions of players in a hockey team, as a method of remembering the order of pronouns in French syntax. This adds some meaning to our operations but it is not a meaning which has anything to do with the French language and its structure. Thirdly, we may attach some meaning to our proceedings by finding a relationship which is inherent in the facts themselves. Thus we may memorize the causes of the French Revolution by reflecting that it was a revolution, and that most revolutions were preceded by acute social distress, lack of peaceful means of redress and so on. But, lastly, we may attach the same pattern to our grouping as our subject does. Only then are we learning to think in the discipline of the subject. Thus, if, on examination, we found that the historian's characteristic pattern of explanation of events like revolutions was to generalize about their common factors, then our third example above would be not only meaningful learning, but a training in *historical* thinking. But if, on examination, we found that this was not the historian's characteristic way of thinking about the French Revolution, then our third example would be an example of meaningful learning, but it could not be defended as a training in historical thinking.

2. One feature in recent years has been the involvement of scholars in the curriculum reform movement. Changes in mathematics and science, for example, are the result of the work of subject specialists rather than teachers.* A striking example of co-operative work between historians and teachers is shown in the publications of the "Committee on the Study of History," a group which survived for a decade from 1961.† Dr. Richard H. Brown, a scholar now at the Newberry Library in Chicago, has described the philosophic background of the Project in a series of articles that have been widely read. In the following extract from an address first given at a meeting of the American Historical Association in Toronto in 1967 he considers the challenge of "inquiry" and "relevance" for the modern historian. In his article he makes reference to Jerome Bruner whose work has caused concern to such Canadian historians as Dr. John Trueman. (See Chapter 7 above).

Historians in America are fond of the metaphor of the frontier. Perhaps because, as practitioners of an established discipline, they have been among the least willing to set out on new ventures, they delight in talking about those who have—and about what happened to them. On the frontier old barriers of class and caste meant little. Many who set out had little idea of where they were going or why; they went primarily because they were dissatisfied with what they left behind. Some flourished, while others died.

*W. K. Richmond, The Teaching Revolution (London, 1967), pp. 87, 105.
†An account of the origins of the group is given in Richard H. Brown, "History as Discovery : An interim Report on the Amherst Project," in Edwin Fenton (ed.), Teaching the New Social Studies in Secondary Schools : An Inductive Approach (New York, 1966) pp. 443-451.

[2] Reprinted from Richard H. Brown, "The Historian and New Approaches to History in the Schools," *Teachers' College Record*, 72, September 1970, pp. 73, 73-75, 78-80 with the permission of the author and of the publisher, Teachers College, Columbia University, New York.

Old institutions were transformed. And eventually what took place on the frontier washed back over the whole of the society, transforming as it did even those who had stayed behind.

So it may be with the frontier of American education, a frontier to be found today in the schools. It is a frontier on which the institutions of American education are being transformed. It is one onto which few historians are venturing. It is rife with opportunity for history to become a more significant discipline than it has ever been before in American schools —measured not in terms of curriculum hours, but in terms of the growth of human beings and the development of those qualities of a reasoned temper, judgment, and perspective which a proper study of history could provide.

*   *   *

What, then, is the nature of this frontier? What defines the challenge? Of all characteristics, two are perhaps most pertinent. One is the hypothesis that people learn best through inquiry—coupled with an insistence that learning, and not teaching, is the chief business of education. The second is an insistence on relevance.

The first modern man on this frontier, of course, was John Dewey. The first in our own day to pick up the pieces of his earlier ventures were people in the sciences and mathematics. They have been joined more recently by scholars and school people in the various disciplines which comprise the social studies domain in the schools—especially by anthropologists, economists, geographers, and sociologists, least of all by historians. Their work has been carried on for the past three or four years chiefly in curriculum development projects, of which there have been perhaps forty or fifty in various social studies fields, twelve or fifteen of them national in scope and influence. The immediate legacy of these projects will be varied both in nature and in quality. Some, such as the Amherst Project with which I have been associated, have concentrated on producing blocks of material or units which could be fitted into an existing course or courses with the hope eventually of transforming these courses from within. Some have been preparing wholly new curricula, along with materials to implement them, for single-year courses, or for four or twelve or even fourteen sequential social studies courses to go from first grade to junior college. Some of the projects have been highly theoretical in their approach and have involved large numbers of scholars analyzing and discussing their disciplines and building new and highly structured courses of study. Others have been more pragmatic, more school-oriented, more interested in the processes of educational change.

How Children Learn

For all their differences, it is what the projects have in common that is most significant, and that best defines the new frontier on which they operate. All are committed in one degree or another to the idea that students learn best what they discover for themselves, and that the most important thing for them to learn, through practice, is how to learn, in order that they may go on learning through life, long after today's facts are outdated. Translated into concrete terms, as has been done most brilliantly by Professor Jerome Bruner of Harvard, this means that students learn best and most usefully when they are asked to play the role of scholars themselves, rather than when they are asked to master the conclusions of scholars about questions which they may themselves only dimly perceive, or which may be quite irrelevant to them. In short, students should be given the raw data of the discipline insofar as possible, learn to ask their own questions, and to move to their own conclusions. The idea is not that we should be training up professional scholars in introductory courses, but that only if we give students an opportunity to do what scholars do will they have a fair shake at learning in the academic disciplines.

Applied to history, the suggestion is that students should learn not so much a set of facts in these introductory courses as what a fact is, how one comes by it, and how one uses it—that they should learn not so much what historians have held our past to be as how and why one engages in the study of history anyway, and how and in what way one can expect to learn from it. Few among the proponents of the "new social studies" would argue that this means that the student must deal exclusively with original sources, any more than the scholar does. Few would argue that it means he must recreate for himself all that men have learned before him and could tell him if he asked. The key thing is simply the notion that he will not really be learning—or will not be learning anything worthwhile—unless he is asking. The model of the scholar learning is thus held to be a proper and usable model for what goes on in a classroom.

Breaking the Boundary Lines

What is most exciting and probably most significant about what is going on in the schools is not so much the new materials and new courses themselves as the assumptions on which they are based. Ultimately, these assumptions turn the world of education, as we have been used to seeing it, on its head. The focus ceases to be what we teach and how we teach it—the "content" and "methods" of the old debates. It comes instead to be how and what students learn. These are not the same thing. They are not necessarily opposite sides of the same coin. The new focus poses for us a host of questions which we are little used to asking, not only about how people learn but about what history is and what its role is in the growth and development of human beings. Because it insists that the best and most useful learning begins with something that each individual learner does, rather than with something that is done to him, the new focus also renders anachronistic our traditional hierarchical view of the world of education—our view that schools are organized for the convenience of administrators and teachers, with the students as objects to be manipulated, and our view that knowledge can realistically be pictured as something that trickles down from the scholar to the teacher and the textbook writer, and from them to the student. The new approaches to curriculum are in fact part and parcel of a host of other experiments in the schools in such things as flexible scheduling, non-graded classes, and programmed learning—all of them having a common core in the idea that learning is essentially something that one carries on independently. Ultimately, carried to its logical conclusions, the new focus breaks down the boundary lines within which, as scholars and educators, we have been used to defining our lives—the boundaries between students and teacher, between teacher and scholar, between college and school, between grade and grade, and between content and method.

*   *   *

What is taking place in the schools has implications not only for the way we think about the role of history in education, but for curriculum-building as well, and for teaching, and for the education of teachers. If learning begins with something the student does rather than with something that is done to him—if in one way or another it begins with the asking of a question—it follows that the most effective curriculum must ultimately be developed in each individual classroom, ideally for each individual student. It will grow out of the questions the students ask and the order in which they are asked. This is not to imply that any old question will do, or that one question is as good as another. If we would inquire with our students into history, it is the great task for history teachers of our time to begin to identify those questions which may profitably be asked of history that are relevant to modern concerns.

These questions, it can be assumed, will tend to have less to do with the building of nation-states and with institutions than the questions we have been in the habit of asking. These were, after all, the questions of past generations, the answers to which built up that store of knowledge that our introductory courses all too often pretend to students is "history." Modern questions will doubtless have more to do with the processes of social change, more to do with human relations, more to do with matters of personal and social and cultural identity. When they are asked, many history courses in the schools will come to look radically different from present ones. Some will doubtless continue to be taught chronologically and to deal with familiar topics. Others will not. Nor is it likely to matter much. What will matter is not the outline of topics to be "taught," but what the student can be expected to do with them; what the questions are, whether they are real or simulated questions, and whether they are relevant to students and profitable for them to consider.

Implications

Ultimately, the new approaches require not only teachers who can put together a curriculum as they go, but scholar-models who are themselves asking modern questions of their discipline. We shall need teachers who know what it is to ask a question, who can think on their feet, harbor an idea, and pursue a line of inquiry. We shall need teachers who are able and willing to see themselves not as pedants but as master inquirers and learners. We are not getting these teachers with consistency today; when we do get them, one suspects all too often that it is because they have surmounted rather than been produced by the system of training we provide for them. We are getting too few teachers who are psychologically equipped to measure the success of a class in terms of what happened to their students, as apart from what they themselves did. We are getting too few who are professionally and intellectually equipped to equate education with inquiry, too few who are equipped to see knowledge and wisdom as elusive commodities to be striven for rather than possessed, and too few who are equipped to see themselves as learners through life, even in their role as teachers.

All too many of these missing dimensions in the education of teachers speak to what is not happening to people in their college history courses —in those courses which alone have it in their province to reflect the real nature of knowledge and the real nature of learning. They suggest how tragic is the loss of human resources when the scholar who devotes his life to learning transforms himself at the classroom door, and offers himself in the classroom as a model of pedantry rather than as a leader in inquiry. To a striking degree the new approaches in the schools breathe new meaning into two tired cliches of American education. One is the idea that fundamentally content and method cannot be separated. The other is the idea that teaching and scholarship are part and parcel of the same thing. Because they do, they suggest that the teacher education of the future will be much more heavily dependent on the contribution of professional scholars in the academic disciplines. It is a contribution that requires professional scholars to think of what they do in terms of the education and growth of human beings. It is a contribution that far too few are equipped to make.

Professor Martin Duberman concluded a recent review of a new book in American history with the telling comment that "Seward's significance, as man and politician, still eludes us. We will discover it only if historians shift their purpose from hallowing the dead to enlightening the living." It is the call to do precisely this that is coming loudly and clearly from the frontier.

3. As the more traditional forms of history teaching came under attack, many proposals for change were made. Among these suggestions can be found certain common features such as the examination of behavioural objectives, use of new materials and rearrangement of class groupings. Professor Neil Sutherland of the Faculty of Education at the University of British Columbia, in reviewing the

[3] Reprinted from Neil Sutherland, "The 'New' Social Studies and Teacher Education," in John Lewis (ed.), *Teaching for Tomorrow* (Toronto, 1969), pp. 25-29, with the permission of the publishers, Thomas Nelson & Sons (Canada) Ltd.

nature of these proposals, poses a number of questions about their application in Canada.

First . . . what are the new social studies? A brief historical digression will, I believe, help us in our search for answers to this question. In the 1950s in both Canada and the United States it became increasingly obvious that the various versions of the social studies produced during the second phase of the Progressive era in education were failing to achieve their lofty goals. They were severely attacked. Out of the heated debate which took place on the social studies there emerged three possible courses of action for those desiring change. There was, first of all, the "great leap backward" which meant, in effect, abandoning altogether the social aims of social studies education and, in their stead, teaching separate academic disciplines (usually history and geography) in a manner guaranteed to have the pupils master the basic facts and concepts of these subjects.[2] The second choice was to retain at least some of the social aims of social studies education but to graft them on to new methods of teaching separate academic disciplines.[3] The third choice was to continue with the integrated disciplines approach which underlay the traditional social studies while making a great effort to improve their effectiveness.[4] By and large, most Canadian curriculum makers and teachers took the second of these choices, while their American counterparts followed the third. The work done by those who took either of the latter two choices was greatly influenced by the concept of "structure," which was first clearly articulated, in 1960, in Jerome Bruner's *The Process of Education.*

In his recent book, *The New Social Studies,* Edwin Fenton provides us with a reasonably clear and systematic account of work which he sees as going on in five broad areas of this domain. First, there are the groups of teachers and psychologists who are trying "to state objectives of instruction in terms of specific mental and physical acts expected from students and to develop tests to determine when these objectives have been attained."[5] Second, there are those who are working to develop new teaching strategies by which the objectives can be achieved. Third, there are the many organizations which are producing new teaching materials across the whole range of the social sciences. Fourth, there are those who are experimenting with various and hopefully more efficient groupings of pupils for teaching purposes. Finally, a smaller group has been trying to improve the preparation of new teachers and to upgrade the talents of those already on the job. . . .

[2] Hilda Neatby's *So Little for the Mind* (1953) is the best Canadian example of this view, and Arthur Bestor's *The Restoration of Learning* the best American.

[3] See, for example, George S. Tomkins, "Geography in the Elementary School," *Journal of Education* (U.B.C.), #6, December, 1961, pp. 87-94, and Neil Sutherland, "Structure in the History Curriculum," *Social Education,* v. 26, #3, March, 1962, pp. 133-136; 140.

[4] Much of the "Project Social Studies" and other curricular reform efforts discussed later on in this paper proceeded from this basic premise.

[5] Edwin Fenton, *The New Social Studies* (1967), p. 3.

TEACHING OBJECTIVES

Long lists of objectives have always appeared at the beginning of curricular guides and they seemed to me, when I was a beginning teacher, to have been specifically and cunningly designed to make me feel completely inadequate no matter how hard I worked. To reduce my anguish, I stopped reading them. Nevertheless, I do not believe that I was then the only teacher in Canada to take such an irreverent step. Now, however, we are attempting to translate these piously hopeful catalogues into behavioral terms so that teachers and school systems may not only know much more precisely *what* they should be doing, but they can also measure with some degree of accuracy whether or not they arrive at their stated destinations.

Let us take from the new forms an example from each of the clusters into which we have traditionally divided our teaching objectives:

Knowledge of Selected Content

The pupil can recall in two minutes the names of the ten Canadian provinces and their capital cities.

Inquiry Skills

In order to extract the geographical relationships expressed in a previously unseen photograph, the pupil can recall and apply the analytical procedures used by him and his class on other photographs.

Attitudes and Values

In a discussion of the present problems in the relationships between French-speaking and English-speaking Canadians, the student defends his opinion with relevant factual and conceptual information rather than with appeals to prejudice or authority.

*   *   *

Between the statement of aims in behavioral terms and the process of measuring whether or not the aims have been achieved lies the realm of teaching strategies. Or, as Fenton puts it, "much of what children learn stems from *how* they are taught as well as what they are taught."[7] Since we have found that the traditional teaching strategies of recitation, teacher presentation, and the so-called "problems" approach are not adequate vehicles for achieving our behaviorally stated aims, we have been forced to develop new teaching strategies. Discovery exercises (such as Senesh's one for primary grades on making gingerbread men in order to teach the economic concept of the division of labour) are but one example of the many developments taking place in this field.[8] In my view, the recent efforts

---

[7] *The New Social Studies,* p. 57.

[8] Three recent examples of books which concentrate on strategies for teaching inquiry skills, for example, are Maxine Dunfee and Helen Sagl, *Social Studies Through Problem Solving: A Challenge to Elementary School Teachers* (1966), H. M. Clements, W. R. Fiedler, and B. R. Tabachnick, *Social Study: Inquiry in Elementary Classrooms* (1966), and Bruce R. Joyce, *Strategies for Elementary Social Science Education* (1965).

to use techniques of social psychology, such as role playing and group dynamics, to teach the attitudes and values traditionally included amongst the social aims of education are potentially the most exciting practical changes taking place in this particular segment of the new social studies.[9] In addition, however, the work of some philosophers of education in what they describe as the "natural history . . . of the behavior of teachers as it occurs under classroom conditions" may in the long run produce a whole range of new teaching strategies.[10]

NEW TEACHING MATERIALS

It is in the third area of change, that of the new teaching materials, where one can see not only the greatest volume of activity in the new social studies, but also the greatest amount of diversity. The central theme is "confusion." In 1965, Fenton and Good reported that there were "more than 40 curricular development projects of national significance" underway in the United States alone[11] and, by October, 1967, the number had increased to more than 70.[12] The major "Project Social Studies" programs, financed by United States federal government funds, are probably the best known of these engines of curricular change, but others involve a great variety of organizations, foundations and curriculum centres. Their products range from the multitude being designed by Educational Development Centre, Inc. (EDC), "the General Motors of Curricular Reform,"[13] to the six unit outlines fashioned by the Naperville, Illinois, Public Schools.[14] Although such work is also underway in many areas of Canada, I am sure that our projects are probably much less extensive than the American ones both in scope and in financing.[15] The lack of a national

[9] For a wealth of practical examples of these processes at work, see Fannie R. Shaftel and George Shaftel, *Role Playing for Social Values: Decision-Making in the Social Studies* (1967) and Mary A. Bany and Lois V. Johnson, *Classroom Group Behaviour: Group Dynamics in Education* (1964).

[10] B. O. Smith, M. Neux, J. Coombs, G. Nuthall, and R. Preciano, *A Study of the Strategies of Teaching* (1967), p. 3. Cf. also P. J. Lawrence, "The Anatomy of Teaching," *Education: A Collection of Essays on Canadian Education*, v. 7. (1968), pp. 43-49, for an excellent overview of this whole new and rapidly developing field.

[11] Edwin Fenton and John M. Good, "Project Social Studies: A Progress Report," *Social Education*, v. 29, #4, April, 1965, pp. 206-227. See also Dorothy M. Fraser, "Annual Review of Curriculum Materials" in the same issue, pp. 228-237; 249.

[12] See "A Directory of Social Studies Projects," *Social Education*, v. 31, #6, October, 1967, pp. 509-11. The United States Office of Education now lists 59 elementary and secondary projects (of which 20 are now completed) and 15 in higher education. In addition, there are now 17 Social Studies and related projects sponsored by other organizations.

[13] James D. Koerner, "EDC: General Motors of Curriculum Reform," *Saturday Review*, v. 50, #33, 19 August 1967, pp. 56-58; 70-71.

[14] Dorothy M. Fraser, "Review of Curriculum Materials," *Social Education*, v. 31, #4, April, 1967, p. 310.

[15] One large Canadian undertaking, the National History Project, may in its proposed second stage rival the size of the larger American efforts. See A. B. Hodgetts, Director of the National History Project, "The Teaching of Canadian History and Civics," a paper presented to the Canadian Education Association, 28 September 1967. The almost completed first phase of this project will cost $140,000.

publication for the social studies in Canada means not only that there is little exchange of information amongst those working in curriculum change but also that there may be some wastage, through needless duplication of effort, of the slim funds available for this work.

The objectives of these curricular projects are as varied as their sponsorship and structure. Some propose to produce materials for a single course in a single discipline, others are preparing units which can be included in courses presently offered in the schools, and yet others are developing entirely new curricula and materials for elementary schools, for secondary schools, or for the whole range of the school system. In the next year or two, the small trickle of materials produced so far by these projects will turn into a flood. From the larger ventures, we will receive coordinated "packages" made up of detailed teacher guides, kits of materials and graded texts of various kinds for the pupils, and a whole range of closely coordinated records, films, film strips, single concept film loops, slide tapes, picture sets, and programmed learning materials. Lawrence Senesh's economics program for primary grades is but a prototype of the inundation to come.[16]

While team teaching and individualized instruction are probably the best known of the new schemes to improve or vary instructional procedures, they are by no means the only developments along these lines which have had, or will have, an effect on teaching social studies. Examinations are underway on school size, on the deployment of teachers—should we, for example, allow elementary teachers to specialize in subject teaching, even in the primary grades?—and on the more effective use of school libraries in social studies and other teaching.[17] I can see the raw material for a potentially explosive debate in plans, which are just beginning to take shape, for grouping pupils in social studies as we have done for so long in reading and in arithmetic. Is grouping in social studies consistent with our aims of developing democratic ideals and giving practice in democratic citizenship? If we do group, do we divide our pupils on the basis of their grasp of knowledge in the disciplines, on their measured ability to use various modes of inquiry, or on the level of their progress in internalizing certain required attitudes and values? Will we have, for example, special remedial classes for those whose moral and ethical systems do not measure up to a standard set by teacher, school, or community? On the other hand, if we consider these as bizarre questions, then are we not also admitting that we are not really serious in all of our palaver about attitudes and values?

[16] Lawrence Senesh, *Our Working World: Families at Work* (1963). In Canada, the National Film Board is just beginning to produce materials such as single-concept film loops, sets of slides and urban kits which it hopes will fit into the products of new Canadian curriculum projects.

[17] For a fuller discussion of these efforts see Fenton, *The New Social Studies*, pp. 93-105. For a comment on the faddish adoption of one of these devices, team teaching, see Jack R. Fraenkel and Richard E. Gross, "Team Teaching: Let's Look Before we Leap!" *Social Education*, v. 30, #5, May, 1966, pp. 335-337.

4. Many curriculum theorists have suggested that traditional history classes are confined too narrowly by chronologically ordered narratives. A Committee reported in 1966 that the scope of the subject should be enlarged and that the range of methods used should be broadened.

History, for example, has tended to be interpreted mainly as political history. But the study of history encompasses more than the political affairs of state. Economic, social, and religious history, history of thought (ideas) and of science, technological history, and a host of other fields have contributed significantly to our understanding of the past and the present. Canada's maturation as a nation and her present role in international affairs has also changed our perspective.

In a little more than a generation, anthropology and sociology have matured as social sciences. All understanding of human behaviour, for example, has been enriched by the concept of culture, the concept of value, and the holistic view of man as a bio-cultural organism. The matured knowledge provided by the sociologist is no less conspicuously missing in the instruction of students in group techniques and the significance of seeing themselves as participants in group settings.

The practical approach to this knowledge is now recognized to lie in placing greater stress on procedural learning, emphasizing method as much as narrowly conceived content. Thus procedural learning is distinguished from substantive learning and is related to both methods and techniques.

Method

It has been suggested that it is possible to establish a habit of learning that will be constant through life. In this approach the strictly factual information is not regarded as an end in itself. The new objectives call for greater emphasis on methods and attitudes and on consciousness of learning to stimulate self-direction.

It has been a common practice in schools to concentrate on a "sound basis of facts" and to leave problems regarding the nature of the facts and the relationship between them to a later stage of education. Much evidence has been amassed within the last several years to sustain the idea that a child can be taught any subject and at any age providing the material is translated into his logical forms and challenges him to exercise his full powers. This may be accomplished by a variety of methods.

One way is to start with present circumstances and then go back into history. Another is to begin with historical materials from an earlier period and then show what relevance these materials have in the present, and how present circumstances are similar to, or are not similar to, earlier experiences; e.g., industrialization and the industrial revolutions.

[4] Reprinted from *Directions : An Initial Inquiry into the Social Studies Program for the Schools* (Toronto, 1966), pp. 26-29 with the permission of The Ontario Institute for Studies in Education. Copyright OISE, Toronto 1966.

162

An article by W. C. Trow[1] suggests these relevant principles of an area-study approach to history.

(1) Coverage includes usual objectives, content, and methods of social study curriculum.
(2) The organization requires that successive stations or observation posts be chosen, each some locale that is at the centre of things during a significant period; e.g., Athens in the Age of Pericles.
(3) For more complete coverage, the flashback and flash forward present the past and future of the period in order to pick up causes and look into results.
(4) There is a meaningful continuity of progression in moving from one of these areas and periods to another through elementary and high schools so that later work can build on what has gone before. Cross-relationships are pointed out to give a realization of contemporaneity of events separated in space, as well as similarities of events separated in time.
(5) Progression is from the familiar to the unfamiliar.
(6) It is also from the simpler to the more complex.
(7) Social science phenomena noted in one period may also be observed in another, e.g., autocracy, arid land.

For an approach to history such as this, there are almost endless possibilities for the use of all kinds of visual aids, including motion pictures and television, to assist in imaginary visits to distant times and places. Field trips to historical sites can be arranged, and to galleries and museums where artifacts and restorations can be arranged and inspected. Encyclopaedias, travel folders, and other sources can be studied. A fictional family of the period might be assembled, with members of which the students can identify, discuss their problems, and study the history that *they* would study for flashback. Both original and secondary sources will be consulted, constructs built, various kinds of role-playing and informal dramatizations used, and even more complicated game theory simulations employed. Anachronistic newspapers can be edited with such headlines as "Sophocles' Oedipus Smash Hit."

Further research is also recommended into the value of some existing testing devices, such as intelligence tests, aptitude tests, and tests of student achievement. It was felt by the committee that these testing devices require specialized personnel and that indiscriminate use by teachers and others not qualified to assess them properly often results in more damage than benefit.

Instruction in history should provide opportunities for students to be actively engaged in investigating experiences. Methods of treating historical materials and the characteristic biases and opportunities of each should be

[1] W. C. Trow, "An Area-Study Social Studies Curriculum", *Social Education*: March, 1965.

explored fully. The limitation of each should be assessed, so that the student understands its validity or significance. The student should have a variety of materials from which to make his investigation rather than textbook materials alone. Instructional materials should be provided at the several levels of perception that characterize a particular study group. These levels may be in terms of degree of vocabulary development or of differing social backgrounds. There must, however, be a progression towards a common level of comprehension.

Effective communication among persons of varying perspectives must be regarded as a major objective in social science education and training in history. Materials should be multi-functional and should be used in a great variety of ways. Resource materials in history would include diaries, letters, log-books, travellers' accounts, minute books, magazines, coins, government papers, treaties, constitutions, as well as the materials of anthropology and sociology.

We do not advocate that every child should begin with a mass of unrelated documents and data from which he must sort out historical truth. But in the process, the pupils must be presented with carefully selected primary source materials chosen by the teacher with conscious appreciation of the choices he has made. The student must be guided by the teacher in making his discoveries, but these discoveries must be his own, based on his own thinking and reading.

Method and process are inseparable from content. It is highly unlikely that a well-planned history program will be lacking in adequate and appropriate content. However, content can and is being provided without thought to an adequate methodology or sound teaching processes. When content, devoid of method, is all the history program has to offer, the educational fare is meagre indeed. Only when method and process are involved, even emphasized, can the schools be said to educate.

5. *Some curriculum theorists have attacked the pre-eminence of history among the social sciences in the school program. In the selection of content "the interests of the community," write Donald Oliver and James Shaver, "and of the student who will live within the community, become the most essential factors."* Working from this premise, Oliver and his associates at Harvard reorganized a standard history course to give preference to the clarification of controversial issues.† From their joint work came a flood of paperback publications on a wide range of historical, social and legal topics.‡*

***Donald W. Oliver and James P. Shaver,** Teaching Public Issues in the High School **(Boston, 1966), pp. 7-8.**
†ibid., **247-255.**
‡**Fred M. Newmann,** Clarifying Public Controversy : An Approach to Teaching Social Studies **(Boston, 1970), pp. 85-232.**
[5] Reprinted from Malcolm A. Levin, "Analysis of Public Issues : An Interdisciplinary Focus for Canadian Studies," *Canadian Journal of History and Social Science,* 5(1), November 1969, pp. 1-2, 5, 6-8, with the permission of the publishers.

A number of Canadians have published collections or original works that draw from the same philosophic well. Macmillan of Canada published for a brief period Canadian Public Issues through Inquiry *and McGraw-Hill Ryerson have twelve titles in a series entitled* Issues for the Seventies. *More directly related to the Harvard Project is the work of Dr. Malcolm Levin, a former student and colleague of Donald Oliver, whose* Dilemma *series was published by Holt, Rinehart and Winston in 1971.*

In the following reading, Dr. Levin, now a member of the faculty of the Ontario Institute for Studies in Education, argues for a new type of Canadian Studies program, outlines how the content should be selected and gives some illustrations of the topics that might be discussed in class.

In brief, I wish to argue for a Canadian studies program organized around contemporary public issues which do (or should) concern citizens of Canada. There are two essential components to the proposed program: (1) the selection, organization and creation of case materials taken from the Canadian experience; (2) the orientation and training of teachers in discussing public controversy in the classroom and in helping students to utilize the process of discussion to develop an understanding of the complexities of public controversy, to clarify and justify their own positions on the issues and to understand positions other than their own. Ideally these two tasks should be related through the involvement of teachers in the organization and development of their own curricula in the schools.[1]

*   *   *

Selection of Content: Past, Present or Future?

The controversial issues framework is applicable to both historical and contemporary problem situations. I wish to argue, however, that discussion and analysis of the problems and issues of today and tomorrow should take priority over the problems of yesterday. In a society where the "generation-gap" in knowledge is expanding so rapidly, and development of advanced technological means has far outstripped our ability to devise rational and humane social ends toward which these means may be directed, the schools must bear some responsibility for developing this ability, or they will become less and less relevant. Serious study and discussion of current and future societal problems should thus become a more prominent in-school activity than the usual once-a-week current events period which serves as a break from the routine of the more serious study of the past. Whether or not it is possible for students and teachers to pursue this task seriously within the schools as they are currently organized is an open question—beyond the scope of this discussion, however.

[1] "Curriculum" is here construed more broadly than simply a set of materials and exercises organized in a particular way. The heart of the "curriculum" is the way that the teachers and students relate to the case materials and to each other. Thus the thrust of the project is as much toward teacher education as to the education of young people in schools.

The idea of making the study of current and future societal problems rather than history and geography the central concern of the social studies curriculum is not new and the objections to it can be anticipated to a great extent. The most frequent objection raised is that one cannot deal with current or future problems without first understanding how they came about —i.e. the genesis and development of the problem through time. While I freely concede at the outset that *some* people have gained useful insights into current social problems from a study of the history of these problems, (just as some people claim an increase in their English vocabulary via the study of Latin), there is little empirical evidence that a study of the past is a necessary prerequisite to an understanding of the present or leads people to make better predictions or choices in matters of public policy.

*　　*　　*

Content and Materials

What are the implications of this position for the selection of content and materials and the role of our suggested program within the broader school curriculum? With regard to the former our criteria are quite different from those of the professional historian or social scientist. We do not seek to establish regularities in social behavior over time. Nor do we wish to focus on identifying trends, cycles or other generalizations and seeking evidence to support them. Others have been, and will continue to be, hard at work on these tasks. Consequently we do not seek to either pre-empt or co-opt the modes of inquiry and findings of the social and behavioral sciences, but rather to provide a context in which students can use them in their efforts to clarify their own models of the real world and their feelings about this world. The addition of basic instruction in the concepts of anthropology, sociology, economics, political science, psychology, etc. is a welcome addition to the secondary school curriculum. However, the argument that a basic grounding in these sciences, like history, is a necessary prerequisite to the discussion of social issues is not persuasive. People, young or old, cannot wait for the verdict of history or for the burden of social scientific evidence to clarify their experience, to make judgments and to take action. The longer schools fail to provide settings and experiences which will allow students to engage in this process of clarifying their own views and feelings about the world, the longer they will remain essentially irrelevant to the social education of students and teachers alike.

With regard to topics and materials a public issues approach suggests a selective contemporary emphasis drawing heavily on the mass media, film, literature and personal experience. The following partial list of topics may serve to illustrate the range of content we see as relevant to our objectives:

Separatism—One Nation or Two? (or 5)
Minority Group Views of Canadian Society—e.g. Indians, Eskimos, Hutterites.
Immigrants—Melting Pot vs. Mosaic

The Right to Strike—Labor and the "Public Interest"
Censorship
Civil Liberties: e.g. Government and the Right of Privacy
Schools and Rights of Youth
Drugs and the Law
Urbanization and the Welfare State
Problems of the Future: e.g. Work and Leisure; Population Control; Organ Transplants; Schools of the Future; Pollution; The Sexual Revolution.
U.S.—Canadian Relations

The question of separatism, both with respect to Quebec and other provinces where the desire for local autonomy often outweighs the value placed on national unity, is more a problem of general political policy than personal conflict. Yet individuals are faced with the consequences whichever course is chosen by Quebec (or for that matter British Columbia or the Maritimes) with respect to Confederation. If, for example, armed conflict followed a declaration of independence one could expect the sort of personal dilemmas that individuals faced at the time of the American revolution and civil war. Separatism can thus be dealt with in futuristic terms as well as in terms of current and past relations between English-speaking and French-speaking Canadians or between the provinces and Ottawa. Among the more salient issues related to this topic are: majority rule vs. minority rights; cultural conflict vs. accommodation; conflicting loyalties; what is a "nation"?

The relationships of members of various minority groups to the community at large and to their own cultural groups poses a host of personal and public issues. Can a person psychologically live in two cultures simultaneously? Is it right for the majority culture to impose its patterns of thinking, language and other behavior on a cultural minority? How do different members of the same "minority group" view their relationship to the societies in which they live? To what extent are cultural differences among groups largely a product of environment vs. heredity? What is "progress"? Does one group have the right to impose its will on another? What is the responsibility of society (i.e. the government) to the culturally "disadvantaged"?

Immigration cannot be treated solely as an historical phenomenon seasoned with bromides about equal opportunity and the superiority of the mosaic to the melting pot. Nor can it be confined to those who enter Canada from overseas—the increase in immigration from the United States in recent years has to be taken seriously within this context. Internal migration must also be treated here as one of the important facts of modern urban society: the farmboy or the Maritimer or the small-town mechanic who moves to the big city may be psychologically more of an immigrant than the American who exchanges Chicago for Toronto. How do the prescriptions of various separatists and federalists fit the facts of the mobile society? Who is responsible for the welfare of the immigrant? Should immigration (and migration) be more strictly regulated and/or curtailed?

Similarly the problem of labor-management relations cannot be dealt with solely in terms of the bread-and-butter issues of the past. As the consequences of prolonged labor-management disputes become more far-reaching, the interests of various publics become a more relevant focus of concern vis-a-vis the special interests of the combatants. Nowhere does this issue come into sharper focus than with the question of the right of so-called service professionals—e.g. doctors, teachers, policemen, students —to strike in support of their demands. As some unions become conservative monopolies in partnership with their corporate counterparts, what of the individual worker? What obligations does the union have to its membership? What rights are the unorganized entitled to? What role should the government play in labor disputes? Are there alternatives to the strike?

6. Great interest has been shown in recent years in the use of new techniques in history and the social sciences. Professor Sutherland has outlined some of these approaches in an earlier section of this chapter. Occasionally, however, a method is devised that seriously challenges the current organizational patterns in classrooms. One of these is undoubtedly simulations.

As a survey of the literature shows, simulations have only recently been applied in any systematic way to educational needs. "The emergence of games in the classroom," writes Elliot Carlson, "can only be understood in terms of new developments in educational theory and a trend towards curriculum reform sweeping many areas of education."* Dr. Stephen Sachs, now a member of the faculty at Indiana University, describes some of the uses — and the dangers — of simulations in history and the social sciences.

The idea of simulation is to make a model of a relevant aspect of the real world that involves the making of choices or decisions and to place the students in the roles of decision makers. For example, we have developed international affairs games involving geographic, economic, political, and military factors in which the participating students act as the governments of nations (historical or fictional). In their roles as planners and statesmen the students make decisions concerning economic and technological development, and carry on foreign trade and diplomacy with as much realism as can be built into the model without confusing the partici-

---

*Elliott Carlson, Learning Through Games (Washington, 1969) p. 15. The best bibliographic guide is Paul A. Twelker (ed.) Instructional Simulation Systems : An Annotated Bibliography (Corvallis, Oregon, 1969).

[6] Reprinted from Stephen M. Sachs, "The Uses and Limits of Simulation Models in Teaching Social Science and History," *The Social Studies*, 61(4), April 1970, pp. 163-164, 165-166 with the permission of the publisher.

pants with over-complexity. In simulation, as in the real world, the problems of decision making are dynamic and involve interaction of the participants: the effect of each player's decisions being the result of his own choices plus the choices of the other players.[1] The games teach effectively largely because the participants are able to see the results of their decisions almost instantaneously.

Games of this kind serve two basic purposes. First, they increase the interest of the student in the material. Simulation games do this partly because they are games which may be challenging and enjoyable, but the student's interest in the subject matter is also increased because the role the participant plays puts him actively into the material encouraging him to identify with the problems he is examining. At Indiana University we have had very good results with stimulating student interest. In some cases students became so involved in the game that they arrived early for classes and it was often difficult to cut off the planning and bargaining precisely at the start of the class period. In other instances in secondary school games we found that students gave up lunch periods in order to carry on negotiations.

The second major purpose[2] of simulation games is to give the students an understanding of the material.[3] Simulation games do not teach facts as such, although they may encourage students to gain factual knowledge. Simulation involves decision-making and develops reasoning power and insight into the relationships of the major components of the problem under examination. Simulation teaches why but not what. Games, like the old fashioned spelling-bee, may be used to make the assimilation of facts more palatable, but this is not the primary purpose of simulation which directly teaches the ability to solve problems but can only encourage attaining of specific data. Simulation games, therefore, should be used to teach the meaning and application of principles. They accomplish this end by placing the participants in a competitive position with each other in which each player can only advance consistently in the game by grasping the principles and their applications. Games, however, cannot teach by themselves. Experience with international affairs games in voluntary extra-curricular activities involving college freshmen and sophomores shows that

[1] Though, for certain purposes successful solitaire models or games can be developed which would be operated by individual students.
[2] There are also other secondary reasons why one may use simulation games. For example, an elementary teacher may use them as a device for developing social behavior.
[3] Cleo Cherryholmes, in "Some Current Research on Effectiveness of Educational Simulations: Implications for Alternative Strategies," *American Behavioral Scientist,* Vol. 10, Number 2, October, 1966, pp. 4-7, stated that a quantitative study made at a high school indicated that simulation does increase student interest, but suggested that students involved in simulation did not necessarily learn more than those who were taught by traditional means. However, this latter result does not agree with this author's experience and discussion with some of the Northwestern University faculty members currently working with Cherryholmes leads him to ask if the simulation games used in this early study were applied in the best way to achieve optimal results, and if the tests used measured the kind of learning that is derived from gaming since simulation teaches understanding and problem-solving ability rather than facts.

in most cases students who engaged in simulation without any previous background in international affairs play poorly and learn very little about the game itself or the principles it aims at teaching unless the participants simultaneously engage in related studies. It is only the especially gifted student whose reasoning powers are keen enough to learn from the game alone. In most cases simulation without something more provides recreation but not education.

The need to supplement simulation does not mean that the student should be told everything. If the games are reduced to mere exercises in which the outcome is predetermined they lose most of their value both in terms of creating and in developing analytical thinking. Such narrowly constructed games require no thought and deny the student the challenge he needs to develop his own thought processes. This has been the trouble with some science courses whose "cookbook laboratories" merely restate what the student already has been told and in which the student does not have to do the experiment in order to turn in an adequate lab report. The point is that in simulation the student needs guidance but he must be left enough freedom of action to think through the problems and principles for himself: to make his own creative discoveries.

What a student needs to comprehend in order to be able to solve problems rationally, are the factors that are involved and their inter-relationship. In simulation the factors and relationships of real world problems are represented in the rules of the game. Each rule in a properly constructed model is a given fact representing some factor existing in the problem or situation being simulated. Therefore, in order for the players to comprehend the game and the problem it describes they need to understand the meaning of the rules and must know why the rules were written into the model.

Understanding of the model and its relation to reality can be taught in a number of ways depending upon the level of the students, the complexity of the model, the purpose of the model in relation to the material to be taught, and the available time. Given sufficient time to work on a project, one of the best ways that we have found to examine a problem using simulation is to examine the various factors one at a time, or a few at a time, allowing the students to help construct the model for the game that will be played out after the initial survey is completed.

*   *   *

A good example of the progressively developing simulation is the following European History program. The class is interested in European development between 1850 and 1860. They begin by examining the geography of the period, constructing a map, locating key cities, industry, raw materials, etc. This study is undertaken in part by dividing the class into national teams each of which researches its own country. When the introductory inquiry is completed and the basic rules of an economic geography game are drawn up, the teams engage in an economic game of foreign trade and internal development. As soon as the economics of the period are grasped, military and political factors are added to make the model a full international affairs simulation of mid-19th century Europe. Then, after the game has been played out with accompanying analysis and related studies a post mortem is held comparing the results of the simulation to what actually happened historically. The recap serves several purposes. To begin with, it counters any tendency of the simulation to teach the wrong history.[5] More important, the closing analysis allows the students to ascertain the limits of the model and to perceive the logic of the actual events.

[5] The paper "Stimulation and Simulation" delivered at the end of the 1967 American Political Science Convention stated that in the author's experience with secondary school classes this was not a problem since young students, who are used to gaming, readily distinguish simulation, role-playing from reality.

7. *A number of recently published curriculum proposals have advocated direct comparison of societies. Byron G. Massialas and Jack Zevin, for example, analyzed the structure and value systems of societies differing both in time and place.* By examining India, China, South Africa and Brazil, Edwin Fenton and his associates have assessed the role of "tradition" and "change" in the complex interrelationships within particular societies.† On a more theoretical level such scholars as William McNeill and Arnold Toynbee and educators like E. H. Dance have supported the introduction of World History courses — with greater attention to what has become known as the "Third World" — into the schools and university curriculum.‡*

In the following reading Robin Winks notes the insights derived from comparative studies and shows how the history of both the United States and Canada may be illuminated by the application of a similar approach. He concludes by commenting upon the relationship of new techniques to the growth of the discipline itself.

By Comparative Studies one now means those efforts to relate, organically and simultaneously, the ways in which developments in similar spheres of human activity take place between two or more cultures. A recent series of essays on Turkey and Japan, using both as examples of underdeveloped nations once isolated from the West which moved with great speed into the forefront of their respective areas of the globe, illustrates how the comparative technique may reveal much about a culture not previously under-

*Byron G. Massialas and Jack Zevin, World History Through Inquiry: Social Structure (Chicago, 1969) pp. 1-65.

†Richard Ford, Tradition and Change in Four Societies (New York, 1968).

‡William McNeill, "World History in the Schools" and Arnold Toynbee, "Widening our Historical Horizon," in Martin Ballard (ed.), New Movements in the Study and Teaching of History, (London, 1970), pp. 16-25, 50-59; E. H. Dance, History for a United World (London, 1971).

[7] Reprinted from Robin W. Winks, "Comparative Studies and History," *The History Teacher* 1(4), May 1968, pp. 40-43 with the permission of *The History Teacher*, University of Notre Dame.

stood. Courses in comparative colonialisms, in which students examine closely why the British, the French, or the Portuguese chose to acquire overseas possessions and then compare and contrast the response of indigenous peoples to those colonial encroachments, reveal much about the process called Imperialism, about the dynamics of the three European nations involved in the comparison, and about the ways in which the Maori, the Tahitian, and the Celebean, to use South Pacific examples only, differed within their cultures, and how those differences led to different responses to the European. When such comparisons are made with respect to problems rather than data, and are carried out for at least three cultures and across a substantial period of time, the easy generalizations of the past slip away, and in the slipping thereof the student can see something of the way in which his discipline takes form.

Perhaps the most relevant recent efforts to apply comparative approaches to History consist of those studies of slavery which attempt to discover how the institution varied from period to period, condition to condition economically, and place to place. The imagination shown by Stanley Elkins in his *Slavery: A Problem in American Institutional and Intellectual Life,* which first appeared in 1959, and which used insights derived from studies of Jewish experiences in German concentration camps during World War II, did more than any other book to promote comparative techniques. Since then, David Brion Davis, Herbert S. Klein, the Peases, Orlando Patterson and H. Hoetink have added convincing studies which have served the dual purpose of revealing more about slavery than we have ever known before and providing a solid base of case studies in comparative techniques from which students of other institutional and social problems may draw methodologies. The American Historical Association recognized the growing trend toward comparative work with several overtly comparative sessions during its 1966 and 1967 annual meetings, and, late in 1967, with the appearance of a superior collection of imaginative essays on *The Comparative Approach to American History,* edited by C. Vann Woodward (New York: Basic Books, 1967), the trend could be said to have become a movement. Woodward's book promises to be widely read and highly influential among teachers, especially at the secondary school level, since the chapters in his book were first presented as radio addresses intended for non-university audiences.

The fact that Canada and the United States share a basically common environment, that they were settled during the same period of time, and that they both began as fragments of European societies, provides those of us who wish to try a comparative approach with an exciting series of opportunities for case studies. Those American historians who have attempted to explain the development of the American character in terms of some central, overriding factor have, when they looked to Canada, found that determinants which seemed to hold promise for universal application to North America fall to the ground. Frederick Jackson Turner's thesis, based upon free land, the rise of democracy from mobility, and the ability of settlers who had occupied land in advance of legal organization of that land to frame their own laws, does not hold for Canada, where mobility has been limited by the Laurentian Shield, where many Canadians have continued to look back to their European roots in a way Americans did not, and where law — in the body of the Hudson's Bay Company — preceded settlement. David M. Potter's analysis of the American character[1] which turns upon our awareness of abundance, giving rise to philanthropy, wastefulness, and optimism, does not hold for Canada, where independence came slowly and by evolution, where a staple economy (codfish, furs, timber, wheat) prevented rapid industrialization, and where dependency upon overseas markets limited the optimism born of abundance. C. Vann Woodward's thesis, expressed in "The Age of Reinterpretation"[2] that Americans outside the Confederate states were shaped by their awareness of free security, does not hold for Canada, where French Canadians feared the English and where all feared the Americans. No more do the theses of Daniel Boorstin, Louis Hartz, Perry Miller, or other scholars who have written sweepingly of the American experience hold for Canada. The Canadian course on this continent has been a unique one.

Thus a series of comparative studies between American and Canadian institutions afford us an opportunity to test again the question of geographical determinism and institutional heredity as applied to the evolution of man's activities. Schools in Ontario borrowed in part from those of New York and Massachusetts for their curriculum and administration but they also leaned heavily upon Britain. Business practices in Canada, as Seymour Martin Lipset has shown, placed less emphasis on innovation than in the United States. Attitudes toward race, ethnic identity, and religion differed in Canada, despite the shared impact in both nations of social Darwinism. In short, while we may not yet have techniques by which we may make meaningful comparisons between nineteenth century Iran and eighteenth century Java, we can begin to explore the legitimacy of the comparative approach by casting American history against the backdrop of its immediate neighbor, where environment was similar and institutions dissimilar, and thereby further illumine both our own national experience and the craft of History itself.

[1] *People of Plenty: Economic Abundance and the American Character* (Chicago, 1954).

[2] *American Historical Review*, LXVI (October, 1960), 1-19.

8. *The Royal Commission on Bilingualism and Biculturalism thought that history teaching should serve a social purpose. In particular, the second volume of its* Report *suggested that the distinct*

[8] Reprinted from "The Teaching of Canadian History in the Context of Two Cultures," *Report of the Royal Commission on Bilingualism and Biculturalism,* (Ottawa, 1968), Volume 2, pp. 282-284, 284-285 with the permission of the publisher. Paragraph numbers and marginal headings have been removed.

cultural differences within the nation ought to be frankly admitted and thoroughly studied in our schools. The theoretical principles outlined in these sections of the Report *may serve as a model for a Canada Studies program.*

An emphasis on the different interpretations of Canadian history could lead to a hazardous over-simplification of the difficulties involved in the teaching of history. History can be taught as a discipline. University students and even senior high school students can read and assess the available historical evidence relating to a past event, can compare ways in which authors select and interpret this evidence, and can come to conclusions not only about the past but also about interpretations of the past. History at this level, like such other disciplines as economics and sociology, is to a large extent an academic training in methodology. The student may study Canadian, Chinese, or Roman history, and although the amount and the kind of historical evidence will differ, the student will still learn to be an historian.

But the primary purpose of teaching history is not always the training of historians. History as taught in our elementary schools obviously has little in common with history as a discipline except its concern with past events. History is placed on the curriculum because it serves a social purpose. This purpose should be consonant with a liberal education, teaching the student about human nature and human society by drawing from experience in the past. The study of the past goes beyond the abstraction of a liberal education, however. Students are taught history because societies believe that it provides a desirable and necessary training for future citizens.

This social purpose determines what kind of history is included in the curriculum. Learning from past experience is too broad an objective; students must learn from experience directly relevant to an understanding of their own society. History, it is assumed, can convey this knowledge by showing the problems and the challenges our predecessors faced, by showing the origins and development of our social institutions, by instilling a respect for our heritage. This social purpose explains why national history has a prominent place in school curricula in all countries. Canada is no exception. Canadian students are exposed to the history of Europe and possibly of the United States, but special emphasis is given to the history of Canada.

The Canadian situation, however, is complicated by the different concepts of Canada. When the history of Canada is narrowed to the history of French Canadian society, the past which is directly relevant is also narrowed; and the social purpose of history becomes understanding French Canadian institutions such as the Roman Catholic church in French Canada or minority-language schools outside Quebec. When the history of Canada is similarly narrowed to the concept of people united in a federal union, the social purpose is restricted by the emphasis on the parliamentary institutions and the development of a national economy. These two versions of Canadian history are different because they represent different cultural preoccupations.[1]

The teaching of history cannot and should not attempt to exorcise these cultural differences. The two versions of Canadian history have not created the cultural division; they merely reflect the fact that there are two major cultural groups in Canada. At the same time, the study of our history should also make students aware of the positive values of the other culture and of our common cultural heritage. The briefs that argued for an official version of Canadian history to be taught in all Canadian schools were obviously concerned with this aim. Understanding must, however, begin with the understanding of one's own society and its institutions. Only then is a child able to appreciate the different institutions and values of another society. In Canada this means that Canadian history should not be taught in the same way to all students. The textbook should build on the cultural experience the student brings to school.

The social purpose of history, however, is not to be confused with propaganda. An understanding of contemporary society is inadequate if it is based on narrow exclusiveness. Even if one thinks solely in terms of French Canadian or English Canadian society, the social purpose of history is best achieved by a conscious effort to explain the different values and aspirations of the two societies when controversies arise. But if any text-book lays claim to being a history of Canada, it must go much further. It must be the history of both societies to the extent that the histories are distinct, and it must also present the history of Canada as a country in such a way as to make the points of view of both groups appear logical and comprehensible. The establishment and survival of French Canada is a significant aspect of Canadian history and so is the establishment and survival of Canada as a political union in North America. Any Canadian history textbook should present both these themes. The result will be a history which may still reflect the unconscious cultural point of view of the author, but it will at least have the merit of trying to explain rather than ignore or even deplore our cultural duality.

*   *   *

We have no intention of suggesting any specific reforms in the teaching of Canadian history. The problems of curriculum and methodology are too complex to be resolved by *obiter dicta*. But we are directly concerned with the image one cultural group has of the other, because stereotypes can inhibit effective communication and so muddy the relations between the two groups. Our research on Canadian history textbooks has shown the need for revising the versions of Canadian history now taught in the schools. We do not believe that the restricted perspectives we have found are conscious or deliberate. No provincial authorities, textbook authors, or teachers would intentionally denigrate one of the cultural groups in Canada. The first step is to become aware of the points of view that are

[1] Nor should it be assumed that the divergence in interpretation lessens at the more senior levels. With one exception, all the citations in this section were taken from secondary school textbooks.

unwittingly being fostered in the students now in the classrooms. Precautions can then be taken to eliminate prejudicial attitudes and to foster an awareness of the distinctive characteristics of each cultural community as well as an appreciation of our common cultural heritage.

It is possible to suggest criteria which might be used to assess the Canadian history taught in our schools. Obviously, disparaging and prejudicial epithets should be avoided. More positively, an adequate history of Canada would include the most important and the most characteristic developments of each society. Events should not be excluded because they are controversial. Such events should be discussed within an adequate historical context so that the attitudes and actions of both societies become comprehensible even if they are not necessarily portrayed as desirable. An historian must offer his interpretation of the past, but if historians from the other cultural group have a different interpretation, some reference should be made to this other explanation of events. In this way, Canadian history may at least help to give students a better understanding of our cultural duality and its contemporary implications.

History is not the only school subject which deals with Canada. Other subjects — such as geography, civics, and social studies — will also make references to the two societies in Canada. Here, as in history, the student will encounter attitudes and value judgments which may have a formative influence. We have not investigated the courses of study in these areas, but it is likely that they enshrine the same conventional attitudes encouraged in Canadian history textbooks, and that they present Canada largely from the point of view of one of its cultural groups. The criteria suggested for Canadian history courses will be equally applicable in these subjects. It is important that any study of the Canadian people should have as one of its aims the fostering of an awareness of the existence and the nature of our two societies.

NINE

IN THE CLASSROOM

Putting new theories into practice has never been an easy task. Some theorists are notoriously indefinite on matters of implementation and only the foolish would underestimate the difficulty of translating complex models into classroom situations that include thirty to forty young people. Teachers in their turn have not been permitted sufficient free time to reflect on new approaches and have suffered from the commonly-held view that they are consumers of pre-packaged materials. Schools often lack equipment and library resources required by new methods and techniques.

Yet despite these difficulties there have been interesting developments in the way history is taught in the nation's schools. A great number of teachers are experimenting with different ways of organizing students for instructional purposes and using a greater range of audio-visual aids than ever before. In the last few years, teachers have turned to theoretical discussions within the discipline itself for inspiration, suggestions and assistance in the planning of new types of courses. This trend towards the study of the philosophy of history has been accompanied by a greater interest in problems associated with how students learn. Teaching history, therefore, is becoming a much more professional task.

Nevertheless, it is clear that the gap between theory and carefully evaluated practice ought to be closed. A reminder of conditions in the classroom may serve as both spur and brake to the aspirations of curriculum designers. Since teachers have been much more readily influenced by successful classroom practice than by volumes of research data, the dissemination of new ideas based on verified performance looms as the major task of the next decade.

1. In the course of his survey of Canadian Studies in the nation's schools,* A. B. Hodgetts and his staff visited numerous classrooms — almost 900 in all. By and large what he has to say about his observations does not make encouraging reading. "Despite the universal disapproval of the assignment method," he writes, "51.3 per cent of all classes . . . fell into this category."† But among the five "categories" of lessons he did find one that had characteristics of which he wholeheartedly approved.

The Ideal Dialogue

The fifth category contained the best classes observed by our staff. For reasons that will become apparent, we called the technique used in these classes "the dialogue." Sixty-one classes (7 per cent of the total) were placed in this category; more than two-thirds of these, in turn, were found in British Columbia, Alberta, and the Protestant school system of Quebec. In our opinion, these classes were superior in every way — especially in the extent and quality of both student participation and content — to those that employed, however skillfully, any of the methods described previously. Although there were variations within each class, all of them revealed the following features.

ONE: The students, within the limits of age and ability, were well prepared. The reading assignments given to them had been planned carefully by a teacher who obviously was competent in his field and knew the sources. The source material to which the students had been guided introduced controversial, opposing or supplementary viewpoints. If not these, then the readings gave additional factual material from which the students themselves developed different viewpoints. The outstanding feature of all these classes, however, was the almost total absence of any factual recall techniques. There was no lecturing by the teacher; no factual question-answer period to check up on what the class had remembered;

*See Chapter 7 for another reading from What Culture? What Heritage?
†What Culture? What Heritage? (Toronto, 1968), p. 46.

[1] Reprinted from A. B. Hodgetts, "The Classroom and What Goes on in It" in *What Culture? What Heritage?* (Toronto, 1968) pp. 53-56 with the permission of The Ontario Institute for Studies in Education. Copyright OISE, Toronto, 1968.

the students did not read their reports aloud to each other. Initially, the teacher assumed that the students had mastered most of the straight-forward factual information for themselves or, perhaps more accurately, that any misunderstandings they might have had would be clarified in *using* the facts rather than in hammering them home through mere recitation. Working from this basic premise, the students were called on to advance viewpoints, defend positions with evidence, and develop general concepts. Thus the entire lesson evolved around a discussion of ideas — ideas, however, that the teacher, or frequently the students themselves, insisted should be supported by relevant factual information.

TWO: The students had developed or were in the process of developing remarkable skill in discussion techniques. In all of these classes, the students did most of the talking. Frequently they spoke back and forth to each other and became so absorbed in what they were doing that the presence of the teacher temporarily faded into the background. Obviously, they had been taught to respect each other's points of view, to keep an open mind and to listen to evidence from other sources. Consequently, there was a genuine exchange of ideas, a true dialogue that might have put to shame the wrangling of many a municipal council. The atmosphere was completely informal and individual students, without any of the nervous tensions so often observed in the teacher-centered, question-answer technique, sometimes spoke at considerable length using a surprisingly good choice of words.

THREE: None of these classes, however, was completely student-centered. At times, the teacher intervened either to bring the class back on topic, to correct an obvious error in fact, or to express his own ideas. To an outside observer, it was apparent that the success of the classes was partly dependent on the fact that the teacher himself was interested and competent in the topic; he seemed to feel that it was important; he respected the opinions of the class but also — and this is an important factor — he was involved enough to have his own views and the desire to participate with the class. Classes in which the teacher interrupted needlessly or attempted to impose his own opinions on the students were not placed in this category. This means that the sixty-one teachers under consideration here were neither grayed-out neutrals nor domineering masters of the class. In our opinion, they used the best possible discussion techniques and, by example, enhanced this quality in their students. These skillful teachers seemed, at first thought, to possess a natural inborn ability to communicate with the students. Certainly most of them . . . rated very highly on our classroom personality scale and had the respect, affection and confidence of the young people in their classes. Even so, we believe that many of their tactics could be taught to those who do not possess this innate ability.

FOUR: Without exception, these sixty-one classes were studying a topic in depth — again, not occasionally as a change of pace but as a regular practice. This was apparent in the wording of the topic (usually phrased to pose a question, a controversial set of viewpoints or a "problem" to be solved), in the nature of the reading assignments, in the depth of discussion, and in the type of notebooks kept by the students. Textbooks may or may not have been used as a basic starting point but there was an air of interest and expectation that motivated the students to travel far beyond the textbook. Although the lessons had been very carefully set up and more prior thought had gone into them than any of the others we observed, there was absolutely no evidence of the rigid "lesson plan," the neat little "review," the "topic development," the "recapitulation," the "introduction to new work," the "time for pupils to work thereon," nor other devices that seem to delight some teachers' colleges. The topics were so rich and the discussions so good that virtually all of these lessons spilled over from one class period to another. They stood out in marked contrast to the great majority of all others that attempted to cut up history (as so many of the textbooks do also) into chronological little segments that can be fitted into a forty-minute period on the timetable. None of the teachers using this technique seemed to have any difficulty in picking up the threads of a topic which carried over from class to class, or in pacing themselves and their students so that the entire time would not be spent on discussion.

FIVE: Another unique feature of the classes in this category was the extent to which they encouraged the development of intellectual skills. By their very nature, they provided the opportunity and the incentives for students to improve their reading ability; to think for themselves; to make the factual evidence work for them; to weigh and evaluate evidence; to increase their powers of oral and written expression. It was apparent to us that these classes had been partly designed for just this purpose and that they were much more successful in this area than any others. It is generally agreed that intellectual skills like these have a transfer value into life situations. As an independent decision-maker in all levels of society, facing complex, rapidly changing situations, the citizen in a democracy needs the tools (as distinct from the knowledge) to make these decisions effectively. For this reason also, we felt that the classes in this category, designed as they were to develop intellectual skills, rated a place at the very top of our scale.

SIX: Finally, it should be apparent from the foregoing that these classes met most of the requirements of the so-called "discovery" or "inquiry" method of teaching. In fact, when the teacher's role was reduced to a minimum, as it frequently was in these classes, the techniques that we have called the dialogue approximated discovery methods. We feel very strongly that the willingness of the teacher to guide and participate (in the flexible ways described above) does not detract from the advantages of the pure discovery method and actually may prevent the abuses of it that we have recorded earlier . . . .

"You can't do much with these kids anyway"

At this point, we can almost hear the reader saying: "But surely these were older and very bright students? You simply cannot use dialogue or inquiry methods with technical, vocational or terminal classes. The students don't have the interest or ability for this kind of quality teaching; they just don't care." According to our observations, this is not a valid justification for the fact that excellent classes in Canadian studies are discouragingly few. Indeed, our evidence indicates that bright academic classes headed for college and motivated by external rewards and competitive examinations are more likely to tolerate any kind of teaching method, as long as they get the necessary facts to pass from one grade to the next. On the other hand, motivation through interest, through self-reward and the development of a feeling of increasing competence is all the more necessary with students "who couldn't care less."

In view of this tendency "to blame the kids" for all of our shortcomings, the statistics in the chapter notes become important.[9] They show beyond any doubt that the natural ability of the students is not necessarily a determining factor in successfully using the dialogue or inquiry techniques. In our view, they also suggest that a great many educators must completely reverse their thinking about difficult or problem classes. As long as the students in this type of class are taught by hastily designed, dull, expository methods based on the assumption that "you can't do much with these kids anyway," they will continue to be unmotivated, uninterested and difficult. Although this is no guarantee of success, perhaps the only way of breaking the vicious circle of leaden teaching and lumpen students is by trying to use methods that approximate the dialogue technique.

[9] Four of the classes placed in our top category were dead-end, two-year terminals; seven were technical or vocational classes; seven others were unstreamed elementary or junior high school classes; thirteen were unstreamed or quite average academic secondary school classes; the remainder, slightly less than half of the total, were specially selected, above-average academic secondary school classes.

2. *The word "inquiry" has been widely used in recent years by history teachers. Largely as a result of the writings of Edwin Fenton,* teachers in many parts of the country have been revising their classroom methods in order to introduce new procedures. In British Columbia, Professor Neil Sutherland has gone so far as to suggest that the teaching of history ought to be "reversed." To illustrate his point, Sutherland describes how a class might be introduced to the question of immigration by reading Ukrainian folk songs and first hand accounts or by examining photographs and statistics. In the following reading, he outlines the theory upon which the method is based and lists some further examples of its use in schools on the West Coast.*

*See Teaching the New Social Studies in Secondary Schools : An Inductive Approach (New York, 1966), The New Social Studies (New York, 1967) and the Holt Social Studies Curriculum Series (New York 1968-70).

[2] Reprinted from Neil Sutherland, "To Teach the New Curriculum We Must Reverse the Teaching of History," *The B.C. Teacher*, 48(2), November 1968, pp. 56, 78-79 with the permission of the author and the publisher.

Since historians apprehend the structure of their discipline through the practice of their unique methodology, students must be taught to study the history we want them to learn by using historical method. Through their attempts to solve historical problems (such as: what was the nature of the second 'great migration'?) the students will learn the skills of the historian and, through using these skills, gain an insight into historical structure.

The historian arrives at his conclusions and derives his generalizations from a study of primary sources — diaries, letters, log-books, travelers' accounts, folk songs, minute books, magazines, newspapers, coins, pictures, the remains of historical sites, historic buildings, government papers, treaties and constitutions. Our students must have these materials so that they can frame their own questions about history and arrive at their own conclusions, not only about the events of the past, but also about the nature of history and historical thinking.

I am not, I should hasten to add, suggesting that we should present each class with enormous boxes of dusty and unselected historical documents from which it must sift out historical truth. But the students, in the process of *becoming* their own historians, must be presented with *carefully selected* primary sources, and must be guided by their teachers in making their own discoveries. The important point is this: the discoveries must be the students' own discoveries, based on their own field work, their own reading, and, most important, their own thinking.

What we must try to do, then, is to reverse the traditional procedure for studying history. Until very recently, good history teaching has begun with the presentation of a narrative (provided either by the teacher or a text-book) and has then turned to the range of teaching materials (historical documents, photographs, and the like) to illustrate or amplify particular aspects of the narrative. To facilitate this method of teaching, narrative textbooks have been written and then various supplementary materials — picture sets, books of readings, records, and the like — have been prepared to help the good teacher to illuminate for his students the conclusions and generalizations he has already made to the class . . . .

To reverse this teaching process, we use the teaching materials as a starting point for inductive study, which leads the students to the generalization previously supplied by the narrative. In our example this is exactly what was done with the folk songs and other primary material. The class or the teacher poses a general question and then, as they work through the materials, other more specific questions are raised—even some which can't be answered. In this study, for example, one class decided that it wanted to know what proportion of the total immigration population stayed happily in Canada, what proportion stayed unhappily because they could not raise the fare to return home, what proportion returned home to stay, and, finally, what proportion returned home and then came back to Canada for a second try. Shrewd, sophisticated questions, you will agree and of course, there is, as yet anyway, no answer to any of them!

When history teachers move into their classroom practice from this theoretical base, all sorts of exciting classroom sessions, field trips and even homework activities are possible. Probably most of the time will be spent in the handling of historical documents of various kinds and in various ways. To many this prospect may seem to imply somewhat less than a series of joyful 'happenings,' but when one looks at the already large and rapidly increasing range of interesting and appropriate materials readily available now for classroom use, his hesitation vanishes. In addition to materials produced by publishers and curriculum centers, however, ingenious teachers have amply demonstrated that they are capable of devising a multitude of interesting and educationally rewarding activities which fit into the general theoretical framework. I shall list only a few of these to indicate the flavor of what is possible.

• A class of learners so 'slow' that many were unable to read or write reconstructed the settlement pattern of Richmond by interviewing pioneers, collecting photographs of housing styles found in the community, and taking a field trip to the UBC library and other resource centers (after they had judged the local library inadequate) so as to put an approximate date to the houses photographed by studying works on the history of architecture.[7]

• A junior secondary class constituted itself into an expanded Canadian House of Commons (containing all the British North American colonies in 1864) and debated Confederation on the basis of the *Confederation Debates* and other primary sources.

• A senior secondary class divided into teams of Crown and defence lawyers to try Louis Riel on the charge of being a rebel.

• A civics class, following up a field trip to a municipal council meeting early in the school year, arranged to receive a copy of the agenda of each subsequent meeting during the year. Each week the agenda was checked against the report of the meeting in the local newspaper and the class gradually and cumulatively built up a list of municipal functions, problems, areas of conflict with other governments, and a general account of living, vital issues of local government in their area.

• A Grade 5 class constructed a series of parallel time-lines—their own lives, their parents' lives, the history of their school, of their community, of their province and of Canada—in an effort to develop in themselves a sense of time.

• An elementary school class, preparing an item for a school concert, decided to present a picture of what Vancouver was like in 1900. Working in groups, the pupils read through two years of the microfilm of a Vancouver newspaper. Their costumes were copied from newspaper advertisements and every word of their sparkling dialog (which they compiled themselves) was made up of items taken from the newspaper columns.

As with all new developments in education, it is only when the planners have finished their job that the really hard work begins, and the classroom teacher does most of it. The new social studies program will not be finally evaluated on the basis of its coherence, relevance or logic, but on how

[7] Charles K. Curtis, Richmond: a Community Study, Vancouver, B.C. BCTF Lesson Aid #807, n.c.

effectively it quickens within our students the feeling of grasping what history is all about. If we tackle our work inductively, we stand a very good chance of success.

3. R. J. Wensley, a member of the Faculty of Education at McGill University, has been interested in the question of organizing historical ideas in the classroom. Inspired by the difficulties experienced by student teachers, he shows that a rearrangement of the historical material, a reorganization of ideas, can revitalize both teaching and learning.

The major premise of this article may . . . be stated [as follows]: a student is truly involved in the study of history to the degree that he perceives those patterns of related historical ideas which give to the discipline form and meaning.[1] The minor premise follows in direct consequence of the major: the most important activity of the history teacher, the very focus of his "activist teaching," is the process by which he organizes and communicates coherent patterns of historical ideas. In passing, it is not intended that these propositions be understood either as a recommendation for a return to the lecture method of teaching history in the schools, or as an argument against the extended use of materials and audio-visual aids. What is often overlooked, however, is that the history teacher's approach to a course in terms of organization of ideas can, in itself, result in a re-vitalization of history. Once the idea-pattern has been well worked out, the materials and techniques essential to student comprehension almost suggest themselves. Yet the materials remain the servant of the ideas, and are never introduced merely because they happen to be readily available.

The general argument advanced above is re-inforced by a consideration of what happens when a topical approach[2] to the teaching of Canadian history is attempted by a well-prepared teacher. By "topical approach"

[1] The question of what constitutes *structure* in the history curriculum is an open one. Jerome Bruner in *The Process of Education* seems to equate structure with patterns of historical ideas. Neil Sutherland, in his article "Structure in the History Curriculum" reaches the conclusion that "structure in history cannot be found in an over-all systematized view of the past, or in revealed laws which govern the rise and fall of civilizations . . . Structure in history can be only partial structure, contained in its *nature* rather than its content." Both views of what constitutes sructure have important implications for teaching method. Perhaps a synthesis is possible. In this case pupils would be involved in historical materials in such a way that they come to "see" an important historical idea with all its supporting evidence. The linkage of ideas provides direction and momentum in a course; the method by which the ideas are approached is essentially historical.

[2] For the material on the topical approach tò history teaching, I am deeply indebted to Dr. Alana Smith, Head of the History Department, Lindsay Place High School, and particularly to her recorded address "A Topical Approach to the Teaching of Canadian History," Audio-Visual Centre, Macdonald College.

[3] Reprinted from R. J. Wensley, "Activist Teaching and the Organization of Historical Ideas," *McGill Journal of Education,* 1(1), Spring 1966, pp. 38-42 by permission of the McGill Faculty of Education, Montreal.

we mean the organization of historical ideas into categories or themes (for example, "Geographical Influences on Canadian History," "Native Peoples," "Immigration, Settlement, and Economic Growth," "The Development of Canadian Government") which are then worked through from beginning to end in such a way that they cut across the normal line of chronology. In the process the student is brought many times into contact with the present which this form of organization helps make meaningful to him. The "native peoples" no longer vanish mysteriously somewhere about page 80 in the textbook, but are discussed as a continuing aspect of Canadian life. The concept of a changing Canadian constitution, with the nature and extent of the change related to the historical factors which helped shape it, is given a deeper meaning. At the same time, teaching method responds to the stimulus of the new organization of ideas. Intensive work in immigration and settlement suggests, if not requires, a field trip to Upper or Lower Canada Village in order to confirm on the ground what has been apprehended only partially in reading and discussion. Furthermore, it is now easier to plan such outings in advance to coincide exactly with the appropriate part of the syllabus. A wise teacher collects in separate files the documents, graphs, statistics, anecdotes, maps, pictures, and other materials which illustrate the development of the topical idea. Most important, the attachment to the single textbook, which has so often marred the teaching of Canadian history in the past, is completely broken. Reference to a wide variety of primary and secondary sources is ordained by the nature of the work and necessitated by the lack to date of any suitable school texts arranged topically. Thus the teacher grows professionally as a consequence of an imaginative organization (or re-organization) of the Canadian history course.

In practice, however, many teachers hesitate to commit themselves irrevocably to a topical form of organization. When they are not really specialized in history, they may feel insecure in the face of the heavier demands made upon a limited fund of time and knowledge. Or they may simply wish to become familiar with the more conventional chronological arrangement of work before coming to grips with the unknown. Under these circumstances, the textbook is accepted as the focus of organization in the course, and the teacher's main function is discharged in "covering" a daily allotment of pages. But herein lies a danger. Not only does method suffer, for the temptation now is to avoid thought and rely more and more on rote, but the student, striving to see some orderly pattern in a welter of detail, becomes at first vaguely dissatisfied, later restless, and finally learns to hate his subject with all the intensity he should bring to the mastering of it.

At this point we contend that it is not only possible, but extremely desirable, for a teacher to think in terms of patterns of organized historical ideas rather than in terms of pages to be "covered," even when the textbook is being used as the major focus of organization.[3] A simple example

[3] For fuller treatment of this idea see my "Employing Concepts in the Teaching of History," *Macdonald Bulletin*, November 1964.

will suffice to make our meaning clear. Faced with a section of the text expounding the course of the French and Indian Wars 1689-1755, it is possible for a teacher to proceed in one or other of the following ways:

Part A—*BY CHRONOLOGICAL HEADINGS*

I King William's War (The War of the Grand Alliance) 1689-1697
—Causes   —Events   —Results
II Queen Anne's War (The War of the Spanish Succession) 1701-1713
—Causes   —Events   —Results
III King George's War (The War of the Austrian Succession) 1740-1748
—Causes   —Events   —Results
         and so on.

Part B—*BY ORGANIZED IDEAS*

The basic cause of the struggle for supremacy in North America lay in the tensions deriving from the relative geographical and political position of England and France in North America.

(a) By 1700 the French penetration of the Mississippi meant the virtual encirclement of the Thirteen Colonies.
(b) Two fortified areas of extreme political "tenderness" were the Ohio Valley and Acadia.
(c) The use of Indian allies by both sides meant "dirty" warfare and lasting bitterness.
(d) The shape of the British and French empires was being "blocked out" in such intermediary settlements as the Treaty of Utrecht, 1713.
(e) One peculiar thing about the struggle was that it was inclined to take its own form, apart from events in Europe, as in the important year 1755.
(f) All the time the struggle was going on, the Thirteen Colonies were learning how to co-operate with each other in political and military matters.

In the first case (Part A), the arrangement of material discourages the adoption of that investigative attitude which generates intellectual excitement. Where the "headings" and the pages in the textbook correspond closely, as they often do, the student feels that he has been plodding resolutely across a bleak and featureless historical landscape unrelieved by any peaks of meaning. Good teaching may improve the situation, of course, but by and large, such an arrangement militates against good teaching. Organization by "headings" usually fails to produce excellence in teaching because it infers that the main function of the teacher is to dispense bundles of appropriately labelled facts, which may be safely passed back by the student at examination time.[4]

The organization of a section of work into a pattern of inter-related ideas (Part B) makes possible quite a different result. The relatedness of the ideas to one another, and to a single central concept, helps the student to comprehend in terms of larger rather than smaller entities. Clearly perceived ideas also constitute the intellectual hooks and eyes which make it easy to fasten one section of work to another. In addition, each idea suggests an appropriate method. The ideas lettered (a) and (b) in Part B above, cry out for the use of maps, number (c) for the narration and interpretation, through discussion of the stark tragedy of the Schenectady and Deerfield massacres, of the truly incredible tales of Tom Quick and Captain Robert Rogers. Nor need the method be entirely dominated by the teacher. Each historical idea can be conceived of as a kind of hypothesis, an end or aim which the student must strive to explore and test for validity at the same time. The main task of the teacher is to involve the student with historical materials in such a way that he comes to "see" the idea with all its supporting evidence. Facts still continue to be of great importance, but now they have been rallied in the cause of a larger meaning and make more "sense" to the learner than they might in Part A.

[4] I am not suggesting here that topical outlines have no value for orientation and review. They do.

4. Teachers have been experimenting with new forms of classroom organization. One of the models has been the University seminar, now used with increasing frequency in the upper grades of secondary school. Terence D. Tait, a Brampton, Ontario high school teacher who is the author or co-author of two texts* has arranged his senior course on French-English relations around basic issues or questions. In the following reading he describes his organization patterns, system of evaluation, and availability of resources.

For the past three years my Grade Thirteen class and I have used the seminar method as the basic weapon to attack Canadian and American history. The central theme is race relations; approximately one-half the year is spent on French-English relations and federalism and the other half on Black-White relations in the United States (and their impact on Canada). I feel that the seminar method is ideal to develop oral and research skills in the students and the increasing emphasis on this device in many Ontario universities, whether they be Arts students or not, has only served to reinforce this contention. What follows is an outline of

*Black and White in North America : Selected Sources (Toronto, 1970) and (with J. T. Copp) The Canadian Response to War, 1914-1917 (Toronto, 1971).

[4] Reprinted from Terence D. Tait, "A Seminar Approach to Grade 13 History," *Canadian Journal of History and Social Science,* 5(1) November 1969, pp. 71-73, 75 with the permission of the publisher.

some of the topics, methods, means of evaluation and resources I have used in the Canadian section of the course.

Topics

1. Was New France essentially an authoritarian society? Was it in any sense "democratic"?
2. Was English rule following the Conquest "tyrannical"? What role did the French Canadians play in the period from 1763 to 1812?
3. Was the Rebellion of 1837 essentially an expression of *Canadien* nationalism? How did the *Canadiens* react to Lord Durham and his Report?
4. On what grounds did Cartier decide to support union in 1864? Why did some French Canadians oppose union?
5. Why did the Fathers of Confederation opt for a federal system in 1867? How balanced was the division of powers?
6. Were there any essential differences in the two Riel rebellions? What impact did Riel's trial and execution have upon the new nation?
7. How did the nature of federalism in Canada change from 1867 to 1896?
8. Why were many French Canadians vehemently opposed to British imperialism? To what extent was Laurier's path from 1896 to 1911 dictated by this opposition?
9. How did World War I affect French-English relations?
10. How did the depression and World War II affect the nature of Canadian federalism?
11. How did World War II affect French Canadians? Does it explain why Duplessis was so successful?
12. Did the "Quiet Revolution" lead naturally to separatism? How does Levesque justify his contention that separation will work?
13. How did the Pearson administration attempt to meet the growing demands of the provinces? What is Trudeau's concept of "Canada"? Is his message succeeding?

Operation of the Seminars

I have seven periods in a six day cycle including a double period on Day 3. This year I have divided the thirty-two students into four groups. Each group meets once a cycle in a seminar and in the large group on Day 3. Seminars are held in separate rooms and my room is open for study, listening to tapes etc. The double period is the only one which is compulsory for the whole class. I've found that these eighty minutes are usually needed for organizational details: reading suggestions, changes in seminar dates, assignment of topics, student interviews, television and radio recommendations, problems etc. However, the double period is most useful for films, video-tapes, speakers or panel discussions. The period on the free day (this year, Day 5) comes in very handy when seminars are cancelled for assemblies, field trips, absenteeism etc. In addition it is worth-while to select one group which has all its members available on one of my "free" periods (e.g. Period 7, Day 4) if we run into a series of cancellations in the "scheduled" History periods.

During a cycle, the topics are discussed by each group in turn, although time limitations force me to have some topics done in written form. I have two formats.

In the first, one person is selected ahead of time to make a ten minute presentation to the group. He is then questioned for about ten minutes by the other members and myself and then a twenty minute general discussion follows. The second format calls for two members to prepare a ten minute presentation. When we get in the seminar, a coin is flipped and the winner (or loser depending on one's point of view) gives his presentation. When he is finished the second "presenter" delivers a constructive criticism of his predecessor. This is followed by a general question and discussion period. I used to assign one person to act as a secretary for each seminar but abandoned this practice last year.

Evaluation

The seminar work is heavily weighted; each term's seminar work is usually worth thirty to forty per cent. I also mark notes each term (a quirk held over from Grade Nine teaching) and if you consider these as preparation for, and feed-back from, the seminars, then group work is worth fifty per cent in some terms. Exams are usually worth twenty-five per cent.

Evaluation of Presentations

The following factors weigh equally in assessing "presenters" in Format One. Some of my considerations are given for the sake of clarity.
A. Organization—are there clear themes? is it analytic? or is it too factual and/or chronological?
B. Delivery—is it audible? is it slow enough for those taking notes? are important areas emphasized orally? is time limit adhered to?
C. Research—is there evidence that a variety of sources have been used? has the question been approached critically from different angles? is there evidence of point of view?
D. Discussion—are questions from other members of group handled well? is additional information and analysis put forward?

In Format Two, Constructive Criticism replaces A. and B. for the person going second.

Evaluation of the Rest of Students in the Seminar

The members of the seminar who are not assigned a special task are obliged to offer one good question or one constructive comment during the discussion period. They begin each term with a mark of five out of ten. This is modified each seminar by a "seminar participation mark".

+2 extremely good question or comment, shows evidence of good research
+1 good question or answer
−1 meaningless noise
−2 no comment
−3 absent

For each seminar I keep a record sheet which serves as a basis for personal interviews with each of the members of the group.

*   *   *

Resources

The primary location of research material is my room. Here I have a large selection of books on Canadian topics. This material is augmented by a good number of newspaper and magazine clippings. A further source of information is tape recordings. Each week I "publish" a radio and T.V. guide for History students in the school. Many of these I tape for future reference.

I am a firm believer in the "de-centralized" library. Having the material near me enables me to be of help to students who are seeking resources. It also enables me to keep track of the books. All History Department books are catalogued and have cards to be filled out. Books used by Grade Thirteen students can be kept out for two school nights and are subject to a fine of twenty-five cents for each day overdue. All books must be returned before 9.00 a.m. so that they will be available for other students during the day. The school library complements the History Department library.

5. *Anthony Barton, a member of the Department of Computer Applications in the Ontario Institute for Studies in Education, has rejected what he calls the discovery or inquiry method. "The discovery method, to malign it slightly," he writes, "consists of attempting to turn the members of a Physics class into thirty Galvanis by supplying each child with a copper hook, an iron bar and a frog's leg . . . and then standing back with narrowed eyes to await the rediscovery of electricity."* Not content with negative criticism, Barton and his associates designed "The Thirties Box" to accompany a series of television films on the Great Depression. Weighing about fifteen pounds, it contains over one thousand items relating to the life of the time, including colour slides, filmstrips, recordings, a tape, postcards, newspaper pages, recipes and postage stamps. Linked to the appropriate audio-visual machinery, the Box transforms a classroom into what they call a psychedelic environment. "The effect," writes David Stansfield, a colleague of Barton, "is a sort of chaotic*

***Soft Boxes in Hard Schools,** This Magazine Is About Schools, 3(1), Winter, 1969, p. 50.

[5] Reprinted from Anthony Barton, "Soft Boxes in Hard Schools," *This Magazine Is About Schools,* 3(1), Winter 1969, pp. 43, 44-50, with the permission of the publisher.

*and random immersion in sounds and images of the Thirties."† In
the following reading, Barton describes the use of the Box in the
classroom and outlines the principles governing its construction.*

David Stansfield and I have been taking a box of multi-media materials
on "The Thirties—The Age of the Great Depression" into school classrooms. It is one of our notions that disorganization has positive educational values. The contents of the box are disorganized, and when the
children are using the box the classroom becomes disorganized. Here is
what one boy had to say about his exposure to the kit:

*Student: Well, you know, feeling of security: walk around, do whatever
you like. You don't know what's going on, so you make the form
for yourself. You come into the room. You're not supposed to
do anything, but you see all this stuff hanging around, and you
say, "Well, it's either going to sit there and do nothing for me
or else it's going to sit there and do something for me," you
know.*

What was the stuff hanging around? Standard equipment from the school
audio-visual room plus the box of materials on the Thirties. I must explain that the materials in the box are soft in the sense that no attempt
has been made to structure them. No labels on the records, no titles on
the filmstrips, no captions on the slides, no step-by-step instructions for
the student. Just $30 worth of raw materials: postcards, stamps, news-
papers, letters, all mixed together: over a thousand items. Something of
individual interest (we hope) to every one of thirty children in a classroom.

What happens? We have tried the kit in twenty classrooms. In one
school, three children are building an airship. A boy in Hamilton, Ontario,
is making a movie about the Thirties. A girl in another school is *reas-
sembling* Guernica. There is enthusiasm, involvement: students are staying in school after hours to find out why food prices are so different today.
In February, our boxes will go into two hundred classrooms to help
follow up four educational television programs on the Depression. . . .

In some classrooms, the children turn the box into a holocaust of light
and sound and recreate the Thirties environment as best they can. Trainee
teachers will go with the boxes to watch what happens.

David is preparing a Teacher's Guide which will request teachers using
the box to say nothing to their students about why and how to use the
materials.

Using a portable tape-recorder, we have obtained many student reactions, often by asking them to interview one another: their reactions are
more varied than those of the teachers, who frequently ask 'For what
grade was this kit designed?'

†**David Stansfield,** The 1930s Multi-Media Kit: A Report on Its Use in
Schools **(Toronto, 1970) p. 16.**

It wasn't. Perhaps nothing should be designed for a specific grade, nor even exclusively for education. To enlarge on that, we have a feeling that there is everything to be said for designing an item of learning material for a child, if you know the child personally; but somehow it does not seem to make sense to design one thing for children, for a mass of children. Take a classroom with thirty pupils and imagine that it is your job to interest every one of them deeply, so deeply that learning takes place. You will never succeed by lecturing, nor by group teaching, nor by showing a film. It is our opinion that your only hope of successfully interesting every child is to provide the class with a range of materials, a range of opportunities, a range of spaces and a range of equipment, and then let them choose for themselves.

NEW NON-STICK PLAN

Choose for themselves is the important phase, for with a range of children you cannot hope to choose on behalf of each and guess aright in every case. So I think there are a couple of lessons for the curriculum planner in our box:

1. *Be more concerned with logistics than design.* Our experiment has driven home to me the disturbing fact that our schools are starved of information (the libraries, textbooks, and audio-visuals are limited, the information channels with the outside world practically dry) and starved of learning materials (think of the scarcity of creative work-stuffs). It is small wonder that many of the teachers with whom we have spoken have been nervous, strict disciplinarians. Behind the thin layer of chalk on their boards lies a vacuum that year by year grows harder and harder to conceal from their charges. Many of them welcome our gradeless box with open arms without knowing why. Give us more, they ask. Give us more.

2. *Stop trying to measure the child.* It seems to me that if it were possible to plot all his variables, Man would have lost the evolutionary race aeons ago. Concentrate instead upon the real problem of meeting the needs of many children all at once. Do not exhaust yourself attempting to define all these needs in advance, be content to define the wide range of interests that must be excited. Think of the full hard-soft spectrum of the requirements of a crowd of children working as individuals. This spectrum *can* be measured, and I believe that there are fat educational rewards awaiting the first researchers in this field. Take your eyes off the child for a moment and look at his environment. Analyse the variety and scope of the materials, measure the availability of information and of workstuffs, investigate the range of the softness of the walls, lighting and seating. Ask yourself for how wide a range of children does *this* school cater? Why does it not cater for all? What is missing? Bring a touch of Jane Jacobs thinking into the scene. Variety is not the spice of life, it is its very essence.

It's not what you put in, it's what you left out.

No spices.

No enrichments.

Build for the continuum.

Many of the children welcome the box. Some are worried by the lack of instructions, some want an outline on the board. One said:

I think maybe that—eh—like the first time like this, it's kind of hard, because it's novelty, you know, and—eh—everybody's you know, wants to do something or other. But if you did this like, you know, every day of the week, like you have normally in class, you'd have to organize things yourself and you—it would be more of a challenge that way. Where just today, it was just like a novelty, you know.

And another said:

Well, this was the first time we'd done it—things were kind of chaotic, but we—like we didn't take it seriously, but if we knew that it was a matter of our passing or failing or whatever, then I think we'd take it seriously, and in the future if we had classrooms designed for this, like, say with a big index file right in the middle of the room, and then branches off, you know, we could get involved in things— people could work in groups and it would be—I, I'd like it better in classrooms.

THE CLASSROOM WITHOUT CLASSIFICATION

Certainly the box respects the student by treating him as an individual, as a person with a mind of his own. The concept of classifying children arose from this respect for the individual, I feel this. How sad that the educators went on to invent grades and streams, to measure I.Q.'s, weights, heights, attendance.

Somehow they lost track of the fact that real learning is a result of deep inward feelings and thoughts, that all else is sham, examination fodder, short-term memory drill. Perhaps the psychologists did not lose track of this, but they were unscrupulous and wished to bare the deep, inward feelings and use them to "motivate" learning, an example of the rat eating its own tail.

Now that grades and suchlike are with us, we cannot sweep them away easily. That sounds as though I were in favour of a rush toward chaos, so let me hasten to explain that I worked for two years writing programs for teaching-machines and those two years convinced me of the value of organizing learning material: I am not an advocate of chaos. I believe *organized material has an educational value equal to that of unorganized material,* though for any given child one kind of material will be more valuable than the other. What I dislike, and what our multi-media something-for-everyone box is an attempt to escape from, is the impression of order dictated from above, something widespread in all walks of education today. Think of Circular 14's textbook commandments, Encyclopedia Britannica's explain-it-all-away filmstrip captions, the so-much-to-do curriculum and the hop-skip-and-jump timetable. I have met many children who have no need of order, it is criminal to impress it upon them; I have met children who thirst for order and to whom bibliographies, electric bells, instructions, classrooms, teaching machines and disciplined lessons should be given whenever they ask for them.

6. The dangers of the "subject centred" curriculum have been underscored on a number of occasions in recent years. The "Hall-Dennis Report," for example, suggested that the interrelatedness of ideas should have precedence, in terms of the curriculum, over the demands of particular disciplines.* Finding a practical alternative, especially in inter-disciplinary studies, is by no means easy. Ian Lister, a former teacher and lecturer in education at York University in Britain, has taught an integrated course on the First World War.

The really active work done by the pupils consisted largely in reading and writing about two books: the first had to be a recent work of popular history. The second had to be an autobiography or a literary work about the war. The most commonly chosen works of popular history were: *August 1914* by Barbara Tuchman; *The Big Push* (about the Somme, 1916), and *In Flanders Fields* by Leon Wolff. The most popular autobiography was Robert Graves's *Goodbye to All That,* closely followed by Sassoon's *Memoirs of an Infantry Officer,* and Blunden's *Undertones of War.* Graves went virtually straight from the sixth form to the trenches and identification with his struggles—against the hearties at school and those officers at the front still lost in an Indian dream—came naturally to most pupils. Many pupils read *All Quiet on the Western Front,* several read *The Good Soldier Schweik,* a few read Hemingway's *A Farewell to Arms* and Lawrence's *Seven Pillars of Wisdom.* The worm's eye views of some of the autobiographies gave the course the human and committed approach that was necessary. And Graves showed that studying societies by studying them at war, analysing the patient in a state of epilepsy, does have some advantages. The British Army in 1914 formalized and sim-

*Living and Learning : The Report of the Provincial Committee on Aims and Objectives of Education in Ontario, **(Toronto, 1968)**, p. 76.

[6] Reprinted from Ian Lister, "The First World War as a General Studies Course," in R. Irvine Smith (ed.), *Men and Societies* (London, 1968), pp. 108-110, with the permission of Heinemann Educational Books Ltd., London.

plified the class structure of civil society, just as the fate of Battenberg typified the clash between extreme nationalism and the interests of an international ruling class.

One cannot say that it was an aim of the course to break down barriers between school subjects: by creating the course from the base up such divisions merely did not arise. Literature illuminated history, and was used to humanize a subject dehumanized by many historians. Thus it was natural, and seen to be natural, to consider the poetry of the First World War. Pupils did a major work of comparison of the poems of Rupert Brooke and Wilfred Owen, and also studied poems by Isaac Rosenberg, Edward Thomas, and Sassoon. A tri-lingual (German, French, English) edition of war poems, *Ohne Hass und Fahne,* helped to show the similarity of the reaction of the sensitive front-line soldiers in the opposing armies.

Later, the course traced events connected with the First World War— the Russian Revolution (where John Reed's *Ten Days that Shook the World* was read by many, an excellent example of "history from below"); Fascist Italy; Nazi Germany (and here several read *Mein Kampf,* noting that Hitler, like Rupert Brooke, was one of those who welcomed the First World War as a release from peace).

Apart from their reading pupils saw a collection of slides of battlefields and monuments of the Western Front; the film *Westfront* (Pabst), which was shown by the School Film Society, and *All Quiet on the Western Front* and *Paths of Glory,* which were shown by local cinemas. Of the last film a contributor in *Culture and Personal Responsibility,* that basic N.U.T. document for all teachers of social studies, said: "The scene of the attack from the trenches is so vivid that I am sure it must bring home to young people the horror implicit in the term 'war of attrition'." Later on during the course several pupils visited the Imperial War Museum (whose Director will arrange special programmes of films for school parties) and a group visited the Joan Littlewood production of *Oh What a Lovely War.* Later, too, the B.B.C. started its series on the war which was seen by the majority of the pupils. There are other possible films which were not used, such as *La Grande Illusion, Battleship Potiomkin,* and *Kameradschaft* (relevant to the international theme), and there are tapes and records which—along with the many cheap paperback books—mean that, from the point of view of materials, a course on the First World War could be done in any part of the country.

7. *A large number of Canadian schools have tried grouping their teachers in teams in order to improve teaching standards. Although patterns differed greatly, the team often tried to combine large group lectures with normal classes, small groups and individual tutorials. In the following reading, G. E. Wiley, a former Head of the History*

[7] Reprinted from G. E. Wiley, "Team Teaching in History," *The Bulletin* 47(1), February 1967, pp. 27-28 with the permission of the author and publisher.

Department, Barton Secondary School, Hamilton, Ontario, who is now with the Ontario Department of Education in St. Catharines, describes one of the more successful experiments with this method of organization in a Grade 11 academic class studying ancient and medieval history.

Our definition of team teaching at Barton Secondary School, Hamilton, was: team teaching is an instructional organization in which two or more teachers work together to plan units of study, to instruct students in large and small groups, and to test the achievements of the programme. And our objectives for using this organization were: (1) to make the special knowledge and abilities of individual teachers available to as many students as possible; (2) to make use of audio-visual aids more efficient and more frequent by using them in large group lessons; (3) to stimulate student investigation and discussion by dividing large classes into small "seminar" groups, and by achieving individual teacher-student conferences; (4) to achieve the presentation of more varied and more effective lessons than are possible day after day in a self-contained classroom; and (5) to promote teacher interaction in planning, teaching, and evaluating the lessons of the team.

Our procedure began, from the teachers' standpoint, with a planning session in the school library in the second period Monday mornings. All four homeroom teachers of the team were present, as well as the librarian, and the art teacher who had experience from the introductory year. The art teacher was a valuable member of the team. We used his specialized knowledge by having him lecture five times during the year, and having him arrange student talks for three other large-group lessons. In addition he was the chairman for student debates and panels on the Thursday large-group classes, and the moderator of an inter-class history quiz competition held on Thursdays during the second term.

From the students' viewpoint, a topic began on Friday. The students were in conventional classes on this day, and after a short introduction they were directed to their textbooks and to other reference books to find information on the topic to be studied. At this point it should be noted that the students were divided into three-person study "teams", each member of which had a different textbook so that different interpretations and information were available to all. On Mondays the classes were again in individual classrooms and the lessons followed up what had been introduced Friday.

We held our large group sessions on Tuesday during the first period. This time had several advantages; special equipment, projectors, maps, amplifiers, and the like could be set up before school began; Tuesday was less likely to be pre-empted by holidays, athletic days, and other special events; and the students had been able to prepare themselves with some background in the topic. Our large groups were held in the auditorium, and consisted of about 140 students. The instruction was most often in the form of a lecture. A lecture was designed to provide information not otherwise easily available to the students, or to raise questions which would stimulate students to further exploration and discussion. At times the instruction came from a motion picture, a student panel, a debate (either students or teachers), and even from plays or skits.

One lecture, for example, was the presentation of the theory: "Maritime States Tend to Develop Democratic Constitutions". In this lecture, some weak, and even false reasoning was offered but it was glossed over with some of the tricks of demagogues or propagandists. The students were warned to watch for the illogicalities, and then in the small groups we had a discussion of these and the tricks of demagogues. The week's topic, of course, was Athenian democracy.

On Wednesdays, the four classes were divided into halves for small-group discussions. Normally, two classes were handled by four teachers at each of two "seminar" sessions during the day. The discussion might arise from the lecture of the previous day, or from a question posed by a member of the group (not always the teacher). At times, some source material would be the focus of discussion. In such a lesson the teacher would ask questions concerning a duplicated document in such a way that the students would be drawn into thinking and discussing the material as historical evidence and eventually relating it to their own experience. For instance, in a document study based on "A Medieval Student's Letter to his Father", the students were asked simple basic questions to get them all involved, and then they were led to question their first answers and to realize that first appearances can be deceiving. Later, they discussed similarities and differences between medieval students and modern university students. In short, the students were encouraged in the small-group meetings to form and express theories and ideas, to refine their ideas, and use their knowledge and experience in discussion. Most students regarded these discussions as the most worthwhile and stimulating part of team teaching.

Generally, there was a large group session in the first period Thursday. These sessions were designed to involve several students, and to be a summation of the week's topic. The activities during this period included debates, panels, skits, dramatizations, quizzes. As mentioned before, the art teacher supervised these periods, leaving the four homeroom teachers free to confer with individual pupils, or small groups of pupils. Either a teacher or a pupil made the request for a conference. And the purpose of the meetings could be to discuss a student's problem, to guide a student in research, to check a student's work, or to organize an activity.

We believe that team teaching was reasonably successful at Barton. There were problems, of course. The facilities were not altered for team teaching, and three of the team members were new to team teaching, and to the school, and two were new teachers. Taken in all, we did achieve our major objectives, especially in the variety of lessons, student involvement, and teacher inter-action.

8. The appeal of audio-visual technology has been hard to resist. As various forms of machinery became more common, teachers found themselves bombarded with appeals, some learned and scholarly but others commercial and highly suspect, to revitalize learning by using the new media in classrooms. In the following article, Mrs. Roberta Charlesworth discusses the use of audio-visual aids in the classrooms of Ontario.

It's a mixed bag, this whole business of audio-visual media in education. For one thing, even the epithet "audio-visual" is anathema. It's anathema to the status-quo-titians who are still hitching old Dobbin to the educational shay in the name of preserving standards and quality and covering the old courses; and it's anathema to those who know where it's at, because the "audio-visual" people have so often been where it's not at, as they have dispensed their post-lesson hardware treats. What's more, audio-visual hardware is expensive, temperamental, non-standard, even obsolescent; prone to being in the wrong place, to losing parts, and to getting stolen. As the song says, "I beg your pardon, I never promised you a rose garden". There are a few problems attendant on moving the world of education into the electronic age. Despite the problems, however, audio-visual media are making possible in education a relevance and an involvement that are sorely needed by a society looking for values and concerned about such issues as survival and identity.

There is no way that the old red school house with a blatant or disguised "Now hear this" operation can survive. There is too much to be known, too much still to be discovered, and too much to be understood for the old learning strategies and old subject disciplines to suffice. Our concerns are not with a finite number of packages of facts but with such present issues as emerging nations, ideologies, ways of life, leisure, face-saving wars, poverty, old age, pollution, communications, racial discrimination, justice, problem-solving, human relations, information retrieval, a sense of community, the megalopolis, lawlessness and brutality . . . Partly as a result of the new technology, reading and writing and mathematics and science are now melting in with linguistics and psychology and anthropology, sociology and ecology. The printed word obviously still has an important place, but other sources of information and—more important—other kinds of information are essential.

Let us pause for a moment to discuss what we mean by the suggestion that other kinds of information are provided by the new media. In a small experimental seminar course conducted at the Glendon College Campus of York University in 1965-66 entitled "Human Communications: the Structure of Interaction", Patrick Watson, one of the resource leaders handed out a typescript of a half hour CBC television interview with Jean

[8] Reprinted from Mrs. Roberta Charlesworth, "It Boggles the Mind :
Audio-Visual Media in the Social Sciences," *The Quarterly of
Canadian Studies,* Spring 1971, pp. 47-51, 51-52, 52-53 with the
permission of the publisher.

Lesage, then Premier of Quebec. The response of most of the thirty participants to the typescript was that of an appalled confirmation of their worst suspicions—"TV's so-called public information shows are nothing but cheap quackery". There was no statement of government policy regarding Quebec's educational objectives, or outline of tax plans, or suggestions of strategies for coping with the radical elements in the party and province. The number of concrete facts gleaned at intervals throughout the program could be tabulated and read in less than one minute.

Then the videotape of the interview was shown and the searched-for facts faded into oblivion. Instead, there was Lesage, the premier, the man who was shaping the fortunes of Quebec, and to a large extent, of Canada. There was the man who was affecting us individually as Canadians, and we could observe personally how he operated. The physical arrangement for the interview suggested the vulnerable position he occupied. Yet, how cleverly he kept himself from being trapped by the probings of the pair of interviewers. The background relationship between the premier and his colourful minister of education became more intriguing as we came to appreciate a master of situational expertise. The course participants became aware of a new involvement in and understanding of a context for the facts they would read about Quebec in the next issue of their newspaper. In other words, the television program provided a deep structure for new surface in-put. Some viewers expect to be able to extract tabulatable facts from every television program. They do not realize that they are receiving non-verbalised information.

Having done actually less than touch on the nature of media information, let us look at some of the contributions audio-visual media are making to the study of social sciences. And let us refer to linguistics —"linguistics"—as an umbrella term to encompass phonology, lexiocology, grammar, semantics, sociolinguistics, anthropological linguistics, applied linguistics. In these areas of study the tape-recorder has been used to capture and make retrievable the spoken word. Audio-tapes have provided language texts which have been accumulated and made available for comparative study, making it possible over the past few years to gain many new insights into the nature and operation of language. Patterns have been discovered, dialects analysed and notions formed about language acquisition. Not only has new information been added to the total body of knowledge about language, but doors have been opened for students of all ages to engage in meaningful and legitimate discovery of their own where they will come up with material that is not "the answer" to a question or to an assignment calling for a return of well established facts. For example, Professor H. A. Gleason of the University of Toronto, tells of a study in an American school where one student of language took his audio-tape recorder into a variety of apartment elevators and rode up and down collecting texts. The student found that as a general rule if people who met on the elevator did not speak to each other within the first thirty seconds, they did not bother speaking at all. He listed the limited number of topics discussed. The world is not going to be a different place in which to live because of this boy's original study of elevator language, but the notion of human language behaviour in situations was being developed and could lead to more significant applications.

One other interesting study of language behaviour could be related to sociology and it also suggests the possibility of an infinite number of companion studies. William Labov describes in his book *The Social Stratification of English in New York City,* a study made in a well-known department store in Manhattan where they found, using audio-tape recordings, that the vocabulary items and pronunciation of both customers and clerks varied from the ground floor to the top floors. Each elevation offered a slightly more exclusive range of merchandise and the level of language used seemed to change correspondingly. Such field studies, using the tape-recorder, can provide the student of Canadian history with new data regarding our ethnic origins and probable migration backgrounds. Neighbourhoods in the larger cities and broader areas of the country such as the Bruce Peninsula and the Kitchener-Waterloo areas of Ontario would be two obvious areas for interesting studies. The two lads from Don Mills C.I. in Metropolitan Toronto who are earning their educational credits this year as they travel to various locations across Canada, could, using models for analysis, make some interesting linguistic observations about Maritime speech, west coast Canadian speech, and small northern town speech. Some nationalists might be interested to know that the influence of American English on Canadian English did not begin with the advent of T.V. and find it interesting to trace vestiges of United Empire Loyalist speech in various locales of the countryside. The study of dialect could profitably be applied to Canadian Literature courses adding a dimension to the appreciation. Similarly, drama students would understand more about the art of drama after comparing a passage of dialogue in a play with a recorded conversation of a similar situation in real life.

Before we turn aside from audio-tape recordings, it would be interesting to estimate how many portable cassette-type tape recorders have been stolen in the past two years—and to consider what the figure signifies.

Videotape, a much more complex medium than the audio-tape, has added elements of practicality, relevance and involvement to academic studies of present day conditions and social behavior. Footage from a few sweeps of the videotape camera will reveal a mosaic of inter-related facets of the physical environment, the economic conditions, the aesthetic level, and the social behavior of any given situation. This mosaic can become the specific information content of the course. In the selection of the material the camera has provided a focus, and a point of view. Verbal discussion and written comment help to clarify and emphasize the comments contained in the tape. The printed word provides a background of principles and theories and guidelines for the applied studies. Several students a couple of summers ago videotaped the student protests that were taking place around the University of Toronto. The videotaping was the cause of some alarm as possibly being intended for sensational use. Such tapes could, however, be analysed as an objective study of the current social phenomenon of protest movements. Who seem to be present? What seems to be their purpose? How do they react to their fellow-participants and to their opposite numbers? Does their attitude change? If so, what seems to cause the change?

The study of group behaviors is greatly aided by the use of videotape. It does not have to centre on more or less spectacular events to be interesting and enlightening. Videotape equipment can unobtrusively and with very little effort be introduced into a group situation, particularly in an informal gathering. Unless a study group has agreed to use its own membership, however, it does not engage in surreptitious taping. This ethical consideration applies particularly in the study of children's social and language behaviour. Data can be gathered for studying gesture and voice inflection patterns, and the language and social behaviour of sets of two or three people within the larger groups.

One group which used its own membership operated under the general auspices of the Ontario Arts Council a year ago. Several inner-city school drop-outs and a peer group from a comfortable suburban area made a videotape record of the interface between the two groups—their initial hostility and the gradual easing of tension as the videotape camera objectified their attitudes.

*   *   *

We have been discussing student-produced audio-visual materials for learning. Professionally prepared tapes can be used for more academic input and serve an entirely different function. Cassette-type tapes are stored in a retrieval system with coaxial cable hook-ups, and television sets as monitors. Independent Study courses can in this way be presented on videotape. A student can go to the area established for monitoring, dial the course and section he wants and get the in-put for his work. Eventually the home TV set will have a hook-up for dial-in programs and there will be no need to go to a school building or a college building for that part of the information. There will still be a need for getting together for discussion and questions, of course. But a student could go at his own pace if he wanted more immersion, not take just two lectures a week in a course. He could ski in the day-time and attend his videotape lecture at night. One centre in California has been experimenting for several years with this type of videotape course. The availability of channels 17 and 19 on our television in the Toronto area, the proposal of co-operative planning on the part of our cable companies and the newly established Ontario Educational Communications Authority are the beginning of a new era in the Canadian education scene.

Film is the last of the audio-visual media which we will discuss at this time. Some of the newer media such as the holograph are not yet readily available for general use and we are concerned here with current possibilities. Moving picture film provides a different kind of information from that presented in videotape and television. There are several reasons for this difference, but the one we are concerned with is created by the respective editing procedures. In general, the major editing of videotape is done during the filming by means of the switching unit. But in cinematography, the editing is a long laborious process that is considered by many film-makers to be as important as the original camera work. In moving picture films only a small percentage of the original footage is used. It is the selection of shots, the sequences, the juxtapositions that make the comment. As we saw earlier, videotape was a marvelous means of collecting information for study. Film, however, because of the selection that has taken place in the editing as well as in the original camera work, provides a unique kind of structured commentary. Videotape captures and transports situations; moving picture films create and imply interpretations. A film on the life of a tribe of Indians would be the result of long hours of study and selection, of filming and editing. The student-made videotape is quite useful in the weekly work. The student-made film is a major essay or final thesis, a compressed statement created out of an accumulation and synthesis of theories, facts, and attitudes.

*　　*　　*

The old ponderous teaching-aid films, shown after the lesson had been taught, are being quietly but firmly discarded. Actually thousands of them should be thrown away to make space for thousands of "art films" and quality documentaries that are now available. The National Film Board has produced hundreds of short films that are or should be primary source material for Canadian students of ecology, environmental studies, political science, anthropology, psychology—and literature. They are in the 16mm format and are reasonably priced. *The Challenge for Change* series with inside studies of Canadian problems, ushers in a whole new concept of personal, local and national enlightenment. For example, *A Non-Rocking Boat Is A Sunken Ship* is a study of the Mohawk Indian Reserve at St. Regis near Cornwall: *St. Jerome* is a study of a community of 35,000 inhabitants, thirty miles from Montreal: *Fogo Island* is a study of the life of a group of Newfoundlanders. All the films were made not *of* but *with* the people of the communities, who are not only the subjects and actors but the co-producers and part of the film crew. Amongst others not belonging to this series, but providing insights into the diversity that is Canada, are the National Film Board productions *City of Gold* (about Old Dawson City), *Cornet at Night* (the prairies during the depression, based on a story by Sinclair Ross), and *Very Nice, Very Nice* (the individual in the chaos of twentieth century events), *Ladies and Gentlemen: Mr. Leonard Cohen, Pas de Deux* (the magic of ballet).

9.　*As a result of the publication of* What Culture? What Heritage? *(Toronto, 1968) a number of curriculum development teams have*

[9] Reprinted from Ralph Sabey, "Project Canada West", *Education Canada* 2(2), June 1971 pp. 19-23, with the permission of the Canadian Education Association.

been formed. One of the first to report was Project Canada West, designed to study the growth of Canadian cities and the problem of urbanization. Dr. Sabey's account of his work may be read in conjunction with Dr. Sellers' article in Chapter 7 and Professor Sutherland's article in Chapter 8.

Project Canada West, a Western Regional Curriculum Centre for Canada Studies, is an integral part of the Canada Studies Foundation. This means that Project Canada West is a direct outgrowth of A. B. Hodgetts' study *What Culture? What Heritage?* This also means that Project Canada West receives the major portion of its budget from the funds raised by the Canada Studies Foundation. With these close ties to the Canada Studies Foundation, it is also evident that the aims and objectives of Project Canada West and the Canada Studies Foundation are similar.

The ultimate aim is to "develop and distribute Canadian studies materials and teaching strategies for use in elementary and secondary schools." There is no thought of producing a "standardized and uniform course in Canadian history." The material and teaching strategies developed will be so designed that decisions regarding their selection and use will remain with the individual provincial departments of education. The materials developed will be designed to give students an understanding of their country and the problems it faces. To accomplish this aim, the materials will utilize the tools of not only Canadian history but of all the social sciences.

With a clear understanding that to meet the broad objectives of the Canada Studies Foundation an organization would require large expenditures of money and time, Project Canada West chose to concentrate upon only one of the "continuing Canadian concerns" cited by Hodgetts—the growth of Canadian cities and the problems of urbanization.

In selecting this theme it was recognized that because of the regional diversity in Canada, urbanization and urban life display a remarkable variability. The urban centres of British Columbia contrast with urban centres in the Prairie region and the frontier urban settlements in parts of Western Canada contrast with the urban settlements in Southern Ontario. Another type of urbanization is existent in Quebec and the Maritimes.

It was also recognized that the effects of urbanization are felt in a dramatic manner by those non-urban dwellers whose small towns are depleted, and by those non-urban minorities, the Indians, who often vacillate between the urban centres and the reserve. In effect, the total aspect of urbanization was considered before this topic was selected from Hodgetts' list of continuing Canadian concerns. It became Project Canada West's objective to devise ways and means to meet the demands inherent in developing materials and the teaching strategies concerned with urbanization.

The first and major thrust was the actual creation of Project Canada West. To organize the project in a manner which would include inter-provincial and inter-institutional educational organizations was no small task. A number of planning sessions did lead to the reality of Project Canada West—an organization to which pledges of support—moral or financial—were given by teachers' organizations, school districts, departments of education, universities and research organizations throughout Manitoba, Saskatchewan, Alberta and British Columbia. In addition, encouragement and financial contributions from the Canada Studies Foundation were obtained.

Project Canada West became a reality just a year ago in June 1970 and a board of directors was established. Membership on the board included people from The B.C. Teachers' Federation, The Alberta Teachers' Association, The Saskatchewan Teachers' Federation, The Manitoba Teachers' Society, the Manitoba Department of Youth and Education, the Alberta Human Resources Research Council, the University of Saskatchewan Saskatoon Campus and the Canada Studies Foundation. An executive director was appointed and the selection of proposals from the 61 submitted by educators in the four western provinces was made. There were four projects selected from British Columbia, three from Alberta, four from Saskatchewan and three from Manitoba.

The proposals to be developed were selected by the following criteria:

(1) The potential contribution which could be made to the study of urban problems as perceived by the Project Canada West rationale. This rationale was developed from the works of Constantinas A. Doxiodis and his study of Ekistics, the study of human settlements. The elements of the urban system to be considered were man, society, shells, networks and nature. The continuing themes of these elements were taken to be individuality, group involvement, inequality of wealth and power, growth, aesthetics, technological systems and future concerns such as pollution.

(2) The strengths of the personnel submitting the proposal.

(3) The assurance of co-operation from the local school system and the universities.

(4) A balance between elementary and secondary education.

Thus proposals dealing with urban government, aesthetics of the urban environment, single resource communities, life-styles and the urban environment, the urban identity crisis, interdependence, urban growth, urban literature, urban education, urban geography, pollution, urban ethnic minorities and the rural-urban migration were selected for further development and for funding by Project Canada West.

Project Canada West devised a five-phase plan for the development of material and teaching strategies associated with each funded project. Phase one, which began in September 1970 and . . . culminated [in] June 1971, was concerned with research and related reading into the selected subjects. The development teams were charged with answering the question: What knowledge—discipline and non-discipline—is available with reference to your chosen subject? This phase necessitated a great deal of association with academic specialists who were helpful in identifying those concepts from the various disciplines which were applicable to the development teams' subject. During this phase, it was also found that an abundant amount of knowledge was suggested by students and by other agents of society. (The full reports of the findings of each development team are now available.)

During phase one it has become increasingly apparent that what was initially viewed as a potential problem has, in fact, become one of the major strengths of Project Canada West: inter-provincial and inter-institutional co-operation.

The board of directors, representing a variety of provincial educational institutions, has been exemplary in its avoidance of inter-provincial disagreements. The hosting of two major conferences and workshops in Edmonton has been successful in developing an esprit de corps among all of the Project Canada West personnel. Provincial jurisdiction over educational matters has been set aside to allow for the unified growth of the project. Educators from all of the western provinces have been working towards the common goal of Project Canada West.

Each curriculum development team also has excellent support from the local school districts. The administrators of each of the 20 school districts have given outstanding support to team personnel who must have released time from their teaching duties to work on their project. The vision of staff development, and hence of the potential value of the team personnel to the district, is stressed. All of the educators who have been contacted express support for Project Canada West's goal of exploring a new role for teachers: the combined teacher-curriculum developer.

In addition to the formal and informal agreements made between Project Canada West and local school authorities about released time for team personnel, there is ample evidence that the personnel and resources of the school and central office administration are offering valuable assistance to the development teams. It is difficult to estimate the value of the actual contributions made by the schools and the school districts to the endeavours of the curriculum development teams.

Another pleasant circumstance is that associated with the contributions of the universities in Western Canada. All faculties of education have given their moral support to the work of Project Canada West, and there have also been people, from all of the universities engaged in assisting the curriculum development teams, who have given their assistance freely, without fees. Professors in the disciplines of education, sociology, anthropology, history, political science, biological sciences, architecture, psychology, economics and geography all have contributed to various curriculum development teams. However, the University of Saskatchewan, Saskatoon Campus, must be specially mentioned as it has assigned two graduate students and part of a professor's time to the project and offered a course in Canada Studies for curriculum development team personnel and others. These services of the universities to Project Canada West are greatly appreciated and it is recognized that without them the curriculum development teams would lack a contribution very necessary to the successful development of curriculum material.

It is not only the educational organizations that contribute their expertise to the projects. Town planners, architects and other professional men have been active in a number of the development teams. Interested parents and businessmen have contributed in many ways too. In fact, it has been both surprising and commendable to find the type of support which is available to those people who are engaged in the development of curriculum material dealing with Canada's urban problems. One is quick to observe that there is not the degree of apathy apparent in these Canadians that one is often led to believe!

Other important contributors are the provincial departments of education. Project Canada West has been in constant contact with the curriculum personnel in the departments. We are seeking their continuing advice and are happy to report that excellent rapport has been established. Although it is impossible for provincial curriculum people to become too heavily involved because they must remain impartial, we in Project Canada West feel that we do have the moral support from the four provincial departments.

Perhaps the most important agency with whom we are co-operating is the Canada Studies Foundation. The Foundation has indicated through its generous financial support that it is interested and encouraged by the direction in which Project Canada West is progressing. The Canada Studies Foundation, through its advisory board, is engaged in a continuing evaluation of the progress of Project Canada West, and it appears that we will continue to work in close harmony with the Foundation.

The success of Project Canada West is contingent upon the success of phase one, for the research and organizational aspect of each curriculum development team will be the foundation for future developments. Phase two is a direct outcome of phase one in that the development of materials and teaching strategies inherent in phase two will be based upon the findings of phase one. The criteria for the selection of the intended learning outcomes for students will be reflected in the material to be produced in phase two.

It is anticipated that the material to be produced will be used for the teaching of discrete units in particular grades. It is not the intention of Project Canada West to develop a course of studies. We *do* intend to develop material: films, slides, video-tapes, textbooks, simulation games and multi-media kits, which will be of value in teaching about a particular aspect of Canadian urban studies in a specified period of instruction. There will be material developed for all school grades 1-12, and the materials will be unique in that they will reflect the concerns and the expertise of the students, teachers and academic consultants from a variety of the social science disciplines.

It is in phase two that there will be an opportunity to develop material from various parts of Canada. The curriculum blue-print developed in phase one will facilitate not only the original Project Canada West team in developing appropriate material, but also will lead to the parallel development of material in different parts of Canada. Thus a Project Canada West team which, for example, has developed a method for looking at urban government in Canada will not rely solely upon its local environs for instrumental content. The final kit of material which results from this study, we hope, will be of such a nature as to encourage comparisons and contrasts in local governments in various regions of Canada and in urban settings of a variety of sizes. It will be material that will be available and useful to schools in all parts of Canada.

In phase three we expect that the materials developed will be used experimentally in a certain number of Canadian classrooms. Those teachers selected to use the material will have been engaged in either the creation of the material or in in-service work to acquaint them with the nature of the material. In this phase, a good deal of teacher interaction throughout various regions of Canada will become necessary. This phase may be viewed as one in which teachers become thoroughly familiar with the materials and one which will probably result in some modification of the material after it has been used in the classroom.

The major implementation of the material to be produced is envisioned for phase four. During this stage the materials, after modification, will be used in more Canadian classrooms. There will be an evaluative component which will seek to measure the success of using the material and the findings of the evaluators will influence the acceptance or rejection of the material as being useful in teaching about urban problems in Canada.

Phase five is not a discrete phase. It will consist of the ongoing evaluation which has already been evident in phase one — both formative and summative evaluation. To this end, Project Canada West is now exploring submissions from various experienced evaluators who have indicated an interest in examining the growth of Project Canada West and the materials being developed. It is anticipated that an evaluative section of Project Canada West will be established and charged with continuous evaluation of all aspects of the project.

It can be said that Project Canada West represents a very ambitious and unique endeavour in the development of curriculum material which will be useful in teaching about a particular Canadian concern — the growth of Canadian cities and the problems of urbanization. It is not the intent of this project to create a chauvinistic view of urban Canada. It is the intent that materials concerned with urban Canada will be successful in allowing students to identify basic concepts of urbanization and to develop a perspective on the urban problems of Canada, of its neighbours and, indeed, of the international community.

Project Canada West seeks to create materials that will let students develop the skills of inquiry, make them aware of the multi-culture basis of Canada and of the country's inherent strengths and weaknesses. The materials developed will be of such a nature that students will become aware of the Canadian heritage, of the Canadian diversity and of the Canadian place in the world community. We want to develop curriculum material that will assist in helping students become rational members of their national and international community.

Another important objective of Project Canada West may be met also. We intend to explore a new role for teachers — as the teacher-curriculum developer. To this end the success of the material produced will reflect the feasibility of such a role. We believe that a partial answer to the student's plea for relevance in education lies with the classroom teacher's perceiving a problem, gaining assistance from academic personnel in planning, organizing and developing material pertinent to the problem, and creating useful curriculum material and teaching strategies for exploring the problem. We do not deny the importance of the academic personnel in the development of a curriculum. We do stress the paramount importance of the professional educator and teacher in becoming more involved in the development of curriculum material.

Project Canada West intends to be successful in meeting both major objectives — the development of material for teaching about the Canadian concern about the growth of Canadian cities and urban problems and in the exploration and development of a new and important role for teachers.

FOR FURTHER READING

For more detailed bibliographies on the nature of the subject and the work of the historian see Martin Klein, "Bibliography of Writings on Historiography and the Philosophy of History" in Louis Gottschalk (ed.), *Generalization in the Writing of History* (Chicago, 1963), pp. 213-247; Patrick Gardiner (ed.), *Theories of History* (New York, 1959) pp. 517-536; and, for more recent writings, Arthur Marwick, *The Nature of History* (London, 1970) pp. 247-253. Oscar Handlin *et. al., The Harvard Guide to American History* (Cambridge Massachusetts, 1961) pp. 1-77 should also be consulted. The periodical *History and Theory* prints annual listings of new writings in the philosophy of history.

Introductory bibliographies for the history curriculum in other countries can be found in J. D. Fines, *The Teaching of History in the United Kingdom: A Select Bibliography* (London, 1969); Henry Johnson, *Teaching of History* (Revised Edn., New York, 1940) pp. 391-460; C. Benjamin Cox and Byron G. Massialas, *Social Studies in the United States: A Critical Appraisal* (New York, 1967) and Leonard S. Kenworthy, *Guide to Social Studies Teaching* (3rd Edn., Belmont, California, 1970). Theses completed after the publication of Walter E. McPhie, *Dissertations in Social Studies Education: A Comprehensive Guide* (Washington, 1964) are surveyed annually in the research review pages of *Social Education*. There is, as yet, no classified bibliography of Canadian publications although some references will be found in Francis C. Hardwick, *Teaching History and Geography: A sourcebook of suggestions* (2nd Edn., Toronto, 1967); John

Lewis (ed.), *Teaching for Tomorrow: A symposium on the Social Studies in Canada* (Toronto, 1969) and Evelyn Moore and Edward E. Owen, *Teaching the Subjects in the Social Studies: A Handbook for Teachers* (Toronto, 1966). "Select Readings in the Teaching of History," an annotated bibliography by G. Milburn, appeared in the *Social Studies Review* Volume 1(9), November 1971 and subsequent issues.

The publications of various curriculum projects are listed in Bob L. Taylor and Thomas L. Groom (eds.), *Social Studies Education Projects: an ASCD Index* (Washington, 1971) and Mary Jane Turner, *Materials for Civics, Government, and Problems of Democracy* (Boulder, Colorado, 1971).

The following journals are particularly useful for recent trends in the teaching of history: *Canadian Journal of History and Social Science* (Toronto), *The Quarterly of Canadian Studies for the Secondary School* (Toronto), *Social Studies Review* (Halifax), *Social Education* (Washington), *The History Teacher* (Notre Dame, Indiana) and *Teaching History* (London).

Chapter 2: How Have Historians Defined History?

E. H. Carr, *What Is History?* (London, 1961)
V. Gordon Childe, *What Is History?* (New York, 1953)
H. S. Commager, *The Nature and Study of History* (Columbus, Ohio, 1965)
G. R. Elton, *The Practice of History* (London, 1967)
H. P. R. Finberg (ed.), *Approaches to History* (Toronto, 1962)
V. H. Galbraith, *An Introduction to the Study of History* (London, 1964)
C. V. Langlois and C. Seignobos, *Introduction to the Study of History* (New Ed., London, 1966)
Henri-Irénée Marrou, *The Meaning of History* (Montreal, 1966)
Arthur Marwick, *The Nature of History* (London, 1970)
Edmund S. Morgan, *So What About History?* (New York, 1969)
Herbert J. Muller, *Uses of the Past: Profiles of Former Societies* (London, 1952)
Allan Nevins, *Gateway to History* (Revised Ed., New York, 1962)
J. H. Plumb, *The Death of the Past* (London, 1969)
G. J. Renier, *History: Its Purpose and Method* (London, 1950)
A. L. Rowse, *The Use of History* (London, 1946)
David Thomson, *The Aims of History* (London, 1969)
George Macaulay Trevelyan, *Clio, A Muse and other essays* (London, 1913)

Chapter 3: Variety in Approaches to the Past

G. Barraclough, *An Introduction to Contemporary History* (London, 1964)

Robert F. Berkhofer Jr., *A Behavioral Approach to Historical Analysis* (New York, 1969)

Robert H. Bremner (ed.), *Essays on History and Literature* (Columbus, Ohio, 1966)

W. H. Burston and D. Thompson (eds.), *Studies in the Nature and Teaching of History* (London, 1967)

Werner J. Cahnman and A. Boskoff (eds.), *Sociology and History: Theory and Research* (New York, 1964)

Thomas C. Cochran, *The Inner Revolution: Essays on the Social Sciences in History* (New York, 1964)

C. D. Darlington, *The Evolution of Man and Society* (London, 1969)

G. R. Elton, *Political History: Principles and Practice* (New York, 1970)

E. E. Evans-Pritchard, *Anthropology and History* (Manchester, 1961)

John Fines, *The History Teacher and Other Disciplines* (London, 1970)

H. Stuart Hughes, *History as Art and Science* (New York, 1964)

Halvdan Koht, *Driving Forces in History* (New York, 1968)

David S. Landes and Charles Tilly, *History as Social Science* (Englewood Cliffs, New Jersey, 1971)

Gordon Leff, *History and Social Theory* (London, 1969)

Seymour Martin Lipset and Richard Hofstadter (eds.), *Sociology and History: Methods* (New York, 1968)

F. Stern (ed.), *The Varieties of History* (Cleveland, Ohio, 1956)

Benjamin B. Wolman, (ed.), *The Psychoanalytic Interpretation of History* (New York, 1971)

Chapter 4: The Historian at Work

Marc Bloch, *The Historian's Craft* (New York, 1963)

Norman E. Cantor and Richard I. Schneider, *How to Study History* (New York, 1967)

Robert V. Daniels, *Studying History: How and Why* (Englewood Cliffs, New Jersey, 1966)

G. R. Elton, *The Practice of History* (London, 1967)

V. H. Galbraith, *The Historian at Work* (London, 1962)

Louis Gottschalk, *Understanding History: A Primer of Historical Method* (New York, 1950)

Louis Gottschalk, (ed.), *Generalization in the Writing of History* (Chicago, 1963)

Carl G. Gustavson, *A Preface to History* (New York, 1955)

J. H. Hexter, *The History Primer* (New York, 1971)

H. C. Hockett, *The Critical Method in Historical Research and Writing* (New York, 1954)

W. G. Hoskins, *Fieldwork in Local History* (London, 1967)

Tom B. Jones, *Paths to the Ancient Past: Applications of the Historical Method to Ancient History* (New York, 1967)

Peter Laslett, *The World We Have Lost* (London, 1965)

Daniel F. McCall, *Africa in Time Perspective: A Discussion of Historical Reconstruction from Unwritten Sources* (Boston, 1964)

Roy F. Nichols, *A Historian's Progress* (New York, 1968)

J. H. Trueman, *The Anatomy of History* (Toronto, 1967)

Robin W. Winks, *The Historian as Detective: Essays on Evidence* (New York, 1968)

Chapter 5: Do Historians Tell Us What Actually Happened?

R. A. Billington, *The Historian's Contribution to Anglo-American Misunderstanding* (New York, 1966)

Herbert Butterfield, *Man on His Past* (Cambridge, 1955)

E. H. Dance, *History the Betrayer: A Study in Bias* (London, 1960)

William H. Dray, *Philosophy of History* (Englewood Cliffs: New Jersey, 1964)

P. Gardiner (ed.), *Theories of History* (New York, 1959)

Pieter Geyl, *Debates with Historians* (Cleveland, Ohio, 1958)

Sidney Hook (ed.), *Philosophy and History* (New York, 1963)

James T. Shotwell, *The Story of Ancient History* (New York, 1961)

Page Smith, *The Historian and History* (New York, 1966)

W. H. Walsh, *Introduction to the Philosophy of History* (London, 1951)

Chapter 6: How Have Historians Told the Story of Canada?

Carl Berger (ed.), *Approaches to Canadian History* (Toronto, 1967)

Michel Brunet, "French Canadian Interpretations of Canadian History," *Canadian Forum,* Vol. XLIV, (519), April 1964, pp. 5-7

Michel Brunet, *La Présence anglaise et les Canadiens* (Montreal, 1968)

J. M. S. Careless, "Nationalism, Pluralism and Canadian History," *Culture,* 30 (1), March 1969, pp. 19-26

W. J. C. Cherwinski, "Bibliographical note: The Left in Canadian History, 1911-1969," *Journal of Canadian Studies,* 4(4), November 1969, pp. 51-60

Ramsay Cook, *Canada and the French-Canadian Question* (Toronto, 1966)

Ramsay Cook, "French Canadian Interpretations of Canadian History," *Journal of Canadian Studies,* 2(2), May 1967, pp. 3-17

Ramsay Cook (ed.), *French-Canadian Nationalism: an anthology* (Toronto, 1969)

D. G. Creighton, "Sir John A. Macdonald and Canadian Historians," *Canadian Historical Review,* 29, March 1948, pp. 1-13

D. G. Creighton, "Confederation: The Use and Abuse of History," *Journal of Canadian Studies,* 1(1), May 1966, pp. 3-11

Michael S. Cross (ed.), *The Frontier Thesis in the Canadas: The Debate on the Impact of the Canadian Environment* (Toronto, 1970)

George Grant, *Lament for a Nation: The Defeat of Canadian Nationalism* (Toronto, 1969)

William Kilbourn, "Canadian History and Social Sciences after 1920: The

Writing of Canadian History," in Carl E. Klinck (ed.), *Literary History of Canada: Canadian Literature in English* (Toronto, 1965) pp. 496-519

W. L. Morton, *The Canadian Identity* (Toronto, 1962)

George A. Rawlyk, "A New Golden Age of Maritime Historiography?" *Queen's Quarterly,* 76(1), Spring 1969, pp. 55-65

L. G. Thomas, "Historiography of the Fur Trade," *Alberta Historical Review,* 17, Winter 1969, pp. 21-27

F. H. Underhill, *In Search of Canadian Liberalism* (Toronto, 1961)

Kenneth N. Windsor, "Historical Writing in Canada (to 1920)" in Carl F. Klinck (ed.), *Literary History of Canada: Canadian Literature in English* (Toronto, 1965), pp. 208-250

Chapter 7: Critical Comment

M. G. Baxter *et. al., The Teaching of American History in High School* (Bloomington, Indiana, 1964)

M. R. Booth, *History Betrayed?* (London, 1969)

C. Benjamin Cox and Byron G. Massialas, *Social Studies in the United States: A Critical Appraisal* (New York, 1967)

E. H. Dance, *History the Betrayer: A Study in Bias* (London, 1960)

E. H. Dance, *The Place of History in Secondary teaching: A Comparative Study* (London, 1970)

N. Frye (ed.), *Design for Learning* (Toronto, 1962)

Edward H. Humphreys (ed.), *Focus on Canadian Studies* (Toronto, 1970)

B. G. Massialas (ed.), *Crucial Issues in the Teaching of Social Studies* (New York, 1964)

M. Mayer, *Social Studies in American Schools* (New York, 1962)

J. H. Plumb (ed.), *Crisis in the Humanities* (London, 1964)

Report of the Royal Commission on Bilingualism and Biculturalism, Volume II, (Ottawa, 1968)

Chapter 8: New Theories

Rodney F. Allen, *et. al.* (ed.), *Inquiry in the Social Studies* (Washington, 1968)

Martin Ballard (ed.), *New Movements in the Study and Teaching of History* (London, 1970)

Sarane S. Boocock and E. O. Schild (eds.), *Simulation Games in Learning* (Beverley Hills, California, 1968)

J. Bruner, *The Process of Education* (Cambridge, Massachusetts, 1960)

W. H. Burston and D. Thompson, (eds.) *Studies in the Nature and Teaching of History* (London, 1967)

Elliot Carlson, *Learning Through Games* (Washington, 1969)

P. Carpenter, *History Teaching: The Era Approach* (Cambridge, 1964)

S. Engle (ed.), *New Perspectives in World History* (Washington, 1962)

Jean Fair and Fannie R. Shaftel (eds.), *Effective Thinking in the Social Studies* (Washington, 1967)

Martin Feldman and Eli Seifman (eds.), *The Social Studies: Structure, Models and Strategies* (Englewood Cliffs, New Jersey, 1969)

E. Fenton, *The New Social Studies* (New York, 1967)

E. Fenton, (ed.), *Teaching the New Social Studies in Secondary Schools: An Inductive Approach* (New York, 1966)

Dorothy McClure Fraser (ed.), *Social Studies Curriculum Development: Projects and Problems* (Washington, 1969)

N. L. Gage (ed.), *Handbook of Research on Teaching* (Chicago, 1963)

Louis J. Hebert *et. al.* (ed.), *Structure in the Social Studies* (Washington, 1968)

Wayne L. Herman Jr. (ed.), *Current Research in Elementary School Social Studies* (New York, 1969)

M. P. Hunt and L. E. Metcalf, *Teaching High School Social Studies: Problems in Reflective Thinking and Social Understanding* (Second Edition, New York, 1968)

Mark M. Krug *et. al., The New Social Studies: Analysis of Theory and Materials* (Itasca, Illinois, 1970)

John Lewis (ed.), *Teaching for Tomorrow: A Symposium on the Social Studies in Canada* (Toronto, 1969)

William T. Lowe, *Structure and the Social Studies* (Ithaca, New York, 1969)

B. G. Massialas and J. Zevin, *Creative Encounters in the Classroom* (New York, 1967)

B. G. Massialas and C. B. Cox, *Inquiry in Social Studies* (New York, 1966)

I. Morrissett (ed.), *Concepts and Structure in the New Social Science Curricula* (West Lafayette, Indiana, 1966)

Fred M. Newmann, *Clarifying Public Controversy: An Approach to teaching Social Studies* (Boston, 1970)

D. W. Oliver, *Teaching Public Issues in the High School* (Boston, 1966)

W. K. Richmond, *The Teaching Revolution* (London, 1967)

Frank Simon, *A Reconstructive Approach to Problem-Solving in the Social Studies* (Calgary, 1970)

Frederick R. Smith and C. Benjamin Cox, *New Strategies and Curriculum in Social Studies* (Chicago, 1969)

Chapter 9: In the Classroom

F. H. Armstrong and H. A. Stevenson (eds.), *Approaches to Teaching Local History Using Upper Canadian and Ontario Examples* (Toronto, 1969)

Tom Corfe (ed.), *History in the Field* (London, 1970)

M. S. Dilke (ed.), *Field Studies for Schools, Volume I: The Purpose and Organization of Field Studies* (London, 1965)

R. Douch, *Local History and the Teacher* (London, 1967)

S. Ferguson, *Projects in History* (London, 1967)

John Fines (ed.), *History* (London, 1970)

N. E. S. Griffiths, *Studying History: Some Practical Suggestions* (Toronto, 1963)

Richard E. Gross *et. al.,* (eds.), *Teaching the Social Studies: What, Why, and How* (Scranton, Pennsylvania, 1960)

F. C. Hardwick, *Teaching History and Geography* (2nd Edn., Toronto, 1967)

J. High, *Teaching Secondary School Social Studies* (New York, 1962)

I.A.A.M.S.S., *Teaching History* (3rd Edn., Cambridge, 1965)

H. Johnson, *Teaching of History* (Revised Edn., New York, 1940)

David F. Kellum, *The Social Studies: Myths and Realities* (New York, 1969)

G. Leinwand and D. M. Feins, *Teaching History and the Social Studies in Secondary Schools* (New York, 1968)

E. M. Lewis, *Teaching History in Secondary School* (London, 1960)

John Lewis (ed.), *Teaching for Tomorrow: A Symposium on the Social Studies in Canada* (Toronto, 1969)

Ministry of Education pamphlet No. 23, *Teaching History* (London, 1952)

Evelyn Moore and Edward E. Owen, *Teaching the Subjects in the Social Studies: A Handbook for Teachers* (Toronto, 1966)

N. M. Sanders, *Classroom Questions — What Kinds?* (New York, 1966)

H. A. Stevenson, *Writing a Historical Essay* (Toronto, 1965)

E. B. Wesley and S. P. Wronski, *Teaching Social Studies in High Schools* (5th Edn., Boston, 1964).

APPENDIX:

ENGLISH TRANSLATIONS

FERNAND OUELLET: History and Sociology: A Historian's Point of View. (Chapter Three, 5.)

For history and sociology it is most likely in the field of social history where exchanges will be most fruitful — at the level of historical concept where attention is focused less on individuals than on groups. Lucien Fèbvre gave this definition of history: "History is the science of man. One must never forget it. It is the science of the constant evolution of human societies, of their never-ending and necessary readjustment to new conditions of material, political, moral, religious and intellectual existence. It is the science of that accord being reached, of that harmony perpetually and spontaneously achieved in every age between the diverse yet simultaneous conditions of man's material, technical and spiritual existence".[8]

To assume this definition of history is to accept the interdependence of the various levels at which man in society evolves. To be sure, economic history is interesting in itself, but it is more so in its social connotations and indeed in its political and intellectual implications. In the same way social history in its pure state, if that is possible, is of limited value and

[8] L. Fèbvre, *Combats pour l'histoire*, p. 31 and following.

does not acquire true perspective unless it is nurtured on economic, demographic, political and intellectual realities. This approach is just as obvious with respect to political and demographic history as it is for the study of ideas, for historical reality is not so easily labelled as might sometimes appear. It is both varied and complex. Ernest Labrousse, Georges Lefèbvre and Albert Soboul accepted this view of a "global" history and the fruitful result is demonstrated in their works on the French Revolution.[9]

Such a view of the historian's craft, far from reducing the concrete demands made on the historian, increases them, since history in fact is tending to become less qualitative and more quantitative. And, moreover, at this level, one document has far less meaning than collections or archives. It is obvious, on the other hand, that measure is more easily introduced in economic history than in other areas. But here also one must guard against all illusions since figures were less important in the past than today. At the beginning of their comprehensive study on *Séville et l'Atlantique* during the century following the discovery of America, Huguette and Pierre Chaunu write: "Is it true that there is no other science than that of the measurable and that history can and should in this sense claim to be a science. . . . It is obvious that satisfactory knowledge of present or past economy cannot be achieved if it is not reduced to some sort of measure. And with no knowledge of living conditions, what knowledge could we have of the past?. . . . And since we generally speak of an Ancien Régime in politics and economics, it is practical, in the context of this outdated system, to speak of an Ancien Régime of measure, designating in this way the centuries for which the historian must be his own statistician".[10] To make measure the keynote of history, not only to gain greater insight into economics but in other fields, is to link history with the other sciences of man. True, measure is not an end in itself, but it enables a deeper understanding of the past as a whole. At the beginning of his quantitative history of Portugal and the Atlantic during the seventeenth century, Frederic Mauro has this to say about his endeavour: "I have tried to meet the standards of the science of contemporary history, that is to write an essay of economic history which would be a geography, a sociology and an economic theory of the past. I have tried to avail myself of the resources of technology and of statistics and of the concepts of the social sciences of today. But I have not used them indiscriminately, for words and systems are a reflection of their times and those of today must not influence the researcher who must create them for his

[9] We should like to draw your attention to a recent book by Albert Soboul entitled *The Parisian Sans-Culottes and the French Revolution 1793-94*. London, Oxford Press, 1964, 280 p. The chapter headings are sufficient indication of the global approach: Mentality and Social Composition, Social Aspirations, Political Leanings, Practical Applications of *Sans Culottes* Politics, Political Organization, Daily Life of the Militant *Sans-culotte*, Popular Movement and Bourgeois Revolution. The works of Labrousse and Lefèbvre are too well-known to warrant full details.

[10] Pierre and Huguette Chaunu, *Séville et l'Atlantique*, 1504-1650, introduction to methodology, p. 6.

investigation and understanding of the past".[11] Such quantitative objectives and the new trend induces the historian to view the study of the past in terms of two basic dimensions which are organization and conjuncture.

To discover the framework, the systems and the unchanging elements in which man evolves is certainly one of the objectives of the historian in search of an adequate explanation of the past. In his search, he should no less evade geographical determinism than ignore economic frameworks, because economics is not an accumulation of unrelated activities subjected to individual whims and having no contact between them. Hierarchies do exist and a pattern of interdependence emerges between various fields as they tend to regroup around one or several dominant activities. Geographical development, though not formally planned, does not come about haphazardly. It can be the result of a general order of things or the product of a system. And the same holds true for society.

Undoubtedly, society is made up of individuals enjoying a certain measure of autonomy, but it is also made up of groups, classes, sometimes castes, each having their own particular interests and sets of values. In every society, even in those which claim a measure of equality, elites do exist and tend to identify themselves with society as a whole and mold it according to their own interests and values. A proper balance of society no doubt depends on purely social factors, but it also finds support in economics as well as in the network of institutions on which it is founded and which are a reflection of it. Solidarity between economics, society and institutions is far from absolute: alterations, dissensions of varying degrees of seriousness occur to demonstrate that no social structure, however rigid it may appear, is immune to change. The creation of the International Commission on the History of Social Movements and Social Structures exemplifies the growing concern of historians over this issue. The same narrow relationship exists between social structure and mentality, so much so that the notion of mental structure and ideology is making its way into the vocabulary of the historian. At the end of his book on modern-day France which can be defined as an essay on historical psychology, Robert Mandrou writes: "This reconstruction of the individual *Weltanschauung* takes on its full meaning inasmuch as it brings about the emergence of a typology enabling the reconstruction of socialized visions; group study is what matters, for it is the group which imposes the full weight of its conformities on the individual".[12] If the historian is brought to think in terms of structures, be they economic, social, political or any other, then he has been compelled to do so in striving to comprehend the past in all its complexity. Furthermore, it is impossible to attain an adequate comprehension of an evolution with sufficient knowledge of the whole complex organization in its state of evolution.

[11] F. Mauro, *Le Portugal et l'Atlantique au XVIIe siècle*, 1570-1670, p. 1.
[12] R. Mandrou, *Introduction à la France moderne*, 1500-1610. Essay on historical psychology, p. 351. See also his book: *Classes et luttes de classes en France au début du XVIIe siècle*, p. 125.

Regardless of their resistance or their age, structures rise and fall, either because of internal necessity, or because of the influence of a particular set of circumstances. The notion of conjuncture, borrowed from economics, has a tendency to acquire far greater meaning in the language of historians. Pierre Chaunu had this to say about it: "It is now a known fact that conjuncture is so inexorable it transcends society, continents and political systems . . . it is all the more so that it is not exterior to man, but is the deepest expression of every human society's own rhythm".[13] Seen in this light, conjuncture is not only economic, demographic, military and political, but involves society and its psychology. In other words, conjuncture is a global phenomenon. It is true that the rhythms or trends of the economy are most significant because economic conjuncture, since it affects the status of groups and classes, confirms certain institutional networks while others are challenged, and sets psychological reactions in motion, has an impact on society, whether direct or indirect. Rare, if any, are the tensions, conflicts, social or political movements that are not linked in one way or another to economic conditions. It is oftentimes during moments of crises that soul-searching is most decisive. The reverse is also true. Even a temporary social change may have economic repercussions. The demographic context which is always important has at certain times forced decisive action upon a group or upon its psychology. Who would dare to deny the many and deep implications of the Loyalist immigration, of the massive arrival of British immigrants after 1815, or of the over-population of the seigneuries of Lower Canada at this same time? The interactions of economics, society and demography are continuous, thereby giving, according to the time, more prominence to one factor or another.

[13] P. Chaunu, *op. cit.*, p. 22. In the comprehensive volume devoted to Atlantic structures in the same series, the author writes: "Any element taken out of the social whole for purposes of scientific analysis possesses duration. The distribution of socio-economic phenomena between structure which is durable and conjuncture which is transient is in no way immutable. Therefore, to speak of structure and conjuncture means nothing more than the wish for classification around the axis of time. Inasmuch as time is a measure of history, that measure which gives it its originality among the human sciences and its superiority in the hierarchy of the social sciences, the breakdown between structure and conjuncture is admirably suited to historical research." P. Chaunu, *Séville et l'Atlantique. Les structures*, p. 12.

MARCEL TRUDEL: Objectivity in History (Chapter Five, 5.)

Objectivity, it must be understood, can only exist inasmuch as there is an object. That is to say the object must preserve its integrity. History, therefore, remains objective inasmuch as it itself remains absolute. Only then, by extension, can we say that the historian is objective if he has respected the integrity of his object. In its absolute requirements, objectivity therefore demands that the past, seen by the historian thanks to an intermediary witness, keep its absolute integrity. Now, under present conditions, it is impossible for the historian to restore the past in its entirety. It is impossible for us to see New France exactly as if we had been senior employees of the Compagnie des Cent Associés and that is why, discouraged and sceptical, some pseudo-historians recommend that we simply limit ourselves to publishing the charter and the ledgers of this Company rather than attempt to bring it back to life, explain it and pass judgment on it. This would no longer be history. And yet, history has its *raison d'être*. It still remains to be written and the historian, of which absolute objectivity is expected, is left as perplexed as before in front of his object.

It must therefore be recognized that a requirement which prevents the object from revealing itself is no longer legitimate, and that absolute objectivity can no longer remain objective when it destroys the object itself. The first step then is to admit that history shall be written through the mediation of a witness. But when history is written, a great number of witnesses that posterity has preserved for us may show up in such large numbers, so easily and as if of themselves: who is going to choose among all of these witnesses? Nothing else and no one else than the historian. Nothing else because here we are not in a laboratory, and no one else because no one else is better equipped in this field than the experienced historian. Thus, and for the second time, absolute objectivity has been diminished, since it is admitted that the historian may legitimately interpose himself between us and the witnesses of the past.

This second intermediary between us and the past, this historian, is a human being, a man of flesh and blood: what will be the posture of this man in the face of the past? Fénelon wrote: "The good historian belongs to no century and to no country." This expression has been cited as an authority in order to restore absolute objectivity and yet, so as not to be misunderstood, Fénelon had at once added that the good historian must not take sides for this one or that one. Since our object here is not to answer Fénelon but those who misuse him, let us nevertheless take the expression as it is usually explained. If the historian is understood to be a living breathing man (and he could not be otherwise), this expression which is being interpreted makes history impossible and pointless. If the historian writes history, he cannot set up his observatory outside of his own time. How could he place himself in a future which he cannot know or in a past which he is precisely striving to know? Turn him out of his own time and the place you give him, besides localizing him more than you blamed him of being, has the disadvantage of being far more dangerous. Can he be anything but of his own country? Let us take as an example a French Canadian historian. It is he before any other who should write the history of French Canada, for no one knows it better than he; his life is enmeshed in it intimately. He will be of French Canada, but of course he will place himself *above* his subject (which does not mean *outside* it). He will respect the integrity of his object, which is French Canada. He will even write the general history of Canada in function of this object. To proceed otherwise would show a true lack of objectivity, since it would imply a diminution of the object itself. And this is how those who oppose a history of French Canada become the greatest opponents of objectivity. They tell us that this history should henceforth be integrated, merged into the general history of Canada. It is difficult to see why such a history would be more objective. One could consequently argue, and with good reason, that the general history of Canada could quite reasonably itself be merged into a history of the Americas. And if one wished to restrict us to a Pan-American history, we could argue further that this Pan-American history should normally be blended into the larger context of European history. And thus, from European history to world history, in our quest for absolute objectivity we have lost our object, or rather the historian is as perplexed as ever before his object. In the light of the principle of objectivity, nothing compels us to forsake the history of French Canada on the pretext that there has existed for eighty years an agreement as artificial as Confederation. The historian will be a man of his time and of his country. These conditions shall provide the requisite ingredients for respecting the integrity of his object, for remaining objective. It should be noted by the way, that we are not speaking of impartiality: objectivity involves only integrity, whereas impartiality belongs to methodology and is not part of the very nature of the object.

INDEX OF NAMES

INDEX OF SUBJECTS